SUCCESS
in Reading and Writing
Second Edition

Kindergarten

Barbara J. Blackford
Betty Cramer

Helen G. Cappleman, Series Editor
With grateful acknowledgment to the late Anne H. Adams,
the originator of *SUCCESS in Reading and Writing.*

GoodYearBooks

An Imprint of ScottForesman
A Division of HarperCollinsPublishers

Cover illustration by Sydney Rives.
Cover design by Amy O'Brien Krupp.
Book design by Carolyn McHenry.

The illustrations used in the charts in Figures 2–2, 2–4, and 2–5 are from *My First Picture Dictionary* (Glenview, IL: Scott, Foresman and Company, 1990). These were drawn by the following artists: 2–2: Diana Magnuson, 2–4: Justin Wager, 2–5: Nancy Munger
The illustration used in the chart in Figure 2–3 is from *My Pictionary* (Glenview, IL: Scott, Foresman and Company, 1990). It was drawn by Linda Kelen. Other art, unless noted, was drawn by Betty Cramer.

Good Year Books

are available for preschool through grade 6 and for every basic curriculum subject plus many enrichment areas. For more Good Year Books, contact your local bookseller or educational dealer. For a complete catalog with information about other Good Year Books, please write:

Good Year Books
Scott, Foresman and Company
1900 East Lake Avenue
Glenview, Illinois 60025

Blackford, Barbara J.,
    Success in reading and writing. Kindergarten/Barbara J. Blackford, and Betty Cramer—2nd ed.
        p.cm.
    "With grateful acknowledgement to the late Anne H. Adams, the originator of Success in reading and writing."
    ISBN 0-673-36000-8
    1. Reading (Kindergarten)—United States—Handbooks, manuals, etc. 2. Language arts (Preschool)—United States—Handbooks, manuals, etc. 3. Teaching—Aids and devices—Handbooks, manuals, etc.
 I. Cramer, Betty.
II. Adams, Anne H. Success in reading and writing.
III. Title.
LB 1181.2.B533 1992
372.4—dc20   91-27589
                                                                                                    CIP

ISBN 0-673-36000-8

 2 3 4 5 6 7 8 9 10 -MAL- 99 98 97 96 95

▶ Preface

Barbara J. Blackford and Betty Cramer, authors

SUCCESS in Reading and Writing is a student-centered integrated reading and writing program that is based on a belief in the capabilities of children and the professionalism of teachers. The flexible structure of the 180 lesson plans insures a balanced curriculum and a daily routine that incorporates reading and writing into each kindergartner's world as naturally as he or she plays, speaks, or listens.

Developed in the mid-1970s by the late Anne H. Adams, *SUCCESS in Reading and Writing* has stood the test of time. For more than twelve years in all kinds of settings, *SUCCESS in Reading and Writing* has proven that valuing literacy and thinking results in literate, thinking students and teachers.

This second edition of *SUCCESS in Reading and Writing* follows in its philosophy and intent the first edition. In the years since *SUCCESS in Reading and Writing* was first developed, we have learned much about process teaching and learning, and a great deal of what Dr. Adams knew instinctively has been researched and proven true. She was able, even then, to outline a structure that insured balanced teaching but was flexible enough that teachers could adapt it to their teaching styles, curricular demands, and, most importantly, their students.

Our goal with this new edition of *SUCCESS in Reading and Writing* was to make the philosophy of the program clearer and the program itself even easier to implement. Perhaps the most apparent change is the incorporation of the oral language strategies into a new Writing module that provides daily opportunities for children to participate in developmental writing and drawing activities related to a five-day theme. Comprehension and higher-level thinking skills are further developed during the Pictures and Words and Storytime modules with the addition of suggested focus questions or guides for each lesson. The Alphabet module has been expanded to include craft activities and Research lessons using magazines and newspapers.

▶ Acknowledgments

SUCCESS in Reading and Writing workshop leaders, who have helped shape SUCCESS as it has developed in classrooms across the country:

Mary Armstrong	Becky Haseltine	Cam Newman
Peggy Bahr	Debby Head	Kathy Newport
Jean Becker	Paula Hertel	Ola Pickels
Patti Bell	Bridget Hill	Libby Pollett
Jean Bernholz	Tina Hinchliff	Karen Powell
Barbara Blackford	Robbie Ivers	Susan Quick
Jill Board	Connie John	Donna Rea
Elaine Bowie	Shae Johnson	Cathy Reasor
Ann Bryan	Delores P. Jones	Patty Redland
Jacqueline Buckmaster	Joanne Jumper	Mary B. Reeves
Helen Cappleman	Janice Keegan	Carole Reindl
Stacey Carmichael	Nancy Kerr	Pat Reinheimer
Kathi Caulley	Dana Kersey	Marilyn Renfro
Betty Cramer	Annie Kinegak	Janice Reynolds
Donna Croft	Barbara Krieger	Marlene Rotter
Suzie Desilet	Esther Lee	Pat Scherler
Bobbi Donnell	Sue Lippincott	Janet Schneider
Marilyn Enger	Lisa Lord	Shirley T. Scruggs
Betty S. English	Kathy Malick	Celeste Singletary
Sandra Fain	Judy Mansfield	Kathleen Smith
Debra Fetner	Howard Martin	Patty B. Smith
Neita Frank	Judy Martin	Pat Sumner
Carol George	Lila Martin	Pam Tate
Randy Gill	Nancy J. Mayhall	Donnye Theerman
Lynn Gori-Bjerkness	Becky Miller	Shirley A. Thompson
Letha Gressley	Debbie I. Miller	Jean Weaver
Andra Gwydir	Debby Miller	Beth Whitford
Carol Hall	Paul Moller	Pat Wong
Mary Harris	Cinda Lee Moon	Michael Wong
Roberta Harrison	Avril Moore	Kristin Zeaser-Sydow

Thanks to Shirley Scruggs and Kathleen Smith for their helpful comments on the preliminary manuscript. Special thanks to Randy and Colin Blackford, Molly Cramer, and Murray for their patience and support. Thank you also to Helen Cappleman for her confidence and guidance. Thank you to the teachers who believe in the potential of all students to read, write, and learn. And finally, thanks to all of the students who make teaching an exciting and rewarding profession.

▶ Art Acknowledgments

The following young artists have contributed to this edition of *SUCCESS in Reading and Writing,* Kindergarten:

Travis Solesbee, Spartanburg, South Carolina
Chris Hart, Matthews, North Carolina
Lambert Mixon, Spartanburg, South Carolina
Erin Grey Senn, Spartanburg, South Carolina
Carrie Walden, Spartanburg, South Carolina
Caitlin O'Connell, Matthews, North Carolina
Julia Dearinger, Louisville, Kentucky
Anthony Pfingston, Matthews, North Carolina
Kyle Poston, Matthews, North Carolina
Noorez Lalani, Spartanburg, South Carolina
Douglas Kiger, Matthews, North Carolina
Dustin Adair, Spartanburg, South Carolina
Megan Chesser, Matthews, North Carolina
Twelvala Robinson, Spartanburg, South Carolina
Sarah Moore, Matthews, North Carolina
Jason Matthews, Matthews, North Carolina
Jamall Geter, Spartanburg, South Carolina
Renell Rawley, Spartanburg, South Carolina
Eugene McGaha, Drayton, South Carolina
Emily Bartos, Matthews, North Carolina

▶ Contents

Chapter 4   The Writing Module   46

Chapter 5   The Alphabet Module   62

SuccesS

in Reading and Writing

Second Edition

Kindergarten

Chapter 1 SUCCESS: The Basic Assumption

The *SUCCESS in Reading and Writing* Kindergarten program capitalizes on the complex world of language and print that the kindergarten-aged child has been exposed to since birth and expands it in an atmosphere that is non-threatening and exciting to children. SUCCESS fosters the excitement of exploring while building the child's self-esteem. An enthusiasm for learning the exciting system that the world uses for rules, advertising, warnings, and fun is strong in the kindergarten-aged child.

"Mrs. Ramsey, I can read! I read the signs all the way back on the bus from the zoo! I read STOP . . . and SLOW . . . and DUCK CROSSING . . . and, DO NOT . . . um . . ."
"Enter."
"Yeah! DO NOT ENTER."

The *SUCCESS in Reading and Writing* framework builds on this enthusiasm. SUCCESS divides the day into four invitations to join more fully the world of language learners and users. The parts of the framework, called modules, welcome the child to formal schooling. A SUCCESS classroom invites students to show off what they know. The framework allows each student to progress without pressure.

The National Association for the Education of Young Children (NAEYC) has published several position papers on developmentally appropriate practices for the young child. These documents state that high quality, developmentally appropriate programs should be made available and that learning strategies should be based on the knowledge of how young children learn. Learning information needs to take place in an environment that allows students to manipulate and explore. Opportunities to interact and communicate positively with other children and adults are essential. All experiences should meet the child's developmental level and foster a child's self-esteem and positive feelings toward learning (NAEYC, 1990).

SUCCESS classrooms provide an environment where all of these qualities exist. SUCCESS is a way of teaching and learning that captures the excitement of the kindergarten child. SUCCESS accommodates children's different abilities, development, and learning styles. The activities in the kindergarten SUCCESS program are designed to provide a learning environment that allows the child to develop to his or her highest potential without the feeling of being pushed or forced to learn.

The SUCCESS teacher is a guide and a facilitator in this learning environment. He or she uses a wide variety of teaching materials and activities that are relevant for the young student. SUCCESS teachers love learning, and they experience true joy when they see young people unlock the mysteries of reading and writing.

Chapter 1

Travis Solesbee

The SUCCESS kindergarten program is based on the belief that young children *want* to learn to read and write. They equate these skills with being "grown-up" and approach them as a form of play. The kindergarten classroom is the perfect place to encourage the desire of young children who want to learn, not to turn off that desire or delay it.

The SUCCESS program incorporates 1) the child's vocabulary, 2) printed words from familiar items in the child's environment, and 3) a flexible structure that enables the teacher to develop a program that varies each day, based on student input.

Although there is little change in the daily lesson format, there is constant change in the students. They change in the way they look at books. They change in their understanding and appreciation of hearing books read. They change in what and how they draw and write. Their awareness and excitement about letters and words grows as they discover the direct correlation between learning and their world. SUCCESS takes into account the changing world of today's kindergarten child.

▶ A Typical SUCCESS Day

In SUCCESS classes, language arts time is divided into four main activities, which are called modules: Pictures and Words, Storytime, Writing, and Alphabet. Each module lasts for approximately twenty minutes daily. The main procedures for each module are very clear:

1. Pictures and Words
  a. The teacher and students discuss and label a picture with words volunteered by students (15 minutes)
  b. The teacher leads a comprehension discussion (5 minutes).

An interesting picture is discussed each day. Children tell about what they see and the teacher labels parts of the picture with their words.

2. Storytime
  a. The teacher and students share books (15 minutes)
  b. The teacher and students discuss the book (5 minutes).

The teacher informally shares the best of children's literature with students each day during a specified listening time. These books often relate to other class activities.

3. Writing
  a. The teacher and students discuss information about the theme (5 minutes).
  b. The students write or draw (10 minutes).
  c. The students share their writing (5 minutes).

Writing is introduced as the expression of the child's own exciting ideas communicated with others in words and pictures.

4. Alphabet
  a. The teacher introduces an alphabetic pattern and related activity (5 minutes).
  b. The students participate in a related activity (12 minutes).
  c. The students share their work (3 minutes)

In an exciting exchange of skills and prior knowledge, children learn and share what they know about the letters of our alphabet.

In addition to these four activities, students read independently for pleasure every day. Most teachers allow students five to ten minutes a day in addition to the other modules.

One of the reasons for the effectiveness of SUCCESS is the predictability of classroom procedures. The basic activities in the modules are the same every day, all year. Students focus their attention on various topics and good things to read, rather than what the teacher has planned for them. They know the excitement of the day will come from exploring printed materials and from the new knowledge they discover. The procedures stay the same; it is the students and what they know that change.

This book is a description of the philosophy behind *SUCCESS in Reading and Writing*, its components or modules, and how they work. Chapters 2 through 5 explain each of the four modules, while Chapter 6 addresses some of the daily details like evaluation, classroom management, and the materials needed. Following the chapters are the outlines of 180 flexible lesson plans, one for each day in a typical school year. Page 6 contains an example of a SUCCESS lesson format. In each module, the *or* followed by a blank line indicates that teachers are encouraged to make decisions about the topics, skills, and materials that are most appropriate for their classes.

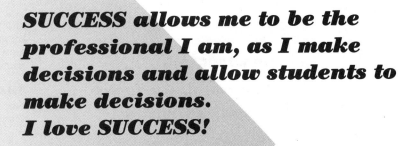

SUCCESS allows me to be the professional I am, as I make decisions and allow students to make decisions.
I love SUCCESS!

Shirley T. Scruggs, teacher

Lesson 7

Pictures and Words

Picture: Adults or _____
The teacher leads a brief introduction of the picture.

CHART DEVELOPMENT
Phase I—Single words The students volunteer words to label the picture and the teacher writes the words on the chart. Most of the labels will be single words. Students draw lines to connect the pictures to the words.

COMPREHENSION FOCUS
The teacher leads a discussion about the picture. Many of the questions will begin with *what*.
The chart is displayed in the classroom.

Storytime

READ ALOUD
Annabelle Swift, Kindergartner
by Amy Schwartz
or _____

DISCUSSION FOCUS
How was Annabelle's big sister helpful to her on her first day in kindergarten? Who were the other characters?

Writing

Five-Day Theme Focus: All About Me or _____

INTRODUCTION
The teacher and the students have a conversation related to the theme.

WRITING ACTIVITIES
While the students are writing or drawing the teacher meets with individuals or small groups to discuss the theme. The student's independent work may or may not relate to the theme. Each student's work is kept in a folder.

SHARING
The students share something written or drawn with another person or the group.

Alphabet

Letters: *F f* or _____

INTRODUCTION—
BRAINSTORMING LESSON
The teacher introduces the letter and demonstrates letter formation. The teacher writes student- volunteered words and illustrations of words containing the letters on the chalkboard.

STUDENT ACTIVITY
On their papers students write
■ examples of the letters
■ their favorite words or illustrations from the chalkboard
■ other words or drawings

SHARING
The students share something written or drawn with another person or the group.
Papers are dated and filed.

Although much about SUCCESS lessons seems the same, the fact is that no two lessons will ever be the same. The experiences and personality of each teacher will come through. The parts one teacher will emphasize will be diminished by another. The materials students use will vary from class to class, so the information they find will never be the same. But most importantly, the students are different in each class. No two groups think the same, act the same, or draw the same conclusions. Yet all can be right. There is rarely one single right answer, one single way of doing the task right. To be right in a SUCCESS lesson, the student has to be able to explain his or her reasoning logically. Those who can defend their ideas are right; those who cannot should try again.

▶ Which Teacher Can Use SUCCESS?

All SUCCESS teachers are literate decision makers who believe children want to read, write, and learn. By making decisions that allow children to be a part of a literary community at school, they know that children can enjoy the same built-in rewards of literacy that adults do.

They truly believe reading, writing, and learning are pleasurable, worthwhile, and even essential for a satisfying life.

They are not adults who have "received" or "completed" an education; they are lifelong learners who are enthusiastic about sharing their ongoing education with younger learners.

They believe that reading, writing, and learning are so rewarding in themselves that the role of teacher becomes one of facilitator, not director.

They want their classrooms to be based on literature or content-area themes.

They see the value of letting children develop reading/writing skills without pressure in an atmosphere where the learning is fun and rewarding.

They want a basic, flexible structure to guide their planning, so that they can save their time and energy for teaching.

▶ The Big Decisions

Any teacher who recognizes the characteristics of a SUCCESS teacher in himself or herself will want to know more about what SUCCESS teachers do every day to carry out this language arts program. SUCCESS is a framework for instruction, and any SUCCESS teacher will be making decisions constantly. What are these decisions?

DECIDING TO FOCUS ON STUDENTS, NOT TEXTBOOKS

Several different programs that are available and being used in kindergartens stress using textbooks and workbooks. Because SUCCESS teachers believe children like to learn and are rewarded by what they learn, they choose to center instruction on their students. They want their children to read and learn more than could ever be included in the

Chris Hart

kits or textbooks for one grade in school. In addition, they don't believe that any body of information is so valuable that it should be "covered" or that there are essential lessons or questions or answers that should be controlled by the teacher and merely received by the student.

SUCCESS teachers choose to focus on the students they teach. They must constantly observe each student to determine his or her needs, interests, budding abilities, and development as a member of the literary community. Many of the decisions SUCCESS teachers make are based on what they learn from their observations.

SUCCESS emphasizes the processes of learning rather than the products of the students' work or the contents of a particular textbook. The emphasis is on the person more than on the subject matter or skills.

DECIDING TO DEVELOP A COMMUNITY OF LEARNERS

SUCCESS teachers decide to think of their classes as communities of learners, with students helping each other and sharing what they are discovering. Motivation and an increase in thinking come along with all the talking and cooperating that students do daily as part of their work. There is little competition and little lonely work. There is lots of explaining and suggesting. The words "What if we . . ." are heard often. Students consider many possible ways to go about their work and know that there is rarely only one right answer.

In SUCCESS classrooms, with the structured, open-ended daily activities, students are expected to do the best work possible for them. In order to do so, they make choices. The fact that students make choices about their own learning, rather than being governed by the choices made by teachers and textbook publishers, matters a lot.

Perhaps because of the community spirit in SUCCESS classes, SUCCESS students are willing to take risks as learners. Students take the initiative because they know that the limits in SUCCESS classrooms have more to do with available time than with a right answer. Many choices are not only acceptable, but valuable. There is more emphasis on process more than on product, and students are not preoccupied with how the teacher judges them. Because of the cooperative approach to learning in a SUCCESS community, students do not feel threatened or afraid. How could they fear failure in SUCCESS classes? With the routine use of everyday materials, the initiative teachers see students take in the classroom in their reading and writing is more likely to show up at home, to be shared with parents and become a lifelong habit.

DECIDING ON A SCHEDULE

SUCCESS teachers are committed to a routine that gives children time they can count on for reading, for writing, and for seeking new information. Extra time is available for reading, writing, and learning in SUCCESS classrooms because very little time is spent telling the class what is going to happen next. Students can dive right into exploring reading, writing, and learning without being confused about directions.

A SUCCESS teacher first needs to determine the time that is available for language arts instruction and choose four twenty-minute periods of time when all, or most, of the students are in the class. Ideally, teachers are able to integrate many content areas within the SUCCESS framework. The four twenty-minute periods of time do not need to be scheduled consecutively.

Teachers choose to teach the modules in various orders. Many begin with the Alphabet module and follow with the Pictures and Words module. After that comes the Writing module. Many teachers prefer to schedule Storytime right after lunch. For others, Pictures and Words is a good way to start the day. The thing that matters is that all four modules, plus read-alone time, are scheduled to happen every day, in any order the teacher chooses.

DECIDING TO MAKE MORE DECISIONS

SUCCESS teachers have made three big decisions already—to think of instruction as student-centered, not teacher- or textbook-centered; to create a community of learners; and to create a framework of time that students depend on for their reading, writing, and learning. Now they prepare to make even more decisions that enhance students' learning. Day by day, they decide what topics and materials to make available and when to include skills instruction or new information. They decide when it is appropriate to integrate content-area topics with language arts instruction and when certain pieces of literature are important for the class. They decide when to ask questions and how to evaluate students' progress. Moment by moment, they decide when to pursue the teachable moments that constantly arise. Many of their decisions differ from year to year because they are learning from different students each year, and their decisions aren't the same as those of other SUCCESS teachers because each teacher and class are unique.

▶ Is It Hard to Teach SUCCESS?

All these decisions! Why would any kindergarten teacher give up grouped center-time activities, commercially made worksheets, or textbooks with teacher's guides? Three things about SUCCESS make the teacher's work easier:

1. Lesson plans for SUCCESS classes are virtually the same every day. The teacher and the students learn the basic procedures for the four modules very quickly, and everyone knows what to do next.

Boring? No, because the topics, skills and materials change a lot. Because the procedures are dependable, the exciting things in class are the books and materials people choose to explore, the new information people learn and share, and the writing produced by the people. Teachers don't spend time duplicating materials or checking papers.

2. Individualizing instruction usually means extra work for the teacher. SUCCESS has helped many students with special needs because of the large amount of individualized instruction that takes place every day. Special needs are met partly because of all the choices students can make, and partly because the teacher is able to spend more time helping students.

During two of the kindergarten SUCCESS modules, Alphabet and Writing, the majority of the lesson time is available for the teacher to work with individual students and their developmental needs. The other two modules, Storytime and Pictures and Words, provide whole-group participation where uniqueness and original thinking are encouraged and all students can be successful.

3. It is easier to make all of these decisions knowing that recent research supports SUCCESS. The most convincing research, though, is what each SUCCESS teacher is able to report about his or her students: how each student learns best, exactly what he or she is able to read and write, what his or her interests are, and so forth.

Educational literature of the 1990s is filled with reports of how some young children are forced into learning too much too fast and how others are not prepared to meet the educational challenges of the classroom. Newspapers report alarming illiteracy rates and sad stories about poor teaching. The good news is that professional journals report about developmentally appropriate activities for the young learner, literature-based instruction, whole language, cooperative learning, process writing, and many other ideas that are integral parts of SUCCESS.

▶ The History of SUCCESS

In 1976, years before terms such as "whole language" and "cooperative learning" were used, SUCCESS was begun by Anne H. Adams to provide an alternative to basal textbook instruction. At that time it was popular to point out all the things that were wrong with basals since the public was becoming aware of the growing illiteracy problem in the United States. Teachers attending professional conferences heard speakers criticizing traditional reading instruction but offer few substitutes.

Anne Adams joined the best of them in trying to persuade people that basals were certainly not solving the problem of illiteracy. She suggested that assigning one more skills worksheet might do more harm than good. Most significantly, she gave teachers a structured, but flexible, daily plan to replace the basals. She gave some reasons that her ideas would work, and she reminded educators that teachers are professionals and should make many decisions every day about how to teach their students.

SUCCESS was used first in Durham, North Carolina. Children who had not succeeded in learning to read and write were indeed successful in SUCCESS classes, and the word began to spread around the country. Anne Adams taught teachers in other states how to use SUCCESS, and more students benefited from this new way of organizing language arts instruction time. Although she died in 1980 before all of the original SUCCESS books were published, the work she had begun flourished because teachers told their colleagues what was happening in their SUCCESS classrooms.

Lambert Mixon

▶ SUCCESS in the 1990s

These days teachers can advocate SUCCESS because of all the things that are right about it, not because it is simply an alternative to basals. Among basals, some of the old problems still exist, but many publishers have at least paid lip service to the complaints of teachers. Some basals even incorporate a whole-language approach. Many teachers have abandoned the basal anyway and substituted instruction that centers around children's books, along with a more hands-on style of teaching, a welcome improvement.

Whatever the case may be with the basals of the 1990s and various forms of literature-based instruction, SUCCESS is a way of organizing language arts instruction that truly helps students. Even though every SUCCESS class is different, after more than a decade of using the SUCCESS framework, teachers can examine the characteristics that SUCCESS classes have in common.

1. Students make many decisions, not only about the substance of their reading, writing, and drawing, but also about how they will use art materials.

2. Students use real-life materials such as children's books, newspapers, and magazines to begin building their reading and writing skills.

3. Students understand that there is rarely just one right answer, and they know they can work with each other to solve problems and seek information; therefore, they are more willing to take risks as learners.

4. The teacher makes many decisions about topics, materials, skills, and the social dynamics of students' sharing and working together.

SUCCESS is effective for me because it allows my children to assimilate the skills and experiences at their levels of ability.

Dana Gasque, teacher

5. Students and teachers focus on the joy of participating, the excitement of discovery, and the processes of learning more than on the final products.

6. A daily routine of reading, writing, and learning allows students extended periods of time for making choices about the books they read, the types of writing or drawing they do, and so on.

7. The teacher strongly emphasizes the importance of communication among students.

8. The teacher's role is to establish the framework within which students can read, write, and learn. Being a creative, energetic teacher in a SUCCESS classroom means observing the strengths and needs of the students and being open to the endless possibilities of what they might learn as literate people working together. A creative SUCCESS teacher learns from and with the students.

SUCCESS is not meant to be used by all teachers. It is recommended for teachers who appreciate the characteristics that make the program work. They must believe that reading and writing are wonderful and that students really do wish to join in the fun of learning and developing as literate human beings. Those who have read this far in the book have considered the main decisions a teacher must make in order to organize language arts instruction this way. The next four chapters explain more about each of the modules. Chapter 6 covers relatively minor decisions the teacher must make: how to get materials; how to evaluate; how to adapt SUCCESS to special situations; how to acquaint administrators, parents, and others with SUCCESS; scheduling for half-day kindergarten programs; and how to keep everyone informed about all the great things happening in a SUCCESS classroom. Finally, in the second part of this book, the Lessons contain 180 outlines for lessons that can be used within the framework of SUCCESS.

Chapter 2 — The Pictures and Words Module

The Pictures and Words module provides children the opportunity to discuss a picture and to name and label objects in the picture. Children will hear, see, and say the letters of student-volunteered words as the teacher writes them on chart paper. A student or the teacher draws a connecting line from the item in the picture to the written word to further develop the reading/writing process. The Pictures and Words module is an excellent opportunity for teachers to integrate numerous curriculum areas and at the same time enhance students' language skill.

▶ Rationale

The Pictures and Words module provides daily opportunities for students to 1) develop the thinking skills that are involved in reading comprehension; 2) increase their oral language ability in a non-threatening environment; 3) see the written form of words they associate with a variety of pictures; 4) observe the formation of letters within the words as they are written; 5) learn new words and concepts; and 6) read the words individually or with the group.

Pictures tell stories. The same relationships among characters and objects that are present in written stories are found in pictures. Through discussion, students develop the concepts of main idea, sequence, causation, real and make-believe, and all of the other elements of reading comprehension. The presentation of familiar concepts in pictorial form provides a focus for students' ideas. Students feel confident discussing items in the picture and exploring their ideas about the message depicted.

Children come to kindergarten being able to speak thousands of words and identify a wide variety of objects. The SUCCESS program capitalizes on these skills and enhances them by combining the oral and written words. Each time a child's word is written as a label for a part of a picture, he or she makes assumptions about the reading/writing process. Students see the written form of words from their spoken vocabulary. As the teacher writes the words volunteered by others in the class and students discuss these words, each student's vocabulary increases.

The fact that students rather than adults volunteer the words used in this module is extremely important. Kindergartners in Portland, Oregon, will come up with words that are different from those volunteered in Charlotte, North Carolina. On the other hand, there is a vast common bank of words used by students in all locations. This module builds on the language of the children in each class, regardless of their backgrounds and experiences.

The Pictures and Words module allows children of all ability levels to be successful. This module enables the child with a very limited vocabu-

Chapter **2**

Erin Grey Senn

lary to participate in the same lesson as a child with an extensive vocabulary. For example, children whose language is delayed will always be able to label some object in the picture, but they will also benefit greatly from learning new vocabulary. Children who come from very enriched backgrounds will begin incorporating their reading and writing skills. Discussions related to the item labeled will provide all students with a better understanding of the meaning of words and concepts.

Using words from the students' vocabulary increases their interest in participating in the charts activity, because it relates experiences from their lives outside school to their school experiences. This shows students that their knowledge is of interest and value to the entire class.

The students hear, see, and say each letter of their volunteered words as the teacher writes the words on the chart. When the teacher writes the words on the chart, the entire class will hear the whole word, see the letters in the word, and voice or echo the name of each letter as it is written on the chart. Students will see how letters are formed as the teacher writes them. They will also begin to make their own assumptions about the sounds and patterns of letters within the context of meaningful words.

During the chart labeling process, the teacher and the students will also read and reread the words that have been written on the chart. Children who are developmentally ready to read these words will do so on their own, while other children will be echoing the teacher as he or she says the words. The lines that are drawn from the picture to the words help students remember what the words are, so all students are more confident about trying to read them.

The charts become a picture dictionary for the children. Children feel ownership of words that they and their classmates have volunteered for the chart. They remember their words above all others because they can personally relate to them. Children frequently refer to previously made charts to read words or to find the spelling of words.

The Pictures and Words module enables the teacher to introduce new knowledge, integrate curriculum, and build a child's feeling of self-worth. Teachers will broaden their students' knowledge base by introducing a wide range of topics and pictures. Children will have the opportunity to name and discuss items that they may not have had the chance to experience on their own.

Teachers can use the Pictures and Words module as a tool for incorporating many curriculum areas. Charts can relate to any area if the teacher has an appropriate picture. Many SUCCESS teachers use the Pictures and Words module to introduce new science, social studies, health, and safety units. Pictures and Words charts can also be very useful for reviewing topics.

The Pictures and Words module provides children many opportunities to increase their feelings of self-esteem. They are able to name the objects and discuss the concepts in a picture. Students spell with the teacher, and some children will read many or all of the words written.

▶ The Elements of a Pictures and Words Lesson

Each Pictures and Words lesson contains three key elements: a Suggested Picture, a Phase Level, and a Comprehension Focus.

SUGGESTED PICTURE

The picture themes chosen for the Pictures and Words lessons cover a wide range of subject areas throughout the school year, assuring a variety in vocabulary, ideas, and opportunities for discussion. The picture themes that are listed in the Lessons are merely suggestions. The teacher decides if he or she will use a picture similar to the one listed in the lesson, or if he or she will substitute another picture that is more timely or appropriate for the class.

When a teacher substitutes a picture, he or she can record the change on the line provided in the lesson. Teachers making frequent picture substitutions should keep a list of the picture themes that they use to insure that they offer a variety of picture themes during the school year.

This book's appendix provides an overview of the Pictures and Words module pictures, listed by lesson numbers. Each fifth lesson is marked by an asterisk, indicating the lessons that are correlated with the Writing module. Teachers may choose to use other themes for the Writing module, but every attempt should be made to have the picture relate to the five-day Writing theme on the day that the theme is introduced.

PHASE LEVEL

Each Pictures and Words lesson includes a phase level. The Phase Levels covered during the school year are: Phase I, Single Words; Phase II, Word Clusters & Title; Phase III, Sentences; and Phase IV, Questions & Answers. These levels denote the developmental sequence of the chart labeling process and are designed to build on previous skills. (Each of the levels is described in greater detail later in this chapter.)

COMPREHENSION FOCUS

The Pictures and Words lesson includes more than merely labeling the objects in pictures; it should also include a discussion of the picture. The purpose of the discussion is to develop understanding and to provide opportunities for oral language development. The discussion provides opportunities for the teacher and the students to consider the pictures as a meaningful whole.

The questions do not always center on the most obvious points of the picture. The teacher uses these focus questions to highlight details and give the students an opportunity to discuss intangibles related to the picture. Feelings, relative positions of objects, and other general association concepts are appropriate and interesting to most kindergarten students.

A Comprehension Focus is suggested for each lesson's discussion. It is a guide for the teacher to insure that he or she asks different types of questions at all levels of comprehension. The focus is simply a question word, such as who, what, when, where, why, and how. Teachers should ask questions that start with the focus word if doing so is appropriate for the picture. For example, if the picture is of people in a swimming pool, possible questions include:

Who is swimming in the pool?

Who has a swimming pool at their house?

Who likes to swim?

Who is having the most fun in the picture?

Who has the beachball?

When did the people get in the pool?

Where is the dog in the picture?

Why does the boy look unhappy?

How many of you have been swimming?

This is just a sampling of questions that might be generated from a single picture. Not all of these questions would be asked.

The Comprehension Focus that is listed for each lesson is a suggestion. The teacher evaluates the picture that he or she chose for the lesson and considers the appropriateness of the suggested focus. The key to making substitutions for the Comprehension Focus is variety; don't rely on the same type of questions for each chart.

▶ How to Teach a Pictures and Words Lesson

SCHEDULING AND PACING THE MODULE

SUCCESS teachers have found the optimum length of this module to be twenty minutes. At times teachers are tempted to continue it longer, but doing so often has negative consequences. Some students tend to lose interest, become a distraction to others, or have difficulty sitting for a longer time. At the beginning of the school year, the entire twenty minutes may be too long to maintain the attention of the class and the teacher may need to adjust the time length. However, as the year progresses, students will improve their ability to listen, wait their turn, locate and name items in the pictures with greater speed, and associate oral language with written words.

The keys to a successful Pictures and Words lesson are keeping the pace rapid and encouraging students to participate. Volunteering words is one way, but it is certainly not the only way. Discussing the ideas presented, drawing a line on the chart paper, adding to a response made by another child, spelling, and reading a favorite word are also ways students can feel a part of the Pictures and Words module.

Keeping the pace rapid and making sure everyone is involved is not easy. There are always students who want to dominate the conversation, others who sit quietly but do not volunteer, and still others who would rather crawl around or bother fellow students.

Teachers have devised different methods to insure that every student has an opportunity to participate. One teacher randomly selects students to participate by picking students' names from a can containing popsicle sticks labeled with each child's name. Another SUCCESS teacher selects a color and every child wearing that color has the first opportunity to name an item in the picture. Every child should have the positive feeling of contributing something to the chart.

Students who are reluctant to volunteer words might be encouraged to do so if the teacher gives them clues about something that they might label in the picture. For example, a teacher might say, "Heather, I see something in the picture that is round and can bounce. Can you tell me what it is?"

The teacher can also provide some "think time" to a child that has not volunteered a word. The teacher might say, "Jamie, I would like you to tell me something that you see in the picture. Think about it for a few minutes and I will come back to you." This gives the student the opportunity to think about the picture without being put on the spot immediately. This technique also works well to draw in the student that is not paying attention to the lesson.

There are three distinct parts to a Pictures and Words lesson. These parts are preplanning, chart development, and displaying charts.

PREPLANNING

Picture selection Each lesson contains a suggested theme for the picture. Select a picture from your picture collection that relates directly or indirectly to the theme. For example, if the theme is "automobile tires," one teacher might choose a full-page magazine advertisement for a car. Another teacher might choose a picture of children playing on a tire swing. A third teacher might choose a variety of different types of tires and make a collage of these pictures on the chart paper. The

SUCCESS has helped tremendously with our discipline system. The emphasis is placed on positive instead of negative feedback.

Dawn Johnson, teacher

Carrie Walden

pictures with much detail encourage more discussion. If a picture of one single automobile tire is chosen, the conversation and words for labeling the picture will be limited.

A fourth teacher may choose a picture related to a content-area theme, a class project, or a book.

After the teacher chooses the picture, he or she notes the Comprehension Focus and decides if it is appropriate for that picture or if a different one would be better. The teacher thinks of several questions he or she could ask that would develop the comprehension skills required for understanding the message of the picture.

Chart preparation The teacher tapes a piece of chart paper on the chalkboard or on a surface that all the children can readily see and reach when writing on the chart. The selected picture is taped or glued to the center of the chart. Some teachers find it helpful to display the chart prior to the actual lesson time. Students soon become aware of the process of the Pictures and Words lesson and look at the picture before the lesson to identify small details.

Displaying the picture ahead of time also provides the teacher the opportunity to encourage a student who may be reluctant to volunteer words. These children can be helped to find an item that they would like to label during chart development time.

CHART DEVELOPMENT

Introduction   The students sit informally in a group on the floor as near as possible to the chart. All students need to be able to see the chart. The teacher then leads a brief, approximately two-minute introduction to the picture. This general introduction to the picture heightens the students' awareness of the picture's content and establishes the direction of the discussion.

The introduction includes the teacher talking about the picture and asking students appropriate questions about some aspects of the picture or its general theme. The teacher may want to use the lesson's Comprehension Focus to facilitate discussion about the picture. In one SUCCESS classroom the teacher used Lesson 16's Comprehension Focus, "why," to build interest for a Fall picture:

> **Ms. Williams:** Why do you think most of the leaves in this picture are red, brown, and yellow and not green? (The teacher calls on Perry who is waving his hand wildly.)
>
> **Perry:** I know why the leaves aren't green! It's because of chlorophyll!
>
> **Ms. Williams:** Perry, that's an amazing word. Do you know what it means?
>
> **Perry:** Well, it means that when the chlorophyll is gone from the leaves, they change colors.
>
> **Ms. Williams:** That's right. The trees know that it is Fall because the sun begins to set earlier and they begin to lose chlorophyll. That makes them change colors. Wow, Perry, I'm impressed! Thanks for telling us about chlorophyll.

This exchange between the teacher and students related the Comprehension Focus to the picture and provided the teacher with a "teachable moment." Perry introduced the class to a vocabulary word and information that is not typically introduced at the kindergarten level. The teacher was able to add further information which some students may remember and others may not. Even more important, Perry felt good that he knew something that no one else knew.

Identifying and labeling objects   After introducing the chart, the teacher asks the class if they see anything in the picture that they would like to name. The students then begin volunteering words for items that they can name in the picture. The teacher asks each student to come up to the picture, point to the item, and say how he or she wants it to be labeled.

The teacher can personalize the chart by asking related questions about the item. This helps give meaning to the words chosen by the student and brings out any special interest a student might have related to an item in the picture.

Mr. Barger: Today we have a picture of many different kinds of animals that would make good house pets. Does anyone see a picture of a pet that they have or would like to have? Billy, what would you like to label?

Billy: I see a dog.

Mr. Barger: Do you have a dog for a pet?

Billy: Yes, his name is Hershey. He is bigger and fluffier than that dog. He has brown spots on his back. Yesterday he ate my cookie.

(Responding to another child's answer, the teacher was able to incorporate information the students learned on a previous field trip to a pet store.)

Mr. Barger: Can anyone name the pet in the picture that can talk like you do?

Pam: There's a parrot just like Pepper that we saw at the pet store. He could say all kinds of neat things.

Mr. Barger: Jerry, do you remember how the bird learned to talk?

Jerry: Ms. Samuels kept saying the same thing over and over to Pepper until he could say it.

Depending on the Phase Level, the teacher assists the student in deciding which word or words from the discussion would be appropriate to use to label the object. As the teacher quickly writes the words, he or she says each letter name aloud, and the students echo or spell with the teacher.

One objective of this module is to afford students opportunities to observe the formation of letters and see that the order of letters is important. As the words are written on the chart paper, the object is not to isolate sound combinations within words or to dwell on the particular sound of one or two specific letters. Instead, it is to hear, see, and say the letter names. Students begin to make their own conclusions about the sounds the letters make within words.

After an item in the picture has been identified and discussed, a student uses the felt pen to draw a line from the item in the picture to the word(s) written by the teacher. Some teachers have found it helpful to place a dot near the word so that the child has a target to draw the line to. This avoids lines being drawn through words. After the first student draws on the chart, another student comes up to the chart, points to a different item in the picture, and the teacher labels the item.

Lesson closure Closing the lesson differs depending on the phase of the lesson within the year. During Phase I, the lesson will conclude with a quick review of all the single words the children have used to label the pictures or they can underline the letters on the chart that are being studied in the Alphabet lesson. During Phase II, the students re-read the word clusters and add a title to the picture. Phase III ends with writing a sentence or two to further describe the picture. During Phase IV, the lesson will close after the students have written a question and an answer in complete sentence form on the chart.

Points to remember

1. Throughout the chart development the teacher should pause occasionally and review the words on the chart by having the students read the words with the teacher.

2. The teacher should write as fast as possible while retaining legibility. This helps him or her keep the students' attention and also allows many students the opportunity to come up to the chart.

3. The flexible nature of the Pictures and Words module provides you with opportunities to insert many kinds of information, not just word meanings and situations in which words are found. Teachers have used the "teachable moments" within the Pictures and Words lesson to comment on matters such as capitalization, plurals, compound words, and contractions. This should be done quickly and not deter from the focus of the lesson. As the year progresses, many students absorb this information and begin to use it in their own writing.

Other possibilities to incorporate knowledge areas might be: counting the letters in the words, matching words with the same number of letters, finding all the words that are plural, or finding labels of objects that use electricity.

4. Do not insist that every student volunteer a word each day. That would result in too many labels on the chart. Especially at the beginning of the year, shy or reluctant students may be asked if they would like to find something in the picture. However, if the response is "No," the teacher should say, "Perhaps you'll want to find something tomorrow." When these students learn there is no threat involved, they will want to give it a try.

5. You should write the words at the beginning of the year. When a student learns to write well, and wants to write—even one letter in a word—you may ask that student to come up to the chart and write the letter while you and the class say it. Eventually, other students in the class will want to write words on the chart paper. Do not discourage this, and do not expect their letters to be "beautifully" formed. Each day during the year, the students' abilities increase. However, having the students write on the charts takes longer than if the teacher writes the word. You should then decide if the pace of the lesson is rapid enough to keep everyone's attention.

To add variety later in the school year, some SUCCESS teachers have allowed the students to use another time of the day to "play school." Individuals or small groups of children enjoy making their own charts and labeling them with inventive spelling.

DISPLAYING CHARTS

When the time limit for the lesson has expired, display the chart in the classroom where it can be seen by all students. If possible, the teacher

Figure 2-1

Developmental Phases

Phase	Content Emphasis	Lessons
I	Single Words	1–20
II	Word Clusters & Title	21–40
III	Sentences	41–140
IV	Questions & Answers	141–180

should place the chart at "finger level" so that the students can touch the words and trace the lines to the pictures.

It is extremely important that the students' words and charts be visible in the classroom—on a bulletin board, beside windows, on the front of the teacher's desk, above the chalkboard, or on the classroom door. Not only are the students very proud of their charts, but they like to return to them on their own time and associate words they know on the charts with the pictures. The teacher should display as many charts as possible.

When the teacher removes the charts from the classroom walls, he or she can tape them onto clothes hangers for easier use by the students. Two charts can be placed back to back on one hanger to provide more stability. The students will use these charts as reference for their writing during other modules or during their free time. At the end of the school year, the teacher might allow the students to take several charts home. Children enjoy sharing the charts with their families and having something that their entire class helped to make.

▶ The Phases

There are four Phases in the Pictures and Words module extending throughout the academic year. Each of the Phases is designed to build on the previous phase. Figure 2-1 lists the lesson numbers and the emphasis in each Phase.

PHASE I

Single Words—Lessons 1-20 In Phase I the teacher writes single words for the items identified by students. That does not mean that the teacher would never write a phrase or even a sentence, if that is what a student requests. The majority of the words written during Phase I, however, will be single words. Figure 2-2 is an example of a chart from a lesson in Phase I. During this Phase, students are learning the procedures of this module. Most important, students are introduced to the reading/writing process as they see the written form of their words and those of their classmates.

During this phase especially, the teacher may need to assist students who want to try but are not sure how to go about it. He or she should ask leading questions such as, "What is the item in the picture that people use to sit on?" and write the child's response, "chairs"; or "Where is the vase of flowers?" and write "table" when the child responds "on the table."

Maintaining a high interest level and good listening behavior is sometimes difficult with beginning kindergarten children. A part of the module format includes students' learning that they will have opportunities to talk and listen to others talk about the picture. Some students take longer than others to learn to become a part of the group, so there may be fewer students who are actively involved in the lesson than there will be later in the year.

PHASE II

Word Clusters & Title—Lessons 21—40   The emphasis in Phase II is on word clusters and writing a title for the chart. Word clusters are two or

Figure 2-2

PHASE I PICTURES AND WORDS CHART

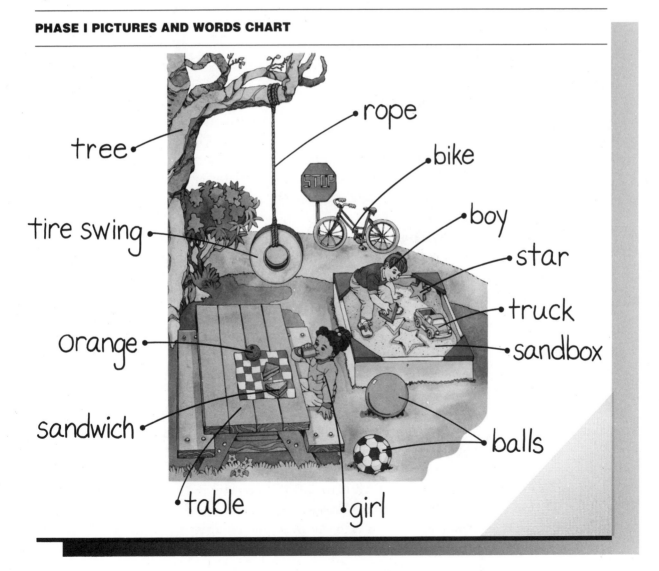

more related words that are not a sentence. During chart development time when the students are labeling the pictures, the students should be encouraged to use word clusters rather than single words. Sometimes getting a word cluster from a student requires some involvement of the teacher:

Caitlin O'Connell

> **Lynn:** That's a flag.
> **Mrs. Evans:** What kind of flag is it?
> **Lynn:** It's a United States flag.
> **Mrs. Evans:** Shall we write United States flag? Class, spell with me. What do you think United begins with? What letter should I write first?
> **Mrs. Evans and the class:** Capital U-n-i-t-e-d (pause); "States," Capital S-t-a-t-e-s (pause); "flag," f-l-a-g.
> **Ms. Evans:** Let's all read this cluster together: "United States flag."

Reading back over the cluster reinforces the concept of word groupings.

If the student cannot think of an adjective or other words related to "flag," the teacher can either have the student call on a classmate for a suggestion or he or she can write the single word on the chart. Figure 2-3 is an example of a chart from Phase II.

In this phase the class also decides on a title for the chart. Some teachers have the students determine a title for the chart before labeling the pictures and some do it after the labeling process. One SUCCESS teacher encouraged the children to suggest a title for a picture of children at a playground before labeling the objects.

> **Ms. Duncan:** Would anyone like to suggest a title or name that we could use for this picture? It should tell us what the picture is all about.
> **Kelly:** The picture has a whole bunch of kids playing on the playground outside. They have swings, slides, and lots of things to climb on. One boy is chasing a girl. When do we get to go outside?
> **Ms. Duncan:** That's right, Kelly, there are lots of things happening in this picture. Can you tell me that again but this time use just a few important words?
> **Kelly:** Playing.
> **Ms. Duncan:** That's a good choice. Would anyone else like to suggest a title for the chart?
> **Becky:** We could call it "Recess Time."
> **Robert:** I want to call it "Playing on the Swings."
> **Ms. Duncan:** These are all very good choices for a title. Why don't we vote on it to see what the majority of the class would like to call the picture?

Figure 2-3

PHASE II PICTURES AND WORDS CHART

On the Farm

red barn

weather vane

white cloud

open door

6 chickens

little kitten

happy pigs

bird house

brown mud

brown and white cow

wooden fence

green grass

The teacher may wish to use a rotating list or some other method to choose the child who picks the picture's title so that everyone in the class gets an opportunity. One teacher reported that he involves a less verbal student by letting him or her be the decision-maker. He calls on someone who has not been saying much to decide which of the choices will be the title. If they do not want to decide, the teacher chooses another student.

During the first lessons in this phase, the students will need the teacher's guidance in determining a brief title. The tendency of the kindergarten child is to "tell a story" or give an entire sentence for the title. The teacher will need to demonstrate how the title needs to be just a few words that "name" what is happening in the picture.

Early in the year, the teacher can use the Storytime module to set the stage for writing titles. The teacher can point out what an author has chosen to "name" a book. The class could discuss how the author might have chosen that title. If the class has discussed titles in Storytime before Lesson 21, the children will have an easier time understanding titles and limiting the number of words in a title. For example, Leo Lionni used the name of the main character to title the book *Frederick*. Another author, Nancy Carlstrom, used a repeating line from the book for *Jessie Bear, What Will You Wear?*

PHASE III

Sentences—Lessons 41–140 Phase III lessons contain all of the elements of previous lessons, but the teacher will be writing at least one student-generated sentence related to the picture at the bottom of the chart. Although single words and word clusters are used to label the items in the picture, the teacher should expand at least one student's response until it becomes a sentence and then write that response on the bottom of the chart. If time allows, the teacher can select another student to add another sentence. Figure 2-4 is an example of a chart completed during Phase III.

The formation of the sentence is done at the end of the lesson and may contain several of the word clusters used on the chart. It is within these sentences and some of the word clusters that the traditional "sight words" such as "and," "is," "when," and "for" are introduced and students may learn to read and spell them. One major difference between the SUCCESS program and some other programs is that high-frequency sight words are used in context, never in isolation or in drills.

During this phase the students will also be exposed to the structure of a sentence. They will see how capitals are used to start sentences, spaces are used to separate words, and punctuation is used to build sentences. This also is done in the context of "natural" sentences, not in isolation. The goal is not that students master the elements of sentence form. Instead, this preliminary work with sentence composing will help the students expand the depth and scope of the reading/writing association process.

In Phase III, as in the preceding phases, the teacher should say the name of each letter as he or she writes it on the chart paper. Students should be encouraged, but not pressured or required, to say letters they know or hear. Gradually, most students will learn to spell key components within words as well as entire words.

PHASE IV

Questions & Answers—Lessons 141–180 Phase IV chart development is the same as in the previous three Phases with the exception of the sentences at the bottom of the chart paper. The emphasis changes from writing any sentences to writing one question and its answer on the chart. This change in emphasis helps the students distinguish between questions and answers. Figure 2-5 is an example of a chart completed during Phase IV.

Many students, even those older than the kindergarten-aged child, have difficulty asking questions. Many of their responses to discussions are centered around "telling a story" about themselves or merely relating facts. During Phase IV the students will learn how to ask a variety of questions—using the "Who, What, When, Where, Why, and How" format—and learn how to respond directly to these questions. This activity will help the students develop good thinking skills and see how the structure of the sentence is changed when asking and answering questions. The teacher may also point out the difference between fact and opinion when answering questions.

Figure 2-4

PHASE III PICTURES AND WORDS CHART

Frog Pond

little bird

flying bug

2 eyes

tall trees

swamp water

spotted frog

lily pads

yellow flower

mouth   feet

The frog is sitting on a lily pad in the swamp. He is going to eat the bug.

Figure 2-5

PHASE IV PICTURES AND WORDS CHART

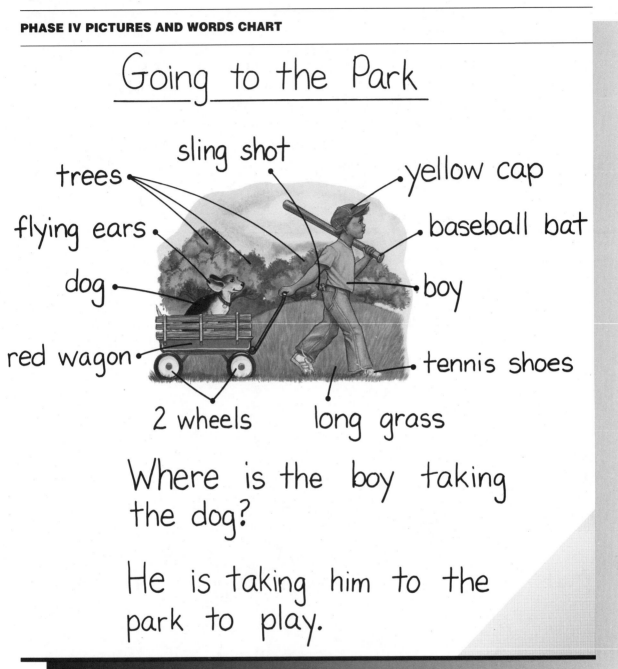

Going to the Park

- sling shot
- trees
- yellow cap
- flying ears
- baseball bat
- dog
- boy
- red wagon
- 2 wheels
- long grass
- tennis shoes

Where is the boy taking the dog?

He is taking him to the park to play.

After the chart labeling process is complete, the teacher can direct the class into forming a question about the picture. For example, if the students have labeled a picture about a boy fishing from a boat, the teacher might direct the class in the following manner:

Mr. Troy: Today we have been talking about a boy who was fishing. Let's count the number of fish the boy has caught. Can anyone in the class give me a question sentence about this?

Vickie: We could say, "How many fish did the boy catch today?"

Mr. Troy: That's a great questioning sentence, Vickie. Let's all spell the words together as I write them on the chart. Now, who would like to suggest an answer for the question?

Randy: The boy caught four fish and one got away. (The answer is then written on the chart in the same manner as the question.)

The teacher may choose to focus or guide the students into using the Comprehension Focus listed in the Lessons or allow the students to choose their own question about the picture. The teacher does need to encourage the use of a variety of question styles.

▶ Materials

Teachers will need the following materials for the Pictures and Words module: a variety of pictures, chart paper, dark-colored felt pens, and a chart rack.

THE PICTURE COLLECTION

Choosing the pictures Pictures used on the daily chart can come from a wide variety of places. Generally, teachers should choose pictures that are large, that contain many details, and whose content is clear and familiar to the students. In addition to magazine pictures, newspapers, catalogs, posters, advertisements, calendars, photographs, napkins, discarded textbooks and teachers manuals, and book jackets are good sources.

SUCCESS teachers have also had some very interesting Pictures and Words lessons using "real" objects. One SUCCESS teacher used a cereal box glued to a piece of chart paper to label. This activity integrated a health unit that the class was studying on food groups. Another teacher used the lid of a game box. The discussion that accompanied the labeling process encouraged students to share how to play the game.

For some lessons the teacher can draw the picture or begin a picture and have the students complete the drawing during the labeling process. Students' drawings or other artwork can also be used for the Pictures and Words lesson.

One teacher could not find a single picture of a toy that was large enough for the entire class to view easily from a distance. He chose to glue a collage of smaller pictures of several different kinds of toys on the chart. He then displayed the chart for a sufficient time prior to the lesson so that the students could note the details of the picture. This helped the students participate in the discussion later.

Occasionally, teachers allow students to choose a picture. If one student has been named "Student of the Week," he or she might be given the opportunity to choose a picture. When a child has been on a trip and brought back a picture, map, or souvenir, that item can be used for the lesson.

*T*he Picture/Word module [now the Pictures and Words module] works best for me because I teach four-year-olds, and it is a much easier concept for them to grasp. They don't write very well, but they quickly catch on to the words associated with the pictures. They love it!

Frances R. Hamilton, teacher

CHART PAPER

Chart paper comes in a variety of types and weights. The common types available through school supply companies are lined, unlined, loose pages, and tablets. The type of paper is determined by the personal choice of the teacher. One piece of chart paper is used for each Pictures and Words lesson.

FELT PENS

The teacher can use either washable or permanent ink felt pens. Permanent ink markers are preferable when using pictures that are laminated or have a glossy coating, because the ink will not bead up on the picture. Permanent ink can be removed from laminated pictures by spraying inexpensive hairspray on the picture and wiping it off. This will enable teachers to re-use a favorite or hard-to-find picture.

Charts should always be legible from a distance. For that reason, dark-colored felt pens such as blue, black, brown, green, red, and purple are preferred. Light colors tend to bleach out and become difficult to read.

CHART RACKS

Chart racks can be used to store charts after they have been displayed on the wall. One SUCCESS teacher likes to place tabs on the side of her charts. The tabs contain the chart title or main idea. This is helpful when she tries to locating a specific chart.

Julia Dearinger

▶
Summary

The Pictures and Words module provides kindergarten children the opportunity to enhance their oral language, build comprehension skills, increase their vocabulary about a wide range of topics, correlate the reading and writing process, build questioning and answering skills, and reinforce the letter formations and letter names. This is accomplished in a positive setting with the children and teacher working together. Every student, regardless of his or her developmental capabilities, is able to participate in the lesson and have a feeling of success.

Chapter 3 The Storytime Module

SUCCESS teachers want students to love to read. They want children to consider books as a source of information, beauty, and pleasure. In the *SUCCESS in Reading and Writing* framework for kindergarten, the Storytime module provides listening and participation experiences with a large number of books from different genres. This module is a daily twenty-minute period for enjoying literature. A number of strategies are used to encourage students to explore a wide variety of fiction, poetry, and informational books in many different meaningful ways.

If you looked in on a SUCCESS classroom during the Storytime module, on most days you would see a teacher reading to the students. Students enjoy the warmth of the class and teacher sharing a book. For many this relates to happy times at home and makes adjustment to school more natural. The students who have not had these experiences with books enjoy and need this time. It is an accepted fact that reading to children positively affects learning to read and becoming a lifetime reader.

▶ Rationale for a Child-Centered Literature Experience

In the field of reading education, there is currently great emphasis encouraging teachers to work from a literature base. The children's books that are available are numerous and varied, and the quality is better than ever before. Kindergarten children are eager to use literature, and each child has varying skills and abilities that they use in responding to the literature.

For example, after hearing the story of Rapunzel, John and Shawn built a bright red castle three feet high. They built it around a box so Rapunzel wouldn't fall down when it caved in. Lee, on the other hand, built her castle by herself. Hers had pink tissue curtains and roses "floating" in the blue crayoned moat. Four other students worked together to build a one-dimensional wall with string-controlled moveable parts.

In another classroom, these children might have colored, cut out, and glued a blackline-master castle. However, in this SUCCESS classroom, they are free to respond to the story in any manner that they wish.

▶ Procedures

The Storytime module consists of two parts: Read-Aloud, when the teacher selects a story and reads it to the class, and the Discussion Focus, when the teacher and students talk about and respond to the story.

READ-ALOUD

During Storytime the teacher selects a book or story and reads it to the class. The children are seated on the floor or at the tables, watching and listening. The teacher and children comment about the story. Sometimes,

Anthony Pfingston

according to the teacher's plan or in response to "Read it again!", the teacher re-reads the story before starting the discussion or an activity.

DISCUSSION FOCUS

The Discussion Focus of the Storytime module suggests a topic for a conversation between the students and teacher each day. The most frequent type of discussion focus suggested is an informal conversation to help students understand a book more fully. These conversations are intended to enhance the child's enjoyment of books. Children bring their interpretations of the stories or facts they have heard to the group, and everyone learns.

The opportunity to talk about books from different aspects over a period of time is sure to heighten students' awareness of different points of view. Hopefully young children will begin to make connections between these ways of looking at books with others and:

- responding as a group: predicting outcomes; participating in the reading of the story; and sharing relevant ideas and experiences
- looking at books alone and responding personally
- communicating with others as a *result* of these ways of responding

Figure 3-1 lists the different Discussion Focus topics that are covered during the school year. There is a Discussion Focus for each of the books listed in the booklist for this module (see the Appendix).

The suggested Discussion Focus is optional as are the specific books listed for a certain day or lesson. SUCCESS teachers enjoy reading and want to be sure that the desire to follow "a plan" does not become more important than meeting the needs and interests of *this* class . . . *this* year.

▶ A Sample Storytime Lesson

The following examples from Lessons 96–100 show how one teacher, Mrs. Hartling, interpreted and implemented the different activities in this module.

During Storytime for Lesson 96, the teacher shared *Chicken Soup With Rice*, a book of seasonal rhymes written and illustrated by Maurice Sendak. The suggested Discussion Focus is: "Children with December birthdays name things they heard in the December verse." The teacher repeated the exercise using several other months (one from each season at least). Several of the children noticed that the book was by the author of one of their favorites, *Where the Wild Things Are*. Louise and Shawn asked the teacher to read the book again. Mrs. Hartling asked all the children with summer birthdays to raise their hands. She re-read the rhymes for June, July, and August. The children chose December next, and those with December birthdays shared stories. The same procedure was followed for several other verses from the book.

Lesson 98 follows with a book related to the Writing module's current five-day dinosaur theme. Two books are suggested in the lesson, and Mrs.

Figure 3-1

Discussion Focus Topics

action words	animals	cause/effect
colors	descriptions	five senses
describing words	humor	funny words/phrases
important events	living things	emotions/feelings
number	objects	comparing characters
opposites	pattern	places
seasons	sequence	prior knowledge
shapes	sizes	rhyming words
sounds	time	characters

Hartling decided to use Byron Barton's colorful book *Dinosaurs, Dinosaurs*.

> **Mrs. Hartling:** This is another book by Byron Barton. Do you remember *I Want to Be an Astronaut?*
> **Aaron:** Yes, but the astronaut book was blue.
> **Erik:** That book says dinosaur! It has a *D*!
> **Mrs. Hartling:** Right! We can read this one together.

Mrs. Hartling read the book through once. The children were "wiggly" so she disregarded the suggested discussion focus and read the book again. During the second reading she asked the children to stand up each time they heard the word dinosaur. The class had a great time because the brightly colored book had the word *dinosaur* on every page and twice in a row at the end.

Lesson 99 features *The Mixed-Up Chameleon* by Eric Carle. The discussion focus is "Can we find real animals in this book?" The teacher read the book. She had chart paper ready to tally the real and make-believe animals. She saved the chart to put in this classroom's reading area along with a few paperback copies of the book.

For Lesson 100 Mrs. Hartling decided to combine the Writing module activity and the presentation of another Byron Barton book. She read the suggested book, *Bones, Bones, Dinosaur Bones*. She decided to delete the discussion focus: "Compare present-day animal sizes to dinosaur sizes. How do we know how big dinosaurs probably were?" She included the focus as she circulated around the classroom while the students were working. For several weeks the children had brought the chicken bones that have been washed, dried, and saved for this day. The children built their own dinosaurs using the bones and clay. Some children used invented spelling to write about their creations. Mrs. Hartling moved about the room helping and having conversations with children. Many of the students gave their dinosaurs a name and labeled them for a class display.

▶ Varying the Storytime Lessons

The following examples show ways that SUCCESS teachers can develop their students' appreciation and understanding of books. All of these types of activities are either suggested in the Lessons or are options for using books during Storytime. Teachers may use any of these to vary the module approach and give children with different learning styles an opportunity to feel successful.

SHARED BOOK READING

During shared book reading, students gather close to the teacher and follow along visually and perhaps verbally with the story. Books with large type or "big books" might be used. The teacher or a child might track the text with a pointer. One variation is to use portions of a favorite story or poem displayed in a pocket chart. Words from the current Pictures and Words chart could also be shared again on a pocket chart.

PARTICIPATORY READING

When using this variation, the teacher or the children choose a book that has repeated patterns, predictable language, refrains, or words that could be read or emphasized in some way. Students join in on certain words, refrains, or patterns. The best application of this would be a strategy decided upon by the students or one that is a natural outcome of the response of the class to the selection.

Mr. Conner has chosen to read *Once a Lullabye* to his class. He likes the illustrations and, if none of the children respond to the repeated refrain, he may decide to call attention to the interesting wallpaper patterns that change according to the animal featured on each page.

> **Mr. Conner:** (finishing a page) Once I was a little sheep, BAA, I fell asleep (turning the page). What animal do you see here? Say it with me.
> **All:** Once I was a little pig, baby pig, little pig. Once I was a little pig. OINK, I fell asleep.

Mr. Conner then asks if anyone would like to tell the class what to say on the next page. A student volunteers, and then most of the class joins in for the rest of the book. The basic refrain for the book is written on the chalkboard with blank spaces where the animals' names were.

> **Mr. Conner:** Could we put in an animal that wasn't in the book?
> **Clara:** Could we use a ghost? (Mr. Conner replies affirmatively and writes "ghost" in the blank space.)
> **Nick:** Let's put in other Halloween guys! How about a skeleton?
> **Mr. Conner:** Great idea, Nick! First we need something for Clara's ghost to say in this bottom space. Any ideas?

All: BOO!

Mr. Connor: Is that O.K. with you, Clara?

Clara: Yes, and I can spell Boo! *B O O . . .*

The class makes a list of some Halloween creatures they'd like to draw for a Halloween book in the manner of the story just read. They make plans for a class book to share with parents at an upcoming Halloween party.

PARTNER READING

I feel my students gain everything from SUCCESS. SUCCESS is a super way to teach because it acknowledges that each child is on a different level and then builds on what he or she knows. SUCCESS believes each child can succeed, and so do I.

Chris Seale, teacher

After hearing a story or part of a story, students might have ten or fifteen minutes of time for enjoying books on their own. The organization of this time will depend on the nature of the class and teacher preference. SUCCESS teachers value the chance students have to share their pleasure in a special book with a partner or a small group. They also want children to have the freedom of an independent choice. The student has to choose for himself or herself and not be influenced by another's preference, even if that person is a favorite friend.

Partner reading could also follow a brief "commercial" for a book or group of books. For example, the teacher might highlight a selection of titles by Donald Crews. A child might share one of the books by reading a page or showing a favorite picture.

John: I like this picture because those trains look like they're moving.

Torie: Yeah, and that color train had two words I know!

Mrs. Kraus: I have another book by Donald Crews that shows something moving. John would you like to choose someone to go to the back table with you? You can look for some more pages to show us.

John: Yes! Can I choose Allison? Come on Allison!

John and Allison: It's going so fast it looks dizzy!

Mrs. Kraus: I think Donald Crews would be very happy to hear you say that. I read that he really likes to have people hear the sounds or see the movement in the pictures he makes for books. Today we have some Donald Crews books from the library. Choose a partner you think you can work with and we'll share the books. Of course, you can look at any other books in our room if you want.

In this classroom the Crews books would be distributed to the partners on the spot. Other children would then select their own books and read or look at their choices without disturbing others.

If only a small collection of books by an author is available, a class can still learn about these important people. The class could be divided into cooperative groups. Some groups could work with books by the designated author. The remaining groups might look at other books. After a brief time the teacher could ask the groups to exchange reading materials.

Figure 3-2

READING AREA

Another option which can be used is a tub or table for the books by a specific author. After reading the day's selection, the teacher distributes the special books to several children. These students look at the books and return them to the "author table" or pass them to another child. Not a speck of dust will gather on these books until all students have seen them.

DRAMATIC PLAY

Poems or stories read to the class would be dramatized informally. A simplified version of reader's theater could also be tried. Most students would be retelling parts of the story rather than actually reading. This approach gives children lots of opportunities to think about sequence and important events and characters. There are many new, beautifully illustrated picture books in which the majority of words in the text are the words to familiar songs. These books have lots of possibilities for drama and puppets of all kinds.

WORD STUDY

The teacher reads the selected story once. He or she might call attention to some category of words in the book. If the children are interested, the teacher asks some of them to contribute words, writing some of these words on the chalkboard to show how they look when written. During a second reading the children might listen for those specific words. The intent of this strategy is to increase awareness of certain kinds of vocabulary or patterns, not to teach mastery of the group of words.

Ms. Morgan has just read *King Bidgood's in the Bathtub* to the class. She asks the group if anyone knows what a "court" is. Chris and Jacob know that a court is for playing tennis. J. T. has seen "Night Court" on television. Hannah suggests a "court" of milk. Ms. Morgan praises Hannah for noticing how much the word "court" sounds like "quart." She re-reads the page in the book where the word "court" is written. Then the class discusses who is in this kind of court and which characters were in the book about King Bidgood.

The exchange in this example was brief, but it proves that it is possible to "teach" some vocabulary in a very short mini-lesson while not detracting from a story that all children seem to love.

EXTENSION ACTIVITIES

Extension activities can include eating a treat related to the book read that day, playing a game, or making an easy craft item to remind the students about the story read. The activity or craft needs to be simple and brief, as time is limited in a twenty-minute module. The extension activity ideas can come from the children. Students hearing the same selection will respond in many ways, and these ideas can be shared.

Mr. Dean used one type of extension activity in his class. He knew that the children in his kindergarten SUCCESS class would enjoy Chris Van Allsburg's *Polar Express*. When he finished the story he simply handed each student a small shiny jingle bell to take home. Many children in the class retold the story to someone that evening!

Kyle Poston

Treats and gimmicks should be used only occasionally. When they are used, the focus may be something other than a material object or a complicated project. One teacher excused her class for recess one or two at a time as she read, "Wild Things, rolling their terrible eyes," or "gnashing their terrible teeth." After reading *Holes and Peeks* by Ann Jonas, another teacher punched holes in file cards to peek through. Partners went off around the room to observe familiar places and objects through their "peeks."

BOOK CENTERS

On some days a teacher might observe a variety of book-related center activities. For example, he or she might see a visiting parent at a table sharing a "big book" with four children. In another area of the classroom, the teacher assistant helps six students with their lines in preparation for a "Pre-reader's" theater presentation of *Jessie Bear, What Will You Wear?* Two boys have a copy of James Marshall's *Goldilocks* and a basket of props to help them carry out their imaginative play. Justin, Andy, and Melissa are painting a picture of Winnie-the-Pooh, which they plan to label and share with the class. The library assistant has come to the classroom to share the reference book requested by a small group. Together they will look for a picture of Tomie dePaola for the bulletin board they are making. The teacher is free to move about the room observing, helping, and facilitating a smooth operation. A good way to begin using book centers is to start with one center carefully modeled, then add others later. Other teachers may wish to use one center (which is changed frequently) to feature books by one author or a grouping of books on the Writing theme.

▶ The Role of the Teacher

FACILITATOR

The teacher in a kindergarten SUCCESS classroom facilitates a lot of reading among his or her students by modeling. The teacher reads for pleasure when the children have free reading time. The teacher shares books with students on a one-to-one basis. The teacher sincerely enjoys reading to the class and shows it. The teacher also deliberately models care for books. There is even a first-aid kit for books in the classroom.

The teacher fills the room (and each day) with current and familiar fiction and nonfiction books, poetry, book characters, authors, and illustrators. Literature is used throughout the day, not just during the Storytime lesson.

SUCCESS teachers challenge themselves to learn about a wider variety of books which will enable them to help children enjoy reading. These teachers try to make good use of the expertise of the school library facilities and publications. They involve the school librarian with the students in selecting books for the class and in searching for information about authors as well.

Exploring the different areas of literature is worth the time involved. Reading nonfiction and poetry for children is important to SUCCESS teachers as readiness for writing as well as for the pleasure of hearing and sharing the language. An excellent range of nonfiction books and ideas is included in Dr. Beverly Kobin's book on nonfiction, *Eyeopeners!*

Kindergartners are interested in the real world, and many of the lesson topics can be enhanced by the use of carefully selected nonfiction. Kindergarten students can look at several different nonfiction books on a subject, do research, and make a picture report.

Reading *Pass the Poetry Please!* by Lee Bennett Hopkins or any book on sharing poems with children, such as the wonderful *Climb into the Bell Tower* by Myra Cohn Livingston, inspires teachers to take time to share a "poetry break" with students. Perhaps, when the class hamster dies, the teacher needs to read aloud that certain short poem from *Everett*

*M*y students gain a positive attitude about the reading and writing process. They learn to read through the discovery method. Many times they don't even realize what they have learned because it is such a natural process. To them reading and writing experiences are fun!

Patricia Reinheimer, teacher

Anderson's Goodbye. It doesn't take long to find an appropriate selection if he or she is familiar with poetry resources. Adults owe children the chance to consider poetry a part of life.

Good audio and video versions of many children's stories are abundant. It is important to preview these materials. Many children's book dealers have copies to preview. SUCCESS teachers want to use the best available version of a poem or story with their classes.

Resources such as the National Children's Book Council, The American Library Association, the National Council of Teachers of English, and the International Reading Association all have excellent information and materials relating to literature for children. Two excellent magazines on children's literature that school libraries often subscribe to are *The Horn Book* and *The New Advocate.* Best of all is the hands-on research you can do at bookstores for children, book fairs, conferences, and children's sections of public libraries.

OBSERVER

The teacher observes, records, and evaluates progress. The kindergarten teacher is usually directly involved in sharing and interacting with children about the selection during Storytime. He or she can record any general observations on a clipboard, providing a series of brief anecdotal records. The teacher writes down (when possible) the times that a child uses reference material. He or she observes when the class has free choice time, noticing when students visit the library corner and the choices that they make. The teacher remembers to make a brief note that Andy stopped building his rocket to come over and hear a poem about dragons. When Meriel retells the entire plot of *Lyle and the Birthday Party* to Robert at recess, the teacher jots it on a Post-it Note™ to attach to the clipboard notes. These observations are made quickly and simply and are very useful when recalling evidence of a student's progress and interests. (See Chapter 6 for more information on clipboard notes.)

COMMUNICATOR

Teachers let parents know what's happening at school. They might use a weekly or monthly class newspaper to "advertise" the author of the week or to publish a dictated "book report." A small booklet, including an author's photograph, encourages the child to introduce the author or illustrator as a real person to those at home. "Book favors" are a great way to encourage students to retell favorite stories heard at school. Making mini-books with words or pictures from a book read in school also promotes sharing. The teacher can encourage students to take books home to share.

Teachers encourage parents to participate with their children in enjoyment of books at home. They encourage parents to volunteer to come and read to small groups or individuals. One SUCCESS teacher features each child's family one time during the year, and often a parent will come and read to the class.

▶ Classroom Organization

A SUCCESS classroom is a place where all kinds of reading materials are appealingly displayed and where there are places to explore books. A library corner that affords comfort, relative privacy, and space for display and storage with easy access encourages children to spend free time with books. Some teachers define this space with shelves, a sofa, or a special book display area. Props for story play and stuffed animals to read to promote enjoyment and sharing about books. Floor pillows and baskets for books of different categories can be as attractive and functional as the most expensive commercial furniture. One teacher designated an inviting reading area with a simple fabric canopy hanging over a bright rug which gave the effect of going into a small room within a room.

Organization of books, rules for use of materials, and checking materials out to take home depend upon the school library policies and the preference of the teacher. He or she should allow students to take part in the planning, book selection, and caring for the center. Children who are involved know how and where to find the materials they want. They choose the book area more often because they are familiar with the materials and are comfortable there.

▶ What if I Don't Have These Books?

This book's Appendix contains a list of the books suggested in the Lessons. These are only a few of the many familiar and recent selections appropriate for kindergarten. Often more than one selection is listed. Hopefully, your library will have at least one of these books. If none of the suggested books is available, another can easily be substituted.

Many of the books listed are available in an enlarged format. These are called "big books." Big books with large print and predictable outcomes

Noorez Lalani

are published especially for use with groups. Many of these are useful in providing a variety of approaches during Read-Aloud. The quality of illustrations and content varies in these books, so careful selection is important.

The books on the list are, in true SUCCESS form, suggestions. There are enough wonderful, well-written, well-illustrated books for children out in the world (that are not even on this list) to choose one (or more) to share with a class every day for several years. The lessons include blank lines for you to add the selections that you find work well with your class.

▶ How Many Books Should I Read?

SUCCESS teachers read more than once a day. They integrate wonderful books into the other SUCCESS modules and into other curriculum areas. They work on being flexible enough to take advantage of a "literature moment," and they are also prepared to read aloud to children on a regular daily basis. These teachers value reading to students so highly that they usually read aloud to all or part of the class three or four times a day. These time periods are often very short—just enough time, perhaps, for a poem from Caroline Bauer's *Poems for a Rainy Day* when the sky suddenly turns dark gray, or for a page from *Ramona the Pest* when someone complains about having to share with an older brother or sister.

The selection does not have to be a picture book. It is not necessary to read an entire book or to use just one book. Two books can be a basis for comparison in story, theme, or illustration. What matters is that each student has enjoyable experiences and an incentive to return to books on his or her own.

▶ Summary

For most teachers the Storytime module is an enjoyable part of the day. *SUCCESS in Reading and Writing* teachers want their students to have many positive experiences with books early in their school careers. Two factors, the classroom environment and the teacher modeling a love for literature, have primary importance in the school setting. These, along with the natural enthusiasm of young children and the wealth of wonderful books available today, make this module an especially exciting time for teachers and students.

SUCCESS classrooms are child-centered classrooms. They are full of eager learners who know and enjoy literature. SUCCESS students are familiar with book characters and authors. Many children in a kindergarten SUCCESS class can retell favorite stories they have heard. A few of the students can already read. Others are just beginning to learn that books are a source of pleasure and information. All of the children in SUCCESS classrooms are a part of the reading world.

Chapter **4** The Writing Module

What to talk about or draw or write about is not a problem for most five- or six-year olds—writing is natural for young children. Consequently, communication and expression happen comfortably in a kindergarten classroom where children are encouraged to interact and explore.

The kindergarten Writing module incorporates oral language and developmental writing, giving students many opportunities to share their thoughts orally, both with a group and with individuals. The module also gives students opportunities to write down those thoughts and ideas for others to read.

▶ Rationale

Much has happened in the area of children's writing in recent years. Public attention has been directed to children's writing from educational and commercial sources. Developmental writing by kindergarten students is much nearer to being the norm than the exception. Schools implement "writing plans" and parents read about expectations for children's writing curricula in newsstand magazines. The exciting part of this change is that children are being given the opportunity and encouragement to write every day.

Lucy Calkins, Donald Graves, Nancie Atwell, and others have been adding to the body of literature about children's writing, and their works have greatly influenced this edition of *SUCCESS in Beginning Reading and Writing*. Following are some of the principles and practices defined by current researchers in the field of process writing on which the Writing module is based.

STUDENTS NEED TIME TO WRITE

All students need time to write, and kindergarten is the time to begin. By this time, many children have been writing in their own way for some time. Thinking and talking about writing; making scribbles; drawing pictures of the circus they visited; writing on clay with a plastic spoon; writing notes to friends; making a list of items needed in the classroom; making a poster for the puppet show or a sign for the store—there is time in the SUCCESS framework for children to do writing activities for at least twenty minutes every day. Children will also have opportunities for writing in the other modules besides Writing. The teacher should take every opportunity to involve children in the writing necessary for classroom operation, such as notes, signs, directions, and labels.

STUDENTS NEED VARIED EXAMPLES OF WRITING

The books in the kindergarten classroom are models for writing and of authorship. Children's books, books made by individual students, and class books are all influential in beginning writing and reading. Books

Douglas Kiger

made by the teacher or older students can be fine models for kindergartners. Above all, there should be a balance of books from all the different genres in children's literature. (See the Appendix for a selected list of excellent books for kindergarten-aged children.)

STUDENTS NEED MATERIALS AND A PLACE TO WORK

Specific materials for this module are described near the end of this chapter. The important thing about these materials is variety. With a variety of pens, pencils, markers and papers, children can try different ways of making their mark in the classroom. A special place to work is nice but not a necessity. The freedom to obtain materials and the freedom of choosing a place to work facilitates risk-taking for a young writer.

STUDENTS NEED A PLACE TO KEEP THEIR WRITING PROJECTS

Each child should have a folder for storing his or her writing projects. These folders should be easily accessible. Children should be able to continue working on a project that is unfinished. They should also have ready access to look at and share what they have done or are working on.

STUDENTS SHOULD HAVE AN OPPORTUNITY TO SHARE THEIR WRITING

There is a short time built into the Writing module for some students to share each day. It is important to assure students that everyone who wishes to share will be able to. From time to time the teachers can point out that there is an opportunity to share if those who wish to show their work can take turns. Avoiding a regular time for "turns" maintains spontaneity.

KINDERGARTEN STUDENTS SHOULD HAVE A CHANCE TO PUBLISH OCCASIONALLY

Publishing a kindergarten student's work can be as easy or as demanding as the teacher chooses to make it. Space for all to put their labeled drawings on a bulletin board is one way of publishing that requires very little teacher effort. Class books are another way to publish written work. Making class books is a suggested activity for several writing projects listed in the Lessons.

Some SUCCESS teachers make enough class books during the year to enable every child to choose one to keep at the end of kindergarten. Some teachers and their students publish a weekly or monthly newsletter. Both the actual making of the newsletter and the showcase it provides for student writing is a great source of parent information and interest.

STUDENTS NEED AN AUDIENCE

Students will have an opportunity to share with their peers every day in some way. Some will share with the whole group. In an average-sized class this can happen once a week for each child. Every day students will share with their peers in small groups and with their teacher as she or he moves about the classroom.

In every school situation there are opportunities for drafting an audience for writers, and older children, especially, often enjoy listening to younger students. Also, among a school's personnel, there are often able, caring people who can make a real difference for certain children.

Parents can help develop their kindergartner's self-esteem by setting aside time to share the materials each week and showing that they value these beginning efforts. It is suggested that the child's Writing projects be taken home on the fifth day of the theme cycle. Parents can also encourage their young writers by providing a place to display writing, showing an accepting attitude toward early efforts, and encouraging a child to find a wider audience by mailing a story or picture to a relative.

▶ General Procedures

The SUCCESS kindergarten Writing module has four parts: a suggested theme, which changes every five days; an introduction to the theme, when the teacher and class have a conversation about the theme; a writing activity based on the theme; and a sharing period, when students share what they have written or drawn with another person.

SUCCESS is effective because it uses ideas from the children's worlds and their vocabulary. It also allows the teacher to pull in skills relevant to the ideas and things the children want to talk about and are interested in.

Kristie Brown, teacher

The themes included in this book are based on activities selected and enjoyed by teachers and children in SUCCESS classes. The topics are planned to include many typical kindergarten areas of interest and to suggest integrating other curriculum areas with SUCCESS in Reading and Writing. The Appendix of this book contains a list of the Lessons' suggested themes and a list of alternatives. Teachers may change the suggested theme if it is not appropriate for a particular situation or group; above all, the teacher should select a theme that his or her class will be comfortable expressing their own ideas about. The next step is for students to observe their ideas and the ideas of others in writing. SUCCESS kindergarten teachers encourage children to draw or write in their own developmentally appropriate way, whenever they can, as soon as they can.

Another consideration in teacher planning for the Writing module is the varying stages of development and progress in a kindergarten class within a given year. Based on these two factors, teachers might want to change the theme if a topic arises that is of greater immediate interest to students. Students should always have the option of writing on a topic other than the theme or continuing a project started at another time.

Figure 4-1 shows the framework for each day in a typical five-day theme cycle. The framework provides students with the security of knowing what their schedule will be rather than waiting to find out what the teacher wants each day. This security gives the students a chance to feel in control of their part of the world and to begin to develop a sense of responsibility for their own learning.

Figure 4-1

Five-Day Theme Cycle

Day 1

Introduce the suggested theme.	(5 minutes)
Students prepare their writing folders and begin writing.	(10 minutes)
Share.	(5 minutes)

Day 2 to 4

Review the theme.	(5 minutes)
Teacher discusses the theme with small groups and records while other students draw or write.	(10 minutes)
Share.	(5 minutes)

Day 5

The students participate in a culminating activity related to the suggested five-day theme.	(20 minutes)

▶ Five-Day-Cycle Lesson Procedures

DAY 1

On the first day of the five-day cycle, the teacher leads a brief conversation related to the theme, correlating both the Pictures and Words module and the Writing module. (The teacher will correlate these two modules on the first day of each five-day cycle throughout the year.) During the discussion, students or teacher may or may not choose to refer to the chart made during the Pictures and Words lesson.

The teacher then distributes letter-size, pocket-type folders to each child. These writing folders usually contain a booklet of paper to be used as a journal or writing book during the five-day cycle. There are baskets on each table with an inviting array of markers, crayons, colored pencils, and lead pencils. There are also containers of glue and glue sticks.

On this first day the teacher might encourage children to prepare their booklets by designing a cover. Some children will begin to draw a picture about the theme just introduced. Others will begin to write about the topic. If time allows, the class meets to share and discuss what they have done. Here is one example from Lesson 21, which is the first day for a theme about birds:

> **Ms. Baker (holds up Julie's folder):** Today there's something extra in your folder besides your writing booklet.
> **Kids:** What is it?
> **Ms. Baker:** There is a piece of brown paper. It's not very big but it should be big enough to make a nest to glue on the cover of your booklet.
> **Leo:** I'm going to make one like the nest on our chart and I'm drawing a robin in it.
> **Julie:** I'm going to cut it up like sticks and build a nest.
> **Sam:** I don't want a nest. I'm going to make a hawk flying.
> **Ms. Baker:** That's fine Sam, If you don't need your brown paper you can put it in the scrap basket. Let's all get started with folders now. You may write, draw, or work on your cover.

The children begin to cut and draw. Some students ignore the cover and begin to write about something related to birds. Evan, who went to the beach yesterday, is writing lines of waves.

> **Evan:** Ms. Baker, these lines say that there was a storm with really BIG waves. It was a really noisy-loud place! I found three shells!
> **Ms. Baker:** Neat, Evan. Are you going to write more?
> **Evan:** No, I'm doing a cover for my writing book.

Ms. Baker records Evan's story on a Post-it™ note and attaches it to her clipboard.

Near the end of the lesson, Ms. Baker asks several children to hold up their work. One or two students tell about their pictures. Ms. Baker comments that every one will get to share during the week. When it is time to stop, Ms. Baker helps the students put their various projects into the writing folders. The children put their folders into the plastic containers that are placed near the worktables.

Here's an example of how a discussion could be extended during Day 1 of the frog theme, which comes later in the year. Mrs. Sherman is sharing a book about a pond to introduce the Writing lesson.

Josh: I've been to a pond like that one before.
Mrs. Sherman: Did you see a frog?
Josh: I saw a lot of them . . . and I caught a big one but my dad made me put it back.
Emmy: Did it look like the one in the book?
Josh: No, it had spots, brown spots . . .
Mrs. Sherman: Can you tell us what it felt like, Josh?
Josh: It was slippery and cold . . . and wet!
Mrs. Sherman: There are lots of different kinds of frogs. This book shows some of the kinds, and Mrs. Rees (the librarian) gave us an old calendar that has twelve different frogs in it (shows a bullfrog picture).
Josh: That looks just like my frog!
Ms Sherman: Let's see what we know about frogs and make a list on the chalkboard of the the parts of a frog like the one Josh caught.
Danny: It has big eyes!
Mrs. Sherman: Great! I'll write the word "eyes."
Susan: The spots on his back are dark brown.
Mrs. Sherman: Super. This is how you write the word "spots."

Mrs. Sherman lists several more names of frog parts on the chalkboard. She then suggests to the students that they may want to draw and label a frog in their writing booklet that day. She then excuses them to begin writing.

Lesson hints Try to keep the sharing time as spontaneous as possible. This is not a question and answer session. These discussions work best when the focus is on "what" is being said rather than whose turn it happens to be. At the beginning of the year, many SUCCESS teachers make a special point to assure students that they *will* have a turn to speak if they wish. Students will learn that the turn might be today, tomorrow, or even the day after that. By the time a few weeks have passed, the children have confidence in the procedure. They will know, too, that they'll also be able to talk with their table groups and to the teacher as he or she moves about the classroom.

Dustin Adair

DAY 2

On Day 2 the teacher meets with the entire class very briefly to share something related to the theme. They continue work from Day 1 or begin a new piece of writing related to the theme. Some children work on topics unrelated to the theme.

The teacher has prepared the children to get their materials and to begin work as they are ready. He or she assists those who need help. When all of the children are settled, the teacher goes to a small group of children and has a two- to five-minute conversation related to the theme. During this time the teacher records at least one word (on a sentence strip or piece of paper) that each student in the group has chosen. The student's name and the date are written on the card. As the conversation ends, the children add their words to a display focused on the week's topic. The teacher continues meeting with small groups during the writing time and repeats this procedure.

The other students continue to draw or write during this time. If there is a teacher assistant or a parent helper available, those children who are reluctant to use invented spelling might dictate their stories or receive help labeling their picture. Near the end of the lesson the students meet briefly to allow several children to share.

Following is an example of how one SUCCESS teacher began Day 2 of the bird theme: Several of the children wanted to share what they had done during Writing time on the first day. The teacher capitalized on this opportunity for some students to have an audience for their writing. Some children shared their own topics. The teacher used some shared examples to re-focus the class on the bird theme.

> **Mrs. Jones:** Who would like to share something you did yesterday?
>
> **Jill:** I made a picture of my doll Ann and I wrote all about her. It's a book!

Jill proudly shares her piece of writing. Martin holds up his cut-out of a bird and a cage. He has labeled the cage and written a sentence by it which he shares.

> **Mrs. Jones:** Your story really tells a lot about birds.
>
> **Martin:** I have a Budgie at home. We let him fly around sometimes. His name is Ben. This is a picture of Ben. I'm going to glue it in my booklet.
>
> **Robert:** My brother found this bird's nest. I drew a bird to put in it. Here's a sign for her. Molly made some blue eggs for the nest.
>
> **Mrs. Jones:** Thanks for sharing your story Martin. Robert, you and Molly can put the nest on our bird table.

The class spends the writing time working on their stories and pictures. Robert and Molly decide to make a sign for the bird display table. Later Mrs. Jones says: "There won't be time to share today, but right now you can each hold up your bird booklet so we can see everyone's cover."

Lesson hints Early in the school year, some teachers put each student's name and the date on the cards to be used for the oral language groups that meet with the teacher. This saves time and also helps the teacher remember who has had a turn. Then the teacher can encourage students who are able to do their own writing as soon as possible.

DAY 3

The format of the lesson on Day 3 is the same as for Day 2. The following example shows how a teacher might vary the brief introduction to Writing time by using the words generated in class groups on Day 2.

The children are seated on the floor near the display area on birds. The teacher is holding one of the word cards made during one of the small group oral language times the day before.

> **Mrs. Conner:** Do any of you see this word anywhere else here?
>
> **Louise:** There it is, three ... No! four times! I think it is "wings"!

Mrs. Conner: Louise! And "wing" wasn't even the word I wrote for you. What was your word?

Louise: I said robin, "The Robin." It's the title.

Mrs. Conner: Does anyone see any other words that are alike?

Several other children call out words. The teacher and students comment on these and then the students leave to begin their regular writing activities.

In Mrs. Strand's class next door, during Day 3 of the money theme (lesson 83), the lesson begins with a few frames from a filmstrip about money. The students discuss what they might write about. Mrs. Strand then checks to see if any children have problems getting started with their writing activity. She then meets with four to six students to discuss the theme using the filmstrip information to start the discussion. A brief conversation follows, during which Mrs. Strand encourages the students to do their own writing, which will go on the papers that are put up in the theme display area. She meets with another group of students, follows the same procedure as before, and posts that group's responses to share. She has time to help individuals and to make a quick list of the students she will meet with on the next day. She is pleased because it seems that there will be time to gather in the display area to share some of the children's contributions.

DAY 4

The format for the introduction and student activities is the same as on Days 2 and 3. In one SUCCESS classroom, Mrs. Murray has brought *The Eyewitness Book of Birds* to read to the class to introduce the bird theme on Day 4. She shows and reads to the class only the part about feathers. She also had many interesting feathers in a basket that is passed around to touch, look at, and discuss. Some of the children chose to draw and write about feathers during their Writing time.

DAY 5

On the fifth day of the theme, the students participate in a culminating activity. The activities suggested in the Lessons are a starting point for the teacher. He or she is encouraged to change the activities to suit the interests and talents of the students. Often the students will have excellent ideas of how they would like to spend the last day of a theme. The suggested lesson for the fifth day in the cycle on birds involves dramatizing a book. Other teachers may choose to visit a nearby pet store to see different kinds of birds, add feathers to a clay bird, make nests from scraps and twigs, or go "bird watching" around the school. The teacher may need to allot more than twenty minute for some culminating activities.

On the last day of the writing topic, the students take home their word cards, writing journal or booklet, and any related projects or materials that they may have stored in their folders or display area.

SUCCESS adds variety and puts pleasure back in teaching. I have been able to reach all children through this approach. My students gain better language development, self-esteem and have become better readers than I thought possible.

Martha Cobb, teacher

The following example shows how a teacher could adapt a lesson to feature words suggested by the students when they meet with the teacher in small groups. On the last day of a topic, the word cards put up by groups of students are usually removed from the bulletin board. Some teachers use a short period of time to share the word cards.

Mrs. Murray directs the children's attention to the words about "castles and dragons" that they have volunteered during the week.

Mrs. Murray: Does anyone want to find a word to tell us about?

Sam: I know one! Here's "moat." They build the moat to keep bad guys out.

Molly: That was my word too. It was on the board three times.

Mrs. Murray: Great! Let's put all these cards together over here. Are there any other words you'd like to choose?

Greg: This moat is a part of the castle and so is a tower. I want to put the tower card up over there.

Molly: We could put all the castle words over there.

Mrs. Murray: Does everyone like that idea?

The class responds favorably. They find all of the words that stand for parts of a castle. Mrs. Murray suggests that the students try to use those words to label the castle that some children painted earlier. They vote to leave the words up for a few more days because the castle is on the wall near the writing center in this classroom and many children have not finished their stories and pictures. When the teacher takes the castle down, the students will take their personal words home to share. (Usually the word cards go home on the last day of the five-day cycle.)

The Appendix contains a list of the suggested fifth-day closure activities that are included in the Lessons.

▶ Some Concerns

"INVENTED SPELLING"

Invented spelling has become one of the main strategies that teachers use to encourage children to put their thoughts on paper. Students can use invented spelling to get their thoughts down faster when they work on rough drafts. For example, a student writing about her new kitten wants to write a word to describe the kitten. She writes down whatever sound she hears in the word she wants to use. In this way, she and other kindergarten students are willing to make their mark without worrying about correct spelling and other mechanics. The more they write or draw, and express themselves on paper, the more confidence they develop as writers.

In the SUCCESS kindergarten Writing module, children's own invented version of conventional spelling is encouraged and accepted. Invented spelling puts the child more in control of his or her own written communication, and SUCCESS teachers recommend this method to children.

Teacher decisions are an important part of encouraging the children to use this strategy while writing. The first decision involves whether a teacher will ask a child to edit his or her own invented spelling, either for publication or for helping the child remember the word later. Some teachers have children edit anything that will be made public. Some teachers write the standard spelling of a child's invented spelling at the bottom of the page or on a note that they attach to the page. Other teachers leave children's invented spellings untouched. Above all, SUCCESS teachers are honest with students about the fact that invented spelling is "for our class to understand. It helps us put our ideas down on paper." They praise the children for their attempts and support the control children gain over their own writing.

Some teachers feel that displaying invented spelling requires an explanation. One teacher might post a sign on a bulletin board that says "Kindergarten Stories Written with Our Own Invented Spelling," while another will be comfortable without a label. Each teacher makes this decision based on what is appropriate for his or her students.

For various reasons, there are always children who are reluctant to risk using invented spelling. Some children will not write unless they know that their words are spelled correctly. SUCCESS teachers honor this fact while continuing to encourage students to become more independent. These children can dictate to an adult or an older student until they gain confidence. Often the motivation comes from seeing others go ahead without needing to wait for help.

By carefully observing a student's writing strategies, the teacher becomes more aware of the child's level of development. The teacher can then work to convince the child that he or she can become more self-reliant. In this way, teachers can give children many meaningful opportunities to *need* to be more in control of their own writing. They invite children to write notes and letters to friends; they ask a child to make a list of things that the class should bring for a party; they have a child make a sign for the new class pet. The students can also use invented spelling while writing a group experience story.

In recent years many teachers and researchers on children's writing have found that there are apparent stages that many children go through if they are encouraged to use "invented spelling." In a SUCCESS classroom, these stages develop naturally as the children observe the teacher writing each student's words on the Pictures and Words chart. Regular sharing of the print in library books and the exploration of letters in the Alphabet module also promote increasing awareness of standard spelling. As the child becomes more aware, he or she views "invented spelling" as a tool. This tool puts the emphasis on the meaning of what the child has to say. The child uses what he or she knows about language, about phonics, and about the larger world to communicate.

SMALL-GROUP CONVERSATIONS

Small-group conversations occur during the first four days of each Writing theme. The teacher meets with a group of three to five students at a time for two to five minutes. He or she plans to have conversations based on the theme with several small groups during the Writing lesson. Following a brief discussion, the teacher uses a wide felt pen to write at least one word that each student has spoken on a card or piece of paper. The student's name and the date are written on the card. At the end of the conversation the children put their words on a display area designated for the current theme.

One small-group conversation might go like this: "What's that, teacher?" asks Louise.

Mr. Brown: "This is a picture I brought to show the group. It's my family. We had this picture taken together as a gift for Grandpa. Do any of you have family pictures?"

All four of the children in the group remember a family picture at home. They tell about who is in their family picture. Mr. Brown writes the name of a family member or another related word chosen by the child on a card for each student. The children proudly go off to put their personal word on the "Our Families" bulletin board.

The purpose of these short meetings is to guarantee experience with oral language and give students the opportunity to see their language written down by the teacher. All of the children in the group see that their words can be written and read by others. As the year goes on, the teacher encourages students who seem ready to write to do their own cards.

DISPLAYING THE THEME

Each week, the words, drawings, and other materials related to the week's theme should be displayed in the classrooms. The display area might be a bulletin board, which can be as elaborate as the teacher wants. One SUCCESS teacher has a student committee make a plan for the board or display area based on the current five-day theme. The children discuss the plan realistically and do the board themselves (with help as needed, of course).

A display table catches children's eyes and meets the needs of the hands-on learner. A three-dimensional space offers many opportunities for sign-making and direction cards. This functional writing can draw in the reluctant child, giving him or her security and self-esteem when he or she is the one to make the big sign, albeit one word (see Figure 4-2).

Another successful type of display for the word cards is to place them around the Pictures and Words chart done on Day 1 of the theme (see Figure 4-3).

USING THE WORD CARDS

The word cards can be useful in the classroom for word-study-type activities based on time and the children's interest. During the week chil-

Figure 4-2

The Display Area

dren who are interested in the words may want to match the cards with words on the chart. Some children may enjoy having a chance to copy words volunteered by other students. A box of paper strips, cards, or small stapled booklets will encourage this activity. Teachers can often get donations of print shop scraps, which are perfect for this use.

The few moments of "wait time" that occasionally occur in many classrooms can be put to good use also. "Does anyone see a card with a *b* word?" "Raise your hand if you see any two words that are alike." These and many other questions and statements will fill those moments and give the teacher some valuable clues to student awareness as well.

▶ Materials

JOURNALS OR WRITING BOOKLETS

To create student journals or booklets, the teacher staples together several sheets of unlined paper (about eight pages) for daily student writing and illustrating. Teachers and students enjoy having different sizes and colors of paper. This short booklet is intended to go home at the end of the five-day cycle. The teacher might make copies of certain work to save, but the purpose of students sharing with an audience is better served if the material is current.

Some kindergarten children will draw in this book every day. Other students may exhibit the early stages of invented spelling using random letters for which they have a long and complex verbal version. Some children, or groups of children, will dictate their stories to a teacher or helper. Still other children will write, illustrate, and be able to read back their pieces of writing to others. The teacher values all of these stages, and because of the flexibility of the SUCCESS framework, he or she has time to share and encourage each child.

Figure 4-3

CHART FOR DAY 1, PICTURES AND WORDS THEME

FOLDERS

The student Writing folder, which will remain at school, is a two-pocket commercial folder provided by the student (or school) to contain the work done by the student during the five-day theme cycle.

PAPER

Paper of different colors, sizes, and shapes provides a way to vary the writing experience. Many school districts or commercial print shops are willing to save the many scraps that accumulate. (This paper is often of much higher quality than usually seen in the classroom.) Some teachers like to have blank books premade or cut and ready to assemble in the Writing Center.

TOOLS FOR AUTHORS

Megan Chesser

Children will be writing for many real-life purposes in a SUCCESS kindergarten classroom. A Writing Center or supplies area should contain various sizes and colors of felt markers, pencils, colored pencils, pens, and crayons for writing and illustrating. Some teachers have these out on tables for all to use at work times. Rulers and templates of various kinds, scissors, glue, and other art materials for illustrators and book makers are an incentive for publishing. Inexpensive date stamps are also useful for young writers and publishers. A paper punch and various kinds of cord, string, and ribbon are interesting additions to the usual stapler for binding books. Commercial bookbinders—the kind with varying sizes of plastic backs—are desirable but not a necessity.

REFERENCE BOOKS

A variety of dictionaries—references, standard, picture, and initial letter type, as well as one adult volume to use as a teacher reference—is best for a kindergarten class. Collections of words around subject themes, such as *100 Words About Dinosaurs*, are also good references, and ABC books make excellent word sources.

CLASSROOM LIBRARY

We know that children come to kindergarten with varying degrees of language experience. Exposure to all sorts of good children's fiction and informational books can enhance every level of progress in communication and comprehension. The child who (during lunch count) says, "I need to go to the cemetery to get a ticket," is substituting one long word that has no particular meaning for him for another. Opportunities to hear words used in all kinds of good books as often as possible will familiarize students with more meaningful spoken and written language.

The children's books present in the classroom on a short- or long-term basis can have a profound effect on children's writing and oral expression. Collections of books, including both fiction and nonfiction which relate to the five-day theme, are very helpful and interesting both as models for good writing and as references.

▶ Summary

During the Writing lesson in one SUCCESS classroom, you might see the whole group of children and the teacher having a conversation together. They might be talking about the theme for the next five days (birds) based on the Pictures and Words chart done earlier in the day. Another teacher in another class might be talking with a group of students about birds, perhaps based on a book read to the class. Words contributed by the children and recorded by the teacher or a child would be placed on a bulletin board or in a display area featuring the bird theme. Students working independently in yet another class might be writing, dictating, or using invented spelling to write about birds or another topic of their choosing.

You would be seeing numerous writing materials. There would be time and space allotted for writing. The encouragement of a cooperative writing community (including the teacher) would be evident. You would be observing the Writing module in action.

Because *SUCCESS in Reading and Writing* is a framework for the goals of both the child and teacher, all levels of development and styles of thinking are honored. The student is in control of his writing because he or she knows that there are many options and he or she knows how to implement those options. The teacher can allow for the child who has had few language-enriching experiences at home, the five-year-old who is a self-taught reader, and the child who, despite having been read to every night, shows no interest in learning to read or write.

The SUCCESS classroom provides a combination of structure and creative flexibility. This combination can help provide an educationally sound kindergarten program which gives students opportunities to feel good about the reading and writing process in kindergarten and later in first grade. This classroom encourages the child to write in some way every day and to know the enjoyment and usefulness of writing.

Chapter 5 The Alphabet Module

The Alphabet module is a daily twenty-minute lesson that provides children with an introduction to the alphabet and various letter combinations. Children will see how letters are formed, where they are placed in words, and how written symbols associate with sounds.

During this module, children can explore the alphabet in a variety of non-threatening activities that accommodate all developmental levels of their abilities. The three types of Alphabet lessons are Brainstorming, Research, and Student Projects.

Brainstorming lessons enable the class to work together to develop an assortment of words that contain specific letters. Students are then allowed individual time to write letters, words, or pictures. Teachers use this time for individualized instruction. The papers are then filed, giving the teacher a longitudinal record of the students progress.

During Research lessons, students search in real-life materials, such as magazines and newspapers, for the specific letter(s) or related items. Research lessons allow students to apply their knowledge of the alphabet to printed material.

The third type of Alphabet lesson, Student Projects, provides children with a hands-on activity related to a letter or combination. In these lessons students use art materials to create a letter-related project that they can take home.

▶ Purpose

The purpose of the Alphabet Module is to introduce students to the written symbols of the English language—how they are formed and how they function in words. The sounds of the letters are taught in context within words in the students' vocabulary. The Alphabet module provides a framework where the reading/writing process is correlated with a student's oral language, object association, art, and literature.

Letters introduced during the Alphabet module are not intended to be mastered by each student. In SUCCESS classrooms students of all ability levels are challenged and encouraged to work to their highest capabilities. The element of pressure is removed from this program because students are not "made" to form an alphabet symbol correctly or "draw" an adult rendition of an object. Students are encouraged to use their reading skills and their understanding of letter sounds to read and write words associated with the letters. During the same lessons students who are being exposed to the alphabet for the first time are equally involved in the learning process by practicing writing individual letters or drawing objects that contain the letters. Both types of students are working at their developmental level and are successful.

While students are making choices about what they would like to write, illustrate, or create using art supplies, teachers are capitalizing on the opportunity to talk with individual children about their choices, giving each child at least one praising comment and one helping suggestion

Chapter **5**

Twelvala Robinson

about their work. Through the variety of methods used to introduce and review letters within this module and the correlations with other SUCCESS modules, the majority of the students will have mastered naming, writing, and making associations of letter sounds by the end of the school year.

▶ General Procedures

LESSON TYPES

In each lesson from 1 to 78, the class spends three days on each letter, and for each letter there are three different types of lessons: Brainstorming, Research, and Student Projects. These lesson types are repeated throughout the school year. After lesson 78, the class spends two days on each letter or sound pattern. When the cycle changes to two days, the first day is always a Brainstorming lesson. The second day is a Research *or* Student Projects lesson.

A TYPICAL ALPHABET LESSON

Each type of Alphabet lesson has three distinct parts. These three parts are the introduction, a student activity, and sharing.

Part One: Introduction The teacher begins each day's Alphabet lesson by introducing that day's letter. Introductions are whole-group demonstrations that are led by the teacher. They involve a variety of activities, such as letter writing practice, thinking of words and objects that contain specific letters, or possibly reading related literature. Depending on the type of lesson, introductions take between five and ten minutes.

SUCCESS helps me to make eager learners and enthusiastic readers. The children actually like to learn. Also, it allows me to be more creative and keeps me from getting in a rut. The students gain a love of reading and reading to learn.

Janet L. Anthony, teacher

On the first day of a new letter or letter combination, the introduction will be longer. On days when Research or Student Projects are involved, the introduction time may be shorter.

Part Two: Student Activity   The second part of the Alphabet lesson involves some type of student activity. This may include students writing and drawing, locating information in research materials, or doing a project related to the Alphabet lesson.

Part Three: Sharing   The third part of the Alphabet lesson includes a sharing activity that will bring closure. On some days students share with a classmate something that they have written or drawn on their papers. On other days students take home materials to their parents.

All students should be encouraged to participate throughout each lesson. Time limits might not allow every student to volunteer a word or assist in the demonstration of a project; however, the teacher should use the student activity time to teach, reinforce, and encourage students who did not get individual attention during the lesson introduction. An Alphabet lesson should be a positive, exciting, and successful experience for the teacher and the students.

▶
Procedures for a Brainstorming Lesson

INTRODUCTION

At the start of a Brainstorming lesson, the teacher and the students assemble near the chalkboard. In some classrooms the teacher stands at the chalkboard while the students are seated on the floor. In other classrooms students may be seated in desks. Everyone should be comfortable, able to see the chalkboard, and feel a part of the group.

The teacher writes that day's letter(s) on the chalkboard and tells the class the letter name(s), then leads the class in a brief demonstration of the letter formation. He or she can choose from several different possibilities for demonstrating how the letter is formed, such as writing the letters in the air, on the floor, on the palms of their hands, on the back of another student, on individual chalkboards, in small boxes with sand or salt, or on heavy-duty locking plastic bags which contain a small portion of finger paint.

In one SUCCESS classroom the teacher began her introduction of the letters *Ll* with the students sitting on the floor in front of the chalkboard.

> **Ms. Stauffer:**   Can you think of a word that has today's letter in it?
>
> **Kathy:**   I see the word "lion" on the chart we made today.
>
> **Ms. Stauffer:**   That's great, Kathy, you used your eyes to help you find an *l* word. Now let's all spell the word together as I write it, l-i-o-n. (The teacher drew a picture of a lion near the word.) Who can think of another *l* word?

Chuck: I hear a *l* in "lollipop."

Ms. Stauffer: That's wonderful, Chuck. Can all of you help me spell it while I write, l-o-l-l-i-p-o-p? We have lots of people who would like to draw a lollipop. Brian, would you like to draw one on the chalkboard?

Lucille: That word has three *l*s.

Mac: Teacher, rabbit has an *l* in it!

Ms. Stauffer: Super. Let's write the word on the chalkboard together, r-a-b-b-i-t. (The class discovers the word does not contain the letter.) Mac, this is a great word. Maybe we can think of an *l* word we could put with it.

Shayla: I know. The word little has an *l*. And there are little rabbits.

Ms. Stauffer: Shayla, the word "little" will work great with "rabbits."

This exchange demonstrates the many different learning situations that can and will take place during an Alphabet lesson. The elements that are a part of this portion of the lesson are:

1. The designated letters can be found anywhere in the word and may represent any sound.

2. As the teacher writes the children's words, each letter should be said out loud and the students echo-spell or spell each word with the teacher.

3. The teacher or students draw simple illustrations of the words written on the chalkboard. These drawings will provide students with visual clues and assist the students who choose to write words on their papers during the student activity portion of the lesson.

4. The words and illustrations of these words should be scattered on the chalkboard and *reviewed periodically* during the introduction.

5. Although the teacher may occasionally volunteer a word, nearly all of the words come from the students' vocabulary. This gives a greater value to the words that are volunteered. Students will show an increased interest if they can personally identify with the words written.

6. Students who volunteer words that do not contain the specific letters should also feel successful. Occasionally, a student will volunteer a word that does not contain that day's letters. In this case the teacher writes the word on the chalkboard and helps the child see that the word does not contain the correct letters. The teacher should try his or her best to incorporate the student's word with a word that could fit the letters for the day, as the teacher in the example did with Mac's word, "rabbit." This makes a positive situation out of a child giving an unrelated word. If no solution can be found, then the teacher and the student should decide what is to be done with the word. One possibility is to erase the word from the chalkboard and encourage the student to remember the word for a day when the letters will work.

Figure 5-1

CHALKBOARD ILLUSTRATION

Above all, remember that the main premise of the SUCCESS program is that all students are successful. There needs to be a atmosphere where students feel free to volunteer without the fear of rejection as a result of a wrong answer.

After reading the brainstorming words for a last time, the students will be excused to their tables to proceed with part two of the lesson. Figure 5-1 shows an example of what the chalkboard might look like at the close of the introduction portion of the lesson.

Teaching dictionary skills   The introduction portion of the Alphabet lesson is an excellent time to introduce the students to the dictionary. Later in the year the teacher should stop at some point during the lesson and have a student look up a volunteered word in the dictionary.

This task is accomplished easily if the teacher guides the student. First, the teacher should have the student open the dictionary. Then the teacher should ask the student to tell the class what the first letter of the guide words are at the top of the page. The class will then tell the student with the dictionary whether he should turn the pages toward the front or the back of the dictionary. This process continues until the student finds the correct page. Higher-level alphabetizing skills are taught as the children are ready. The dictionary will become a valuable tool in your class. Many students will choose to look at dictionaries on their own time.

STUDENT ACTIVITY

Before the students return to their tables after the introduction, a child, teacher's assistant, or parent helper should place a blank piece of paper at each student's place. That allows the class maximum use of the ten- to fifteen-minute student activity time during every Brainstorming lesson. During this time, the teacher and the students are faced with many choices:

Student choices   The students choose from a variety of activities. The students might wish to copy illustrations or words from the chalkboard or practice writing the day's letters. The students may also choose to color their pictures or add new ideas to their papers.

A few students might choose to write or draw something totally unrelated. Children not interested in words or those who do something unrelated to the letter(s) are telling the teacher that they are not aware of sound-symbol relationships yet. Requiring these students to copy items from the chalkboard will only frustrate them. Children will begin making sound-symbol relationships when they are developmentally ready.

The teacher's role   During the student activity time, the teacher's responsibility is to make this a positive experience for every child in the classroom, no matter what the child has decided to put on his or her paper. The teacher becomes the facilitator who encourages the children to work to their highest capabilities.

During this time, the teacher moves around the class and talks with each child about his or her work. In these conversations the teacher needs to find at least one specific item to praise and one item that gives a helping suggestion. The items of praise could be as simple as "Joey, it is great that you remembered to put your name on the paper," or "Sally, I am very impressed that you knew another word that had today's letters," or "Misty, that's a really neat *r*." There will always be something specific in the child's work that the teacher can find to praise.

The teacher should also find one item on the child's paper that could use some improvement. This can be called a helping suggestion. The teacher should look for the most important suggestion for that particular child. For one child it could be help in forming a letter or remembering to put his or her name and date on the paper. Another child might be developmentally ready to use invented spelling and could use some encouragement so that he or she will write a word or sentence to go with an illustration.

Each student's needs are different, and it is the teacher's role to identify these needs. Conversations between the teacher and students in SUCCESS classrooms help the teacher meet the individual needs of each child.

Figure 5-2

ALPHABET ILLUSTRATION

Students should be encouraged to use the entire allotted time to continue to work on their papers. Every classroom has at least one child who writes one thing on his or her paper and announces, "I'm done." Avoid the trap of telling the students that they have to put a certain number of words or illustrations on their papers. For the child that needs continuing reinforcement about the number of items on his or her paper, the teacher might simply respond, "I don't know how many things you should draw. Show me what you can do. We have about twelve minutes." Many teachers have found it very helpful to set a minute timer so that the entire class knows when time is up.

As the year progresses, the teacher may find that the students will need little encouragement to keep writing during the allotted time. Instead, the teacher will be more likely to hear a chorus of, "I'm not done yet!" or "Can't we have five more minutes?"

Figures 5-2 through 5-4 show examples of students' Alphabet Brainstorming papers from throughout the school year. Notice that papers from the beginning of the school year have very little written on them. Papers from the end of the school year show numerous examples of letters, words, and illustrations.

SHARING

During the last few minutes of the Alphabet lesson when the students have completed writing letters and pictures from the chalkboard, they are given a few minutes to share their information with someone. This is done quickly and everyone should be involved. There is not enough time for each child to share in front of the entire class. It is just as effective, however, if students share something on their paper that they are especially proud of with a person sitting close to them. All children need many opportunities to show off their work.

Filing papers   The papers are placed in the students' file folder. All students have their own file folder for storing their Alphabet papers for the entire year. Many teachers teach their students how to file papers; others choose to file the papers themselves.

The benefit of the teacher filing papers is that it gives him or her another opportunity to review each student's work and make notes about improvements or areas of concern. One SUCCESS teacher chose to keep a notebook or clipboard notes to record his findings regarding the student's work. Another teacher used a checklist format to periodically assess if students were achieving the required kindergarten skills for her district's curriculum. Post-it™ notes are useful to record something important about the paper without marking on the student's work. Whatever the system, teachers need to make sure that they regularly review and record the students' development.

Figure 5-3

ALPHABET ILLUSTRATION

In SUCCESS classrooms where students file their own papers, there are many techniques that the teacher can choose from to make this process quick and easy for the students. Some techniques that have been used in SUCCESS classrooms include using color coded folders, using picture clues or stickers to decorate the folders, or assigning each child a number for his or her folder. Whichever method is chosen, the filing process is speeded up greatly if several file boxes or "filing stations" are set up in different locations in the room to eliminate congestion.

Why should I keep these papers?   Keeping the students' Brainstorming papers for the entire year provides a longitudinal record of the progress of each individual student in the class. These folders are extremely helpful in parent-teacher conferences and in teacher assessment of an individual student's progress.

When papers are sent home on a daily basis, teachers, parents, and especially, the students forget how much progress is made in the course of a school year. Parents seldom save all of their child's work. By keeping the papers at school and periodically reviewing them, everyone involved is enlightened and encouraged. Teachers are able to pat themselves on the back and say "SUCCESS really works!" Parents can see how much their child has learned during the year. The child will respond to their early papers, "I didn't do this—I don't write like that!" As they look through the remaining papers, they will beam with pride at what they can do now.

Figure 5-4

ALPHABET ILLUSTRATION

Each student will accumulate approximately seventy-two Alphabet papers. Some SUCCESS teachers feel that this is too cumbersome to keep in one folder, especially if students are doing the filing. Often these teachers choose to remove the papers from folders at the end of each grading period and save them. Some teachers send home every third or fourth paper at the end of each grading period, but they always keep a large majority of the papers at school. Cleaning out the folders during the school year is *never* recommended. To do so would rob the teacher of all evidence of a child's growth.

Papers should go home with the children at the end of the school year. The children and their parents will be delighted and astonished at the progress made throughout the year. Some SUCCESS teachers like to show the importance of the Alphabet papers by having the students design covers and binding them into books or wrapping the papers like gifts before presenting them to their parents.

Helpful Hints   Teachers are encouraged to keep the parents informed about the letters being studied during the Alphabet module. This can be done with simple class newsletters or by periodically sending home photocopies of the student's work. (For more information about newsletters and communications with parents, see Chapter 6.)

Dating the papers before they are placed in the folders is extremely important. At first, the teacher will need to date each paper, but if the date is written on the chalkboard each school day, many students will learn to do this fairly early in the year. Still other teachers have found it easiest to use an inexpensive date stamp which they purchase at office supply stores.

▶
Procedures for a Research Lesson

INTRODUCTION

On Research days the teacher's introduction time can be brief. A maximum of five to seven minutes is all the time that is needed. The teacher should have the students assembled for a whole group presentation, remind them of the day's letter(s), and review how the letter(s) looks and how it is formed.

In Research lessons students use magazines and newspapers to locate information related to the day's letter(s). The teacher will make many choices on how to introduce the letters and materials.

One SUCCESS teacher introduced an Alphabet lesson using a magazine by cutting out an example of a letter and a picture of a related object for that day's letter. She then glued the pictures onto a piece of chart paper which developed into a class chart. On another day this teacher chose to vary the lesson by gluing these items on an $8\frac{1}{2}'' \times 11''$ piece of paper to show students how they could record their own findings. Another teacher introduced a newspaper Research lesson by having her students use a yellow highlighter pen to mark the day's letter(s) on a page from the newspaper that was taped to the chalkboard.

After either of these kinds of introductions a teacher and his or her students can orally brainstorm other possibilities of items that might be found in the research material before being excused to begin the next step, the student activity.

STUDENT ACTIVITY

The student activity portion of Alphabet Research lessons is very exciting for both the teacher and the students and should take the majority of the lesson time. Most SUCCESS teachers allow ten to fifteen minutes for this portion of an Alphabet lesson. Students will use this opportunity to apply their knowledge of the day's letter(s) to the use of real-life materials, and teachers are able to aid the students in learning basic research skills while at the same time expanding students' knowledge of the reading/writing process.

SUCCESS allows the freedom to create and generate new ideas. Children "think," not just repeat given information. All areas of the curriculum can be integrated. The whole language approach becomes a reality.

Deborah Weber, teacher

What are students learning?   Regardless of the materials used for Research, there are many benefits that result from doing this activity:

1. Students learn to scan for information. This skill is usually not learned until higher grade levels, but kindergarten children (with guidance in the beginning) can learn how to scan and look at the details of the pictures or words.

2. Students are encouraged to develop higher-level thinking skills as they are given the opportunity to look in a variety of materials.

3. Students learn that there isn't just one right answer. The open-ended research format allows them to apply their previous knowledge in locating information. As long as they can relate the item to the day's letter, the teacher will accept it.

4. Since the students are frequently exposed to a variety of magazines and newspapers, their fear of not being able to read is eliminated. They soon discover that they can read lots of things—even pictures or individual letters.

5. Each student's feeling of self-worth will increase as each discovers that he or she can be successful in locating many different kinds of information.

Choices   There are many choices for both the teacher and the students to make during Research time. The teacher chooses whether the activity time will involve producing a class chart or individual papers, or if a combination of the two methods will be the finished product. Students make numerous choices about what items to cut or tear out of a magazine and what letter(s) to highlight in the newspaper. Following are examples of different approaches to Research Alphabet lessons.

Making class charts with magazines   One SUCCESS teacher, after leading a brief introduction and review of the letters *Gg*, chose to have her students create a class chart. She excused the children to go to their tables, where a parent helper had placed an assortment of magazines. As the students looked through the magazines, they cut out the letter *Gg* or objects they knew were spelled with a *Gg*.

The parent helper assisted students during their search. Some students found pictures of items that contained the day's letter and some students looked for the letter in different type styles. When one student found an item in the magazine, she took the item to the teacher, who was standing near the chart. The student told the teacher what the item was and glued the item onto the chart. She then watched as the teacher wrote the word near the picture.

Mrs. Forbes: Jeanetta, what did you find?

Jeanetta: I found a picture of a giraffe.

Mrs. Forbes: That's great, let's put glue on the back of the picture and you can choose where to put it on the chart. Now let's write the word "giraffe."

Nancy: Look I found a big "G."

Mrs. Forbes: Super, you can put it with the other *g*'s on the chart.

Tom: Teacher, does hamburger have a *g* in it?

Mrs. Forbes: We can write the word on the chalkboard and check. You were right, Tom. Where do you see the letter *g*? Is it in the beginning, the middle, or the end of the word?

Tom: In the middle.

Chris Hart

Figure 5-5

CLASS CHART ILLUSTRATION

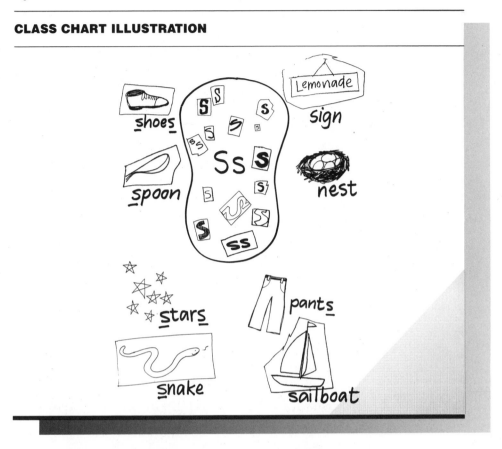

Mrs. Forbes: Right again. Let's put your picture and word on the chart.

Carmine: I found two giant *g*'s that are red. Here, teacher, you glue them on. I have to go find some more.

Colin: I have a picture of a horse.

Mrs. Forbes: Let's write *horse* on the chalkboard. Colin, do you see a *g* in the word *horse*?

Colin: No, but horses can gallop.

Mrs. Forbes: That's wonderful. Now we can write "horses gallop" on the chart.

Figures 5-5 and 5-6 show examples of two completed class charts.

Individual papers and magazines   Research lessons in which students record their findings on their own papers are conducted in the same manner as the method described for making a class chart. The only exception is that the items are glued onto individual papers.

During this type of Research lesson, the teacher, parent volunteers, or teaching assistants help individual students locate items in the magazines. Some children may need more help than others. There are always students who quickly flip through magazines and proclaim, "This magazine doesn't have anything." With the help of the teacher or parent volunteer, students can be guided, not told or shown, how to find an item that they could put on their papers. The adult can give this type of child hints such as: "I see the letter at the top of this page," or "Let's look in the magazine and see if we can find something that will remind us of an animal that has today's letter."

These activities are more complicated than class charts because the students have so many materials to manage at the same time. They will need magazines, scissors, glue, and blank paper. One tip is to have the students glue down items that they find as they go, so that the cut-outs are not lost. The completed papers should go home with the student. Figures 5-7 and 5-8 show examples of Research papers using magazines.

Combining the class chart and individual papers   Some days teachers may vary the magazine Research activity by combining the class chart and individual papers. During these lessons, students choose one or two of the items that they find to glue onto the class chart. The other examples of the letters and objects are glued onto their individual papers that go home with them.

Newspaper research activities   The newspaper lessons most frequently involve locating letters or parts of words. This activity works very nicely if the students use highlighter pens to mark the letters or words containing the letters. Light colored crayons can be substituted for highlighter pens.

Newspaper activities are easier to manage if the students are given pre-cut 9″ × 12″ sections of the newspaper. These do not have to be precisely cut, and everyone in the class will not have the same section of newspaper.

Figure 5-7

THINGS YOU CAN BAKE

Figure 5-8

PETS

The students will locate as many examples of the letters as possible. Because of the fine print in newspapers, the teacher may have to direct students having difficulty finding the letter(s) to a line or area on the newspaper that contains larger type. For some students it may be helpful to select sections from the newspaper, such as ad supplements that many grocery stores and car dealers use. These pages always have many words printed in larger type. Figure 5-9 shows an example of one student's completed newspaper Research paper.

Helpful research hints

1. Discoveries made during the student activity time are very rewarding to the students, and frequently their excitement can become very vocal. The children will want everyone to know what they have found. This excitement is contagious. The teacher knows from this excitement that the students are involved, learning, sharing their knowledge and enjoying what they are doing. Students doing Research activities may be noisy, but they are also productive.

Conversation should be encouraged, but it will need to be monitored so that it stays within the teacher's noise limits. Some SUCCESS teachers have signals to let the children know when they are approaching this limit.

2. It is helpful to demonstrate how items found in the research materials can be cut or torn out more easily. Frustration is eliminated or lessened if a teacher shows the students how to tear out the entire page of a magazine and then cut out the wanted item. This also helps keep the magazines tidy and easy to store.

SHARING

The sharing portion of the lesson needs to be brief, lasting only a few minutes. This time allows the teacher an opportunity to bring closure to the lesson. The teacher will choose the type of sharing that best suits each Research lesson.

Class charts   At the end of an Alphabet lesson that involves making a class chart, the class might briefly discuss the items placed on the chart.

The chart is then displayed on the classroom wall. The students will refer to these charts because they contain words and items that are important to them. The charts can be sent home with the students at the end of the school year.

Figure 5-9

NEWSPAPER REPORT

Individual papers When the lesson has involved the students making individual papers with magazines or newspapers, the teacher should direct the students to show a classmate something interesting on their paper. These papers can either be filed with the Brainstorming lesson papers or they can go home with the students to share with their parents.

▶
Procedures for a Student Project Lesson

LESSON PREPARATION

Prior to Student Projects, the teacher will need to make the following decisions:

1. Shall I use the suggested activity listed in the Lessons? What substitution shall I make, if any?

2. What materials will be needed for the activity?

3. Should the activity be conducted with the whole class, or as a center activity?

4. How much time is required for the activity?

SUGGESTED ACTIVITY

In each lesson of this type, there is a suggested activity. These are merely suggestions, and teachers are encouraged to substitute a different activity, if they feel it is more appropriate for their students.

The suggested activities listed in the Lessons are frequently shown with a simple drawing. The teacher will often make choices about how to create this article and what materials will be needed.

The Student Project activity needs to be simple enough in design that students can easily complete it in the ten- to fifteen-minute time. The teacher might choose to adjust the schedule to allow for more work time for more complicated activities or the students might be allowed to complete the activity at another time.

MATERIALS

The teacher will decide what materials best suit the activity. One SUCCESS teacher might choose to use construction paper to create the boats suggested as an activity in Lesson 112. Another teacher might choose to use crayons and watercolor paints. Still another teacher might choose to have the students make three-dimensional boats out of milk cartons. Some Student Projects will be art activities. Other Alphabet module projects will involve listening and following directions for the use of special materials.

This is an opportunity for SUCCESS teachers to model ways to honor the efforts of other people. If a teacher constructs a sample project, he or she might say, "This is one way to make a turtle. We can get good ideas from each other but our turtles won't all look alike."

Another teacher might say "Here are some materials that we can use today. Does anyone have an idea how we could use these materials to make turtles?" This process encourages children to value each other's ideas, work together, and use problem-solving strategies.

As the children are working, show or comment on the interesting way a child is folding the paper. Ask a student to hold up his partly finished dog to show how he glued the ears. Praise children who make positive comments about someone else's work.

GROUP SIZE

The teacher decides the size of groups that will work together to complete the project. Some activities lend themselves easily to the whole class creating one object, such as a mural. Other activities involve having the entire class working at the same time on individual creations. Still others are more manageable if they are done in small groups during the scheduled Alphabet time or during center time.

INTRODUCTION

When introducing a Student Projects lesson, the teacher reviews the letter(s) focus and demonstrates how the Student Projects can be completed. Keeping the introduction brief allows maximum time for students to create their projects.

One SUCCESS teacher began the introduction portion of Lesson 36's Student Project by reading the book *Funny Bones* by Janet and Allan Ahlberg. The class discussed the different types of animal skeletons that were seen in the book and talked about how x-rays show pictures of bones. This teacher showed the class several x-rays of human bones and then demonstrated how the children could make their own x-rays by drawing the bones of different animal skeletons with white chalk on black construction paper. He then excused the students to go to their tables to begin their own activity.

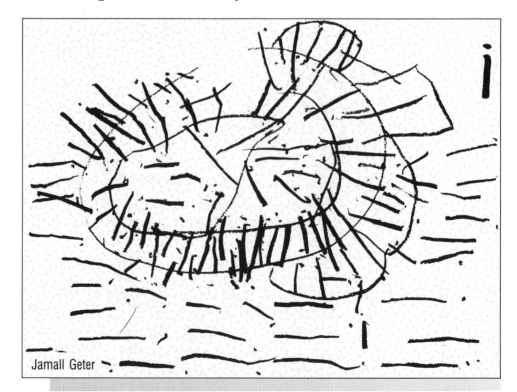

Jamall Geter

STUDENT ACTIVITY

The Student Activity portion of an Alphabet lesson constitutes the majority of the lesson time, ten to fifteen minutes. During this time the students are not only creating, but they are interacting with their peers by helping each other and talking about the uniqueness of their own articles.

While the students are working, the teacher moves around the classroom and assists children. One child may need help managing his glue, another may need guidance in a decision about what could be added to her creation, and others may be asked to talk about their object.

In one SUCCESS classroom the students were using multicolored scraps of construction paper to create fish from Lesson 8. On this day, Mr. Drake chose not to lead the class in a step-by-step demonstration of how a fish might be made, but instead talked about the different sizes, color, shapes, and body parts of fish. He then released the class to make their own fish.

Mr. Drake: That's okay, you don't have to make a fish. What would you like to make?

Rick: Can I make a rocket?

Mr. Drake: Sure. Maybe you would like to add something to the bottom of your rocket that has the letter *f* in the word. I'm thinking of something that is very hot.

Rick: Yeah! My rocket will have fire shooting out of the bottom.

SHARING

After the students have cleaned up their spaces, they can share their materials with each other and talk about what they have made. Sharing time is the last two to three minutes of the module. The teacher may also wish to save the projects to use for a bulletin board or hall decoration or send them home with the student that day. Eventually the projects will go home with the student.

▶ The Developmental Phases

There are four developmental phases in the Alphabet Module. Each phase contains a different approach to introduce students to letters. The basic format found in the preceding section should be followed to teach each Alphabet lesson. The only differences between the developmental phases is the letter(s) emphasized. Figure 5-10 is a list of the emphasis in each phase and the lessons where the emphasis is found.

PHASE I: UPPER- AND LOWER-CASE LETTERS—LESSONS 1–78

During Phase I, the first seventy-eight days of the SUCCESS program, the emphasis is on single alphabet letters. The upper- and lower-case forms of each letter are introduced at the same time. Three days are

Figure 5-10

Content Emphases

PHASE LEVEL	CONTENT EMPHASIS	LESSONS
I	Upper- and Lower-Case Letters	1–78
II	Rhyming Words	79–122
III	Object Labeling	123–132
IV	Letter Clusters	133–180

spent studying the same alphabet letter. On the first day the letter is introduced to the class. The teacher and class brainstorm words containing either the upper- or lower-case letter in any position within the word. The second and third days are either Research activities or Student Projects.

Students are not expected to master all there is to know about letters and letter-sound relationships. Instead, they will achieve these skills as they are developmentally ready.

PHASE II: RHYMING LESSONS—LESSONS 79–122

Beginning with Lesson 79, the emphasis changes to rhyming patterns in words. Two days are spent studying each rhyming pattern. The first day of the rhyming pattern uses the brainstorming technique used during the first day of Phase I lessons. The second day of the rhyming pattern involves Research or Student Projects activities.

To introduce the rhyming word, the teacher might write the rhyming starter word on the chalkboard. In Lesson 79, this word is *mat.* Then the teacher could ask the students for words that rhyme with *mat,* such as *fat, bat, cat, flat, splat,* and *hat,* and write those words on the chalkboard. The teacher might add illustrations of the words. Occasionally, a student will volunteer a word that has the same rhyming sound but does not have the same spelling pattern. These words should also be written on the chalkboard, and, depending on the class, the teacher should decide how much attention to give the difference in spelling.

Students who are having difficulty identifying rhyming words might be guided by the teacher. For example, one teacher might ask her students, "Which of the following two words sound most alike: *cat, shoe, flat*? That's right, *cat* and *flat* sound the most alike."

PHASE III: OBJECT LABELING—LESSONS 123–132

Beginning with Lesson 123, the emphasis is on single letters within whole words. During these lessons, the teacher and students brainstorm names of items within the classroom that contain the letters for the day. The students then label each object with flash cards. The "Object Labeling" lessons should be taught in the following manner:

1. The teacher introduces the letters that will be the focus for the day. Students volunteer words that contain at least one of the day's letters, and the teacher writes these on the chalkboard. Each word does *not* have to contain both letters for the day. When the students cannot think of a word, the teacher guides them with hints of items containing the letters. The class says the name of each letter as it is written. It is not necessary to have a large number of words on the chalkboard. For example, the letters for Lesson 123 are *b* and *n*. Students might identify the names of objects in the room that contain these letters: book, necklace, box, Bobby, banana, table, paint, sand, and bear.

2. During the student activity time, students make their own word cards out of small pieces of paper or index cards. On each card students write one of the words on the chalkboard or another word that the student has thought of that contains either of the letters for the day. Although each student should make at least one flash card, many students may make several cards. Often they write the words are written with developmental spelling. The students place or tape their cards either on the object or near it. There may be twenty cards on the same object, if twenty students write the same word. Students may draw a picture of the object on the flash card. When students have finished labeling objects, they may also choose to use the remaining lesson time to write some of these words on a larger sheet of paper that can be filed or taken home.

3. The teacher can have the students take the word cards down before the next Object Labeling lesson, or he or she can leave the word cards attached to the objects throughout the series of lessons. The word cards can either be attached to a larger sheet of paper and filed in the student's Alphabet folder or sent home with the child.

PHASE IV: LETTER CLUSTERS—LESSONS 133–180

In this last phase, Letter Clusters, the emphasis is on words containing two-letter combinations, usually at the beginning of words. These letter clusters, or blends, will introduce the students to decoding sounds together. This phase of the Alphabet Module should be taught in the following manner:

1. The teacher introduces the Letter Cluster for the day using the brainstorming techniques described earlier in this chapter. In Lesson 133, for example, the Letter Cluster is *br*, so the teacher writes *br* on the chalkboard. Then he or she writes a word with the letter cluster, such as "brother."

The teacher then pronounces the word, slightly emphasizing the letter cluster, and asks students to say the word too until someone thinks of a word that has the *br* sound in it. If no one volunteers a word quickly, the teacher writes a second word, such as "bring," and the class reads both words. Although most of the words will have the letter cluster in the initial position of a word, some students may volunteer words that have the letters near the middle or ending of a word. The teacher writes these words also since they do contain the correct letter combination.

2. The teacher completes the lesson following the student activity and sharing portions of a Brainstorming lesson.

The second day for each Letter Cluster combination is either a Research activity or a Student Projects lesson. The procedures for these lessons are the same as discussed earlier in this chapter.

▶ **Materials**

Teachers will need the following materials for the Alphabet Module: chalkboard, chart paper, unlined paper, pencils with erasers, crayons, one file folder per student, a cardboard box to hold the file folders, newspapers, magazines, highlighter pens, and assorted art materials. At the beginning of the school year, the teacher should decide how these materials will be managed. The materials should be located in an readily accessible place. A shelf or bookcart can easily be used to store the supply of blank paper, magazines, and newspapers.

The chalkboard is used to record student-volunteered words and illustrations that are generated during the brainstorming portion of the letter introduction. Chart paper is used to create class charts.

Primary pencils or regular-sized lead pencils can be used by the students. Often SUCCESS teachers like to provide both kinds of pencils and let the children decide which type they like.

Each child needs a file folder to hold some of the work completed during the Alphabet module. The papers created on the *first* day of each new alphabet letter, rhyming word, or letter cluster are filed. Some SUCCESS teachers also choose to file individual Research papers. A sturdy card-

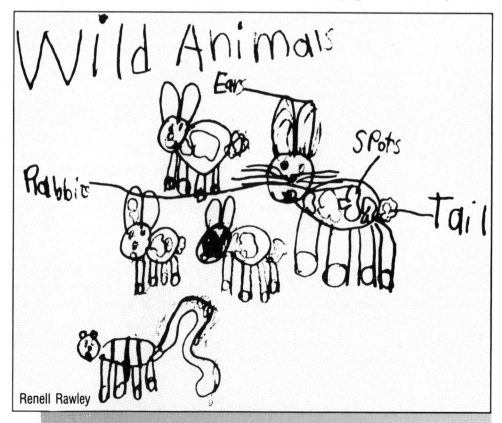

Renell Rawley

board box or small crate can be used to store these files. (For more information on filing techniques refer to Chapter 6.)

Magazines are used during the student Research activities. During these activities students will be tearing or cutting from the pages of the magazines; therefore the supply will need to be replenished frequently. Magazines do not have to be current editions. Providing a variety of magazines stimulates the students' interest and offers a wide range of information. SUCCESS teachers have seldom had difficulty keeping a stock of magazines. Many SUCCESS teachers notify the parents of their students and members of the community when the magazine supply is getting low. People are generally very willing to offer their used magazines, if they know of your need.

The newspapers that are used during the Alphabet module do not have to be current issues, although many SUCCESS teachers get a subscription to a daily newspaper. The students will be using the newspapers to highlight letters or words, locate pictures of items, and other related Research activities. Cutting the newspaper into $9'' \times 12''$ pieces makes the newspaper a manageable size for the kindergarten child.

▶ Summary

The Alphabet Module is a unique opportunity for kindergarten-aged children to explore the world of words, increase their vocabulary, develop early research techniques, follow directions, enhance listening skills, learn letter formations and names, and make individual associations of letter sounds. All of this is accomplished in a non-threatening manner. Each child is able to advance as far as he or she is developmentally ready, in an atmosphere of learning that is fun and natural.

Chapter 6 Scheduling, Evaluation, Communication, and Materials

This chapter is about the general, everyday details that concern teachers who use *SUCCESS in Reading and Writing*, such as schedule adjustments for half-day kindergarten, record-keeping and evaluation, communicating with parents and administrators about student progress, and effective use of teacher assistants and volunteers in the classroom. Also addressed is a list of the myriad materials suggested in the Lessons and suggestions about room arrangement.

▶ Whole vs. Half-Day Kindergarten

Kindergarten teachers are often confronted with very strict time limits and unique scheduling difficulties. Teachers with the opportunity to have their students for an entire school day have little difficulty following the complete SUCCESS program, while other teachers are forced to offer their students a well-balanced program in a half-day. For the half-day kindergarten teacher, the demands may seem overwhelming as he or she tries to combine SUCCESS with the other required curriculum.

Both full- and half-day SUCCESS schedules are currently being used throughout the United States, and both have stood the test of time. Questions that need to be considered are: How much language arts time is available in my schedule? In what order should I teach the modules? Is it possible to integrate other kindergarten curriculum areas into SUCCESS? How can I display two sets of charts and student projects? Is there a way to use SUCCESS and keep the centers that I am currently using?

▶ Scheduling

A SUCCESS teacher conducting all modules will need four twenty-minute blocks of time a day. These time blocks do not need to be sequential. Each teacher has his or her own preference about the order of modules that works best with his or her students. Special classes and other curriculum areas need to be considered when deciding the module sequence. Some teachers like to begin the day with a large group activity, such as Pictures and Words, followed by Writing, which often requires more movement. This same teacher might then take her students to a special class such as music, p. e., or the library. The students might then return to the classroom for the Alphabet and Storytime modules.

Kindergarten children are very much creatures of habit. Once the students are used to a routine, any change is often disruptive. The students quickly learn what procedures are used for each module. They know what is expected of them and how their time will be spent. This eliminates a lot of "*What are we going to do next, teacher?*"

For the half-day kindergarten teacher, there are choices to be made in regards to scheduling. If it is impossible to have four separate twenty-

Chapter **6**

Eugene McGaha

minute time blocks, the teacher will need to be a little more creative with scheduling. The teacher might choose to omit one of the modules (a different one each day) or combine two of the modules.

Although all of the modules are important to insure a balanced language arts program, it is possible to omit one each day if time is a constraint. The modules that can be taught less regularly are Alphabet and Pictures and Words. These two could be alternated each day. All students need time daily to express their thoughts freely, both orally and in writing. Further, no kindergarten activity is more important than sharing books. For this reason, Storytime and Writing should be scheduled every day.

Most SUCCESS teachers frequently combine two of the modules. Even those who have a whole-day kindergarten have days when time is tight. The majority of the Lessons simplify combining modules because the topics are related. On most days two of the modules are correlated. Every five days the Pictures and Words picture theme is used to introduce the Writing lesson; therefore the Pictures and Words discussion can replace the introduction time in Writing. Immediately after Pictures and Words, students can begin their Writing activity. On other days the Storytime book and discussion can serve as the introduction to Writing or the Alphabet activity. The combination of possibilities is limited only by the teacher's resources and imagination.

Occasionally, less than twenty minutes is needed to complete a module lesson. A book selected for Storytime or a picture chosen for Pictures and Words may be completed in a shorter length of time. The teacher has the choice of using this extra time during one of the other modules or in another activity. Teachers choosing to shorten the module time need to make sure that they are not taking all the time from the student activity portion of the lesson.

▶

Integrating Curriculum

The SUCCESS format makes it extremely easy to integrate other curriculum areas. Each of the modules provides different approaches that may be used to correlate curriculum areas. For example, the teacher may wish to introduce students to bicycle safety. The Pictures and Words module could provide an opportunity to label a picture of a bicycle and discuss its safety features. The Storytime module is the perfect choice to read a collection of fiction and nonfiction books related to bicycles. The Alphabet research activity for letters *Bb* might be changed to looking for safe places to ride bicycles. The Writing theme for the week could also be changed to Bicycle Safety. The blank line in each SUCCESS module lesson provides a place for teachers to record these important changes.

Integrating curriculum areas such as science, social studies, and health with SUCCESS modules also gives the teacher additional time for other activities and relieves the teacher's frustration that there is not enough time for everything.

▶ **Centers**

SUCCESS can be integrated into classrooms that are using centers as part of the daily routine. A balanced kindergarten program needs to offer children all kinds of opportunities to play and freely explore as well as build beginning reading and writing skills. SUCCESS activities can be included as a center choice along with blocks, painting, a sand table, or home living.

Alphabet and Writing activities, for instance, can be completed at a center. After the teacher introduces the lesson to the whole group, the students can complete the activity during center time. An adult will need to be available to assist and converse with the children in the Alphabet or Writing center.

Later in the year children can work together in a center to complete a Pictures and Words chart. Their labels will be in developmental spelling. Also, reading centers where students explore books independently can contain a collection of books related to themes discussed in any of the modules.

▶
Evaluation and Assessment

All teachers must gather evidence or documentation of students' progress. Beyond gathering information, teachers have to assess the strengths and weaknesses of each of their students and then be able to communicate each student's progress to parents, the principal, and the students. Kindergarten achievement reports in some school systems require little more than checks for social, emotional, and behavioral areas, while others are extensive lists of sub-skills on which the child is checked for mastery. A few kindergarten teachers give letter grades. Teachers who choose to participate in the SUCCESS program actually have far more documentation of students' true progress than they typically do with other approaches to teaching.

SUCCESS teachers have more opportunities to know their students and how they think, as well as their academic strengths and weaknesses, because they spend 75 percent of the language arts teaching time interacting with individuals. The written documentation of the students' progress consists of longitudinal records and clipboard notes about every student.

STUDENTS' FOLDERS: LONGITUDINAL RECORDS OF PROGRESS

Papers produced in the Brainstorming lessons of the Alphabet module are always filed in each student's folder. These papers provide the teacher with documentation of the student's progress. The teacher will have little difficulty in assessing growth for the student by reviewing these papers. The papers serve as a record of the development of the student's handwriting; details in drawings; awareness of letters, numbers, words and sentences; associations of letter sounds; rhyming; patterns and knowledge of subject areas. Although most Writing papers are sent home at the end of the cycle, teachers are encouraged to keep a photocopy of a representative sample of students' writings.

TEACHERS KEEP RECORDS

Besides the Alphabet folder and some occasional Writing papers that are kept for each student, the teacher can maintain records of progress by methods such as clipboard notes or checklists.

Clipboard notes These are anecdotal notes recorded by the teacher during school that include information about individuals or the whole class. Whatever the teacher notices that attracts his or her attention should be written on the clipboard. The notes may reflect academic achievements or frustrations, social conflicts or examples of teamwork and mutual respect, and emotional highs and lows. Many teachers report this is their most valuable tool in assessing not only academic growth but social and emotional growth. The notes become a diary of progress for each student.

Each day the teacher begins with a new set of clipboard note forms. SUCCESS teachers have found keeping these notes during the Alphabet and Writing modules to be most useful. Teachers use many styles of forms. The most common element in all of them, however, is that they have the students' names pre-printed beside or in a space large enough for the teacher's notes. Many forms have spaces for the teacher's objectives for that module. For instance, the teacher may want to be particularly aware of who works with whom during the Alphabet Research lessons. In the Writing Module the teacher may want to focus his or her attention and notes on the students' use of inventive spelling. Teachers often try to record one strength and one weakness for each student they talk with or observe.

The teacher will not make notes for each student during each module. There may be days when there are no notes on a student. Many teachers star the names of students they have made fewer notes about recently or that they want to be sure and notice for some other reason. Following are samples of notes from teachers' clipboards:

"Shawna wrote her name today without a helping card."
"J.R. very excited. He kept blurting out words that we could have written on the chalkboard for letter *Mm*."
"Randy can not stay in his seat for more than two minutes."
"Brandon quietly working while everyone at his table is talking."
"Sarah wanted to know how to spell *snowman*. She wrote *snomn* by herself. What a smile!"
"Dominique can't keep her hands to herself today."
"Taylor spent the entire time looking at a book about dinosaurs and didn't write."

Teachers read over their clipboard notes regularly. Although some of the things they have recorded seemed innocuous at the time, patterns usually emerge that are invaluable for teachers as they increase their knowledge of each student and modify their teaching to accommodate their new insights.

Periodic checklists SUCCESS teachers also use checklists to assess students' progress. Often these checklists may contain the objectives, skills, or graded areas on report cards that a teacher is required to document. The information for these checklists can come from several areas. The teacher can gather information from filed papers, clipboard notes, or conversations with the students.

One SUCCESS teacher was required to mark on the first quarter report card whether the students understood the concept "top" and "bottom." He talked with his students during an Alphabet Research activity, asking each child to point to the tops and bottoms of many different objects in magazines and the classroom. This information was recorded on a checklist. Another teacher needed documentation of whether her students could recognize particular letters. While they were looking at library books, she asked her students to point out these letters. Still another teacher used information from filed papers and clipboard notes to mark on the checklist whether her students could clearly write their names.

SUCCESS is effective for me because it gives me the freedom to teach the children in a style I am comfortable with. It also allows more student involvement, which keeps them more excited about what they are doing. SUCCESS is wonderful for a child's self-concept. I love it!

Kris Dowling, teacher

Pen

Megan Chesser

▶

Communication with Parents and Others

Teachers need to be in constant communication with the parents of their students and the administrators to whom they report. The following section contains several strategies for keeping parents and others informed about what is happening in SUCCESS classrooms.

PARENTS

Teachers should worry more when parents do not ask questions about their philosophy and teaching practices than when they do. The more teachers and parents understand each other and work together, sharing their knowledge, the more the students will benefit. Teachers, therefore, should take the initiative to establish this type of relationship. Instead of waiting for parents to ask, teachers should inform parents of what is happening at school and why.

Often teachers who use this program are a minority within their school staff. If they are breaking away from the way others are teaching, they must know why and be able to explain it to anyone who asks. People will ask, "What is SUCCESS?" "How is it different?" "Why have you chosen to teach this way?" "What do you expect to accomplish?" "What can I do to help you and my child?" Teachers need to be confident and have plausible answers to these questions.

There are several ways SUCCESS teachers keep parents informed. First, they write letters at the beginning of the year explaining their goals and outlining the procedures they will be using. They plan Open House programs, invite parents to visit during school hours, and many send home regular newsletters. But most important, each day teachers send home students who are excited about learning and who are growing in their awareness of the world around them and their important place in that world.

Letters to parents   At the beginning of the year teachers are encouraged to send a letter home to parents explaining their philosophy and how SUCCESS works. The following are some hints from veteran SUCCESS teachers that will make those first letters more effective:

1. *Be brief.* Parents don't want to hear your whole philosophy of education. Nor do they want to read a detailed description of what happens in your language arts block. Just include a summary of what your goals are and an outline of the program in a one- to two-page letter.

2. *Be positive in your description of SUCCESS.* Remember it has stood the test of time. Avoid such words as "new," "innovative," and especially, "experimental." Describe what your students will be doing, instead of what you will *not* be doing.

3. *Invite them to come to school in a couple of weeks to see the program in action.*

4. *Inform them in a positive way that they are welcome to look at the papers in their child's Alphabet folder at any time.*

5. *Request that they read to or with their child nightly.*

6. *Ask them to donate magazines and occasional recyclable materials for projects.* Some parents may subscribe to a magazine as a gift to the class; others will send old magazines from home.

Open house   The best way to understand SUCCESS is to experience it. For their Open House presentation many teachers do abbreviated SUCCESS activities with the parents functioning as their students. One teacher wrote that he had his students bring their parents to the program. The parents sat in the students' desks and the children sat in chairs beside their parents. During the lessons, the children helped their parents when they had difficulty. Examples of the student's works should be readily available to the parents. Books, charts, and other key materials should be visible. Above all, concentrate on the students, not the program.

Newsletters   There are many better ways to keep parents informed than by sending home papers. One way that many teachers have found effective is a weekly newsletter. The goal of these newsletters is to stimulate discussions between parent and child about what happened at school that week. A format that takes relatively little of the teacher's time is to scatter around the page blurbs about such things as the Writing topic for that week, the letters studied in the Alphabet lessons or sample words from some of the charts, book titles the teacher has read, and the many questions and discoveries made by the students during the week. Some teachers write these blurbs in what they call "clouds" that surround a student-drawn illustration. Others write them in different shapes, such as leaves in the fall or hearts around Valentine's Day. Teachers that have access to photocopies that make reductions can simply assemble a collection of sample papers that different students produced during the week. Teachers often like to list the topics, letters, and special events will be taking during the next week at school. Parents learn to expect these letters weekly. One parent said to her child's teacher, "Since I work during the day, I can't come into the classroom. The weekly newsletter makes me feel like I am in touch with what is happening at school. The newsletter lets me know what I can do to help my child. It also gives us some great conversation starters."

VISITORS

Parents, administrators, and other teachers are encouraged to visit a SUCCESS classroom in progress. Whenever these adults are present, they are not permitted merely to sit in the back of the room and watch. Instead they are encouraged to circulate around the room and talk with students. They may answer students' questions, listen to students read or discuss their books, comment on students' Writing folders, or simply ask the students to explain what they are doing. Visitors are usually impressed not only at the competence of the students, but also at the students' confidence in themselves.

ADMINISTRATORS

Support from administrators is usually very important to the confidence teachers feel about trying new teaching strategies. SUCCESS is just as scary for some administrators as it is for some teachers. Many administrators are not familiar with SUCCESS and are wary of having some of their teachers organize their language arts instruction so differently from the others on the staff. In cases where administrators are not encouraging teachers to try strategies like SUCCESS, teachers should make an appointment with their administrator(s) to discuss their request. Those who have been in this situation recommend teachers do three things:

1. Take the time and initiative to *write down* your reasons for using the program. Don't be negative about other programs; be positive about SUCCESS.

2. Agree to abandon the SUCCESS framework if, after a minimum trial of twelve weeks, it is not working for your students.

3. Invite the administrator to come into your classroom frequently to be an active visitor—after two to three weeks. Allow yourself time to get your program underway.

Administrators can show their support of teachers who use the SUCCESS program by providing the necessary materials and by visiting their classrooms often, talking with their students, and browsing through student's folders. Whenever an administrator visits a classroom, he or she should:

- see the teacher circulating around the room talking with individual students,
- see students looking at books or working in groups,
- hear a buzz of purposeful activity,

- see many current Pictures and Words charts hanging around the room,
- see boxes containing Alphabet folders,
- talk to students about what they are doing, and
- feel the excitement of learning in progress.

Most importantly, administrators can show their support for these risk-takers by patting them on the back regularly. These teachers have gone out on a limb to do something different because they are convinced it is for the good of their students.

▶ Teacher Assistants and Parent Volunteers

SUCCESS teachers spend 75 percent of their language arts time working directly with individual students. If this time is divided equally among the students, the individual teaching time is much higher than with other teaching techniques. If kindergarten teachers are able to have full or part-time teaching assistants or volunteer parent helpers, then the adult-to-student ratio time dramatically increases, as does the quality of the learning that takes place.

Teaching assistants and parent volunteers are an extremely valuable asset to the classroom. They can do almost everything that a teacher can do when helping children with their reading and writing. Teaching and learning are a team effort. Everyone, including the adults in the classroom, learns from each activity. Everyone, including the students, teaches and helps each other during every activity. SUCCESS classrooms are a community of learners, where everyone works together toward a common goal. That common goal is that learning be fun and worthwhile, and that it continue throughout one's life.

Emily Bartos

Teacher assistants and parent volunteers may need some training or guidance from the teacher before working with children. A "training meeting" is often organized by SUCCESS teachers at the beginning of the school year. At this meeting the SUCCESS teacher might discuss the philosophy of the program, demonstrate sample lessons, and give examples of typical ways that the adults can help the students. In their eagerness to be helpful, parents frequently forget that they are there to guide the students into discoveries and not merely do the work for them. The SUCCESS teacher should model how the adult helpers might encourage students' inventive spelling, guide students into looking closer at a magazine or newspaper for research, or discuss with students different ways that they might complete their projects.

▶ Materials

The materials needed for a SUCCESS classroom are, for the most part, common, everyday materials. Although they are far less expensive than workbooks, basals, or even duplicated materials, they are nonetheless important. In each of the preceding chapters there has been some mention of the materials used specifically for each module. Following is a comprehensive list.

1. *One to two SUCCESS manuals.* If two are purchased, the second can be loaned to parents and others who are interested in learning more about the program.

2. *Many, many children's books (thirty to fifty library books that can be rotated every two to three weeks.)* Teachers also supplement the library collection with books from their classroom collection, basal literature books, and any other source they can find.

3. *Magazines.* Most of the magazines used in the activities are written for adults (*Life, People, Good Housekeeping, Ebony*, etc.). Classroom subscriptions to children's magazines are recommended whenever funds allow. Parents may also with to contribute to a subscription for the classroom.

4. *Newspapers.* The newspapers used in Research activities do not need to be current. However, many SUCCESS teachers like to have a daily newspaper to discuss current events at some time during the day with their students.

5. *Lined or unlined chart paper.* One sheet of chart paper (18″ × 24″ or larger) is used each day in Pictures and Words. Occasionally some may be used in other modules for group displays, Research charts, and such.

6. *Many dark-colored, wide-tipped felt markers.* Charts need to be visible from a distance. Teachers have noticed that some colors are hard to read and some markers fade easily.

7. *Masking tape* or other devices for hanging Pictures and Words charts.

8. *Dictionaries.* In a SUCCESS classroom an assortment of dictionaries is preferable. The teacher needs a good, current dictionary. Students need a small assortment of pictionaries and elementary dictionaries that they can use effectively, with guidance, for looking up spellings of words and definitions. Having only pictionaries will teach students that dictionaries are not very useful, because they do not have the words in them that students need.

9. *One file folder per student.* These sturdy folders are stored in boxes or plastic crates in several stations around the room. The collection of papers goes home at the end of the year.

10. *A supply of blank 8½" × 11" paper.* Students will use the blank paper for writing booklets, Alphabet Brainstorming lessons, Research activities, and drawing.

11. *Assorted construction paper and re-cycled materials.* Many of the Alphabet Student Projects use various colors and sizes of construction papers. Re-cycled materials such as egg cartons, milk containers, meat trays, or tubes may also be needed for several projects. Refer to the Lessons for the specific materials needed.

12. *Maps.* A United States map, a world map, and a state map should be displayed in the classroom at all times. Students will learn a lot about geography and map reading skills as they look up places they discuss.

▶
Classroom Arrangement

The most important factor in arranging a SUCCESS classroom is that all students need to feel a part of the group. Can everyone see the chart as the teacher writes on it? Can the chart pictures be viewed easily? Can they comfortably see to copy parts of the chart or chalkboard? Can everyone hear the teacher read during Storytime? Can they see the pictures? Is it easy for students to interact with each other during the modules?

In SUCCESS talking to others is essential. That does not mean that there is chaos, but is does mean that few modules, if any, are absolutely quiet. Conversation during the modules is important. Students need to talk to others about what they are doing. The wonderful thing about most beginning kindergarten children is that they talk—constantly—often without the need of an audience.

The way the room is arranged helps encourage interaction without the need for extensive movement. Desks, tables, or work areas need to be arranged so that students can have easy access to materials. Filing stations, as well as other materials, might be placed in several locations to avoid bottlenecks.

Teachers who have four to five students help pass out paper, Writing folders, or other materials find that less time is spent getting ready for a lesson, leaving more time for the actual project. Teaching assistants and parent volunteers can also perform this task while the students and the teacher are involved in large-group discussion of the activity.

Another consideration in room arrangement is that space is available on the floor for large or small group gatherings. Most teachers gather their students around them for Storytime and other module introductions. A carpeted area is a wonderful thing to have. Students often move to the floor when working on Research or Student Projects. Some students prefer to look at books while sitting on the floor, in windowsills, or under desks.

SUCCESS classrooms should appear to be as student-centered as the instructional practices are. Students' words and ideas fill the room. The most recent charts from Pictures and Words are everywhere. Class books, murals, and student projects are proudly displayed. The teacher is usually not immediately evident to the visitor, because he or she is somewhere among the students, conferring about something of immediate concern only to that student. *Learning is happening*.

▶ A Community of Teachers

Just as students work and plan together, SUCCESS teachers are encouraged to work together. In many areas groups of SUCCESS teachers have formed regional networks. They meet regularly to share ideas, solve problems, and inspire each other. On a smaller scale, when like-minded teachers in the same building or in the same district get together frequently to plan and confer, the SUCCESS teacher feels like a member of a community.

The framework of SUCCESS not only allows, but depends on, teachers making decisions that focus their program on their students. The reinforcement of a group is important in building and maintaining confidence. Whether the gathering is an informal meeting in the teachers' lounge or a follow-up workshop, teachers learn that there is always more to learn about teaching and learning the SUCCESS way.

Lessons

Walls, roof, and floor alone do not make a house a home, but the people inside certainly count on the building's firm framework. Similarly, these lessons do not constitute a rich language arts program in themselves, but the SUCCESS framework gives students and teachers freedom to form literary communities in schools.

The lesson plans are centered around themes that are highlighted in two or three of the modules. Blank lines indicate many opportunities for teachers to substitute different themes, either relating the activities in a day's lesson more closely, or making them more diverse in their themes.

Books are suggested in most lessons for the teacher to read aloud to the class. There is no prescribed list of books for SUCCESS. Teachers should read their own favorite books and investigate new books that become available to them. They should read some books over and over throughout the year, and they should consider scheduling books for reading aloud that enhance the class's study of a particular theme. Most important of all, the teacher should read aloud to the class every day.

Lesson 1

Pictures and Words

INTRODUCTION
Picture: School or _____
   The teacher leads a brief discussion about the picture.

CHART DEVELOPMENT
Phase I—Single Words: The students volunteer words to label the picture, and the teacher writes the words on the chart. Most of the labels will be single words. Students draw lines to connect parts of the picture to the words.

COMPREHENSION FOCUS
The teacher develops comprehension of the picture by asking questions, many of which will begin with *how*.
   The chart is displayed in the classroom.

Storytime

READ ALOUD
The Story About Ping
by Clare H. Bishop
or _____

DISCUSSION FOCUS
Ping "missed the boat." Discuss what happened.

Writing

Five-Day Theme: School
or _____

INTRODUCTION
The teacher and the students have a conversation related to the theme. Reference might be made to the Pictures and Words chart made earlier in the day.

WRITING ACTIVITIES
While the students are writing or drawing, the teacher meets with individuals or small groups to discuss the theme. The student's independent work may or may not relate to the theme. Each student's work is kept in a folder.

SHARING
The students share with another person or the group something they have written or drawn.

Alphabet

Letters: *L l* or _____

**INTRODUCTION—
BRAINSTORMING LESSON**
The teacher introduces the letters and demonstrates letter formation. On the chalkboard, the teacher writes student-volunteered words and illustrations of words containing the letters.

STUDENT ACTIVITY
On their papers, students write
■ examples of the letters
■ their favorite words or illustrations from the chalkboard
■ other words or drawings

SHARING
The students share something they have written or drawn with another person or the group.
   Papers are dated and filed.

Lesson 2

Pictures and Words

INTRODUCTION
Picture: School bus or _____
 The teacher leads a brief discussion about the picture.

CHART DEVELOPMENT
Phase I—Single Words: The students volunteer words to label the picture, and the teacher writes the words on the chart. Most of the labels will be single words. Students draw lines to connect parts of the picture to the words.

COMPREHENSION FOCUS
The teacher develops comprehension of the picture by asking questions, many of which will begin with *who*.
 The chart is displayed in the classroom.

Storytime

READ ALOUD
School Bus
by Donald Crews
or _____

DISCUSSION FOCUS
Talk about a day in the life of a school bus.

Writing

Five-Day Theme: School
or _____

INTRODUCTION
The teacher and the students have a conversation related to the theme.

WRITING ACTIVITIES
While the students are writing or drawing, the teacher meets with individuals or small groups to discuss the theme. The student's independent work may or may not relate to the theme. Each student's work is kept in a folder.

SHARING
The students share with another person or the group something they have written or drawn.

Alphabet

Letters: *L l* or _____

INTRODUCTION—STUDENT PROJECTS LESSON
The teacher reviews the letters and letter formation. The class discusses construction of a ladybug from egg carton sections or construction paper.

STUDENT ACTIVITY
The students make their own version of a ladybug.

SHARING
The students take their projects home.

Lesson 3

Pictures and Words

INTRODUCTION
Picture: Animals or _____
The teacher leads a brief discussion about the picture.

CHART DEVELOPMENT
Phase I—Single Words: The students volunteer words to label the picture, and the teacher writes the words on the chart. Students draw lines to connect parts of the picture to the words. Most of the labels will be single words.

COMPREHENSION FOCUS
The teacher develops comprehension of the picture by asking questions, many of which will begin with *what*.
The chart is displayed in the classroom.

Storytime

READ ALOUD
Leo the Late Bloomer
by Robert Kraus
or _____

DISCUSSION FOCUS
How did Leo feel before he "bloomed"?

Writing

Five-Day Theme: School
or _____

INTRODUCTION
The teacher and the students have a conversation related to the theme.

WRITING ACTIVITIES
While the students are writing or drawing, the teacher meets with individuals or small groups to discuss the theme. The student's independent work may or may not relate to the theme. Each student's work is kept in a folder.

SHARING
The students share with another person or the group something they have written or drawn.

Alphabet

Letters: *T t* or _____

INTRODUCTION—RESEARCH LESSON—Magazines
The teacher reviews the letters and letter formation. The teacher leads a discussion about words for objects that may be found in magazines which contain the designated letters.

STUDENT ACTIVITY
The students cut or tear the letters or related objects from magazines and glue them on individual papers or the class chart. Some of the objects may be labeled.

SHARING
The teacher and students discuss items on the class chart. The chart is displayed in the classroom.

Lesson 4

Pictures and Words

INTRODUCTION
Picture: Furniture or _____
The teacher leads a brief discussion about the picture.

CHART DEVELOPMENT
Phase I—Single Words: The students volunteer words to label the picture, and the teacher writes the words on the chart. Most of the labels will be single words. Students draw lines to connect parts of the picture to the words.

COMPREHENSION FOCUS
The teacher develops comprehension of the picture by asking questions, many of which will begin with *where*.
The chart is displayed in the classroom.

Storytime

READ ALOUD
Action Alphabet
by Marty Neumeier and Byron Glaser
or _____

DISCUSSION FOCUS
Discuss the pictures the authors chose for each letter. Why were they chosen?

Writing

Five-Day Theme: School
or _____

INTRODUCTION
The teacher and the students have a conversation related to the theme.

WRITING ACTIVITIES
While the students are writing or drawing, the teacher meets with individuals or small groups to discuss the theme. The student's independent work may or may not relate to the theme. Each student's work is kept in a folder.

SHARING
The students share with another person or the group something they have written or drawn.

Alphabet

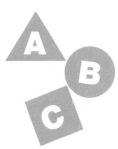

Letters: *L l* or _____

INTRODUCTION—BRAINSTORMING LESSON
The teacher introduces the letter and demonstrates letter formation. On the chalkboard, the teacher writes student-volunteered words and illustrations of words containing the letters.

STUDENT ACTIVITY
On their papers, students write
■ examples of the letters
■ their favorite words or illustrations from the chalkboard
■ other words or drawings

SHARING
The students share with another person or the group something they have written or drawn.
Papers are dated and filed.

Lesson 5

Pictures and Words

INTRODUCTION
Picture: Food or _____
The teacher leads a brief discussion about the picture.

CHART DEVELOPMENT
Phase I—Single Words: The students volunteer words to label the picture, and the teacher writes the words on the chart. Most of the labels will be single words. Students draw lines to connect parts of the picture to the words.

COMPREHENSION FOCUS
The teacher develops comprehension of the picture by asking questions, many of which will begin with *when*.
The chart is displayed in the classroom.

Storytime

READ ALOUD
My Teacher Sleeps in School
by Leatie Weiss
or _____

DISCUSSION FOCUS
Talk about the clues the class found and where they found them.

Writing

Five-Day Theme: School
or _____

INTRODUCTION
The teacher leads a class discussion about points of interest generated during the first four days of the theme and introduces the student activity.

STUDENT ACTIVITY
Tour the school and record things seen. Make a picture of a place in the school that you think you will like.

SHARING
Display the pictures on a bulletin board and later bind them into a class book.

Alphabet

Letters: *T t* or _____

INTRODUCTION—RESEARCH LESSON—Magazines
The teacher reviews the letters and letter formation. The teacher leads a discussion about words for objects that may be found in magazines which contain the designated letters.

STUDENT ACTIVITY
The students cut or tear the letters or related objects from magazines and glue them on individual papers or the class chart. Some of the objects may be labeled.

SHARING
The teacher and students discuss items on the class chart. The chart is displayed in the classroom.

Lesson 6

Pictures and Words

INTRODUCTION
Picture: Children or _____
   The teacher leads a brief discussion about the picture.

CHART DEVELOPMENT
Phase I—Single Words: The students volunteer words to label the picture, and the teacher writes the words on the chart. Most of the labels will be single words. Students draw lines to connect parts of the picture to the words.

COMPREHENSION FOCUS
The teacher develops comprehension of the picture by asking questions, many of which will begin with *how*.
   The chart is displayed in the classroom.

Storytime

READ ALOUD
Box Turtle at Long Pond
by William T. George
or _____

DISCUSSION FOCUS
Where does the box turtle live? Does he always stay in one place?

Writing

Five-Day Theme: All About Me
or _____

INTRODUCTION
The teacher and the students have a conversation related to the theme. The conversation might include a reference to the Pictures and Words chart made earlier in the day.

WRITING ACTIVITIES
While the students are writing or drawing, the teacher meets with individuals or small groups to discuss the theme. The student's independent work may or may not relate to the theme. Each student's work is kept in a folder.

SHARING
The students share with another person or the group something they have written or drawn.

Alphabet

Letters: *T t* or _____

INTRODUCTION—STUDENT PROJECTS LESSON
The teacher reviews the letters and letter formation. The class discusses making a turtle from paper plates and construction paper.

STUDENT ACTIVITY
The students make their own version of a turtle.

SHARING
The students take their projects home.

Lesson 7

Pictures and Words

INTRODUCTION
Picture: Adults or _____
   The teacher leads a brief discussion about the picture.

CHART DEVELOPMENT
Phase I—Single Words: The students volunteer words to label the picture, and the teacher writes the words on the chart. Most of the labels will be single words. Students draw lines to connect parts of the picture to the words.

COMPREHENSION FOCUS
The teacher develops comprehension of the picture by asking questions, many of which will begin with *what*.
   The chart is displayed in the classroom.

Storytime

READ ALOUD
Annabelle Swift, Kindergartner
by Amy Schwartz
or _____

DISCUSSION FOCUS
How was Annabelle's big sister helpful to her on her first day in kindergarten? Who were the other characters?

Writing

Five-Day Theme: All About Me
or _____

INTRODUCTION
The teacher and the students have a conversation related to the theme.

WRITING ACTIVITIES
While the students are writing or drawing, the teacher meets with individuals or small groups to discuss the theme. The student's independent work may or may not relate to the theme. Each student's work is kept in a folder.

SHARING
The students share with another person or the group something they have written or drawn.

Alphabet

Letters: *F f* or _____

INTRODUCTION—
BRAINSTORMING LESSON
The teacher introduces the letter and demonstrates letter formation. On the chalkboard, the teacher writes student-volunteered words and illustrations of words containing the letters.

STUDENT ACTIVITY
On their papers, students write
■ examples of the letters

■ their favorite words or illustrations from the chalkboard
■ other words or drawings

SHARING
The students share with another person or the group something they have written or drawn.
   Papers are dated and filed.

Lesson 8

Pictures and Words

INTRODUCTION
Picture: Feet or _____
   The teacher leads a brief discussion about the picture.

CHART DEVELOPMENT
Phase I—Single Words: The students volunteer words to label the picture, and the teacher writes the words on the chart. Most of the labels will be single words. Students draw lines to connect parts of the picture to the words.

COMPREHENSION FOCUS
The teacher develops comprehension of the picture by asking questions, many of which will begin with *who*.
   The chart is displayed in the classroom.

Storytime

READ ALOUD
Feet!
by Peter Parnall
or _____

DISCUSSION FOCUS
Compare the sizes of the feet in the illustrations with the feet of the actual animal. Discuss the relative sizes of the "off in the distance" part of the pictures.

Writing

Five-Day Theme: All About Me
or _____

INTRODUCTION
The teacher and the students have a conversation related to the theme.

WRITING ACTIVITIES
While the students are writing or drawing, the teacher meets with individuals or small groups to discuss the theme. The student's independent work may or may not relate to the theme. Each student's work is kept in a folder.

SHARING
The students share with another person or the group something they have written or drawn.

Alphabet

Letters: *F f* or _____

INTRODUCTION—RESEARCH LESSON—Newspapers
The teacher reviews the letters and letter formation.

STUDENT ACTIVITY
The students use highlighter pens or crayons to mark the letters in newspapers.

SHARING
The students share something they have marked on their newspaper with another person or the group.

Lesson **9**

Pictures and Words

INTRODUCTION
Picture: Automobiles or _____
   The teacher leads a brief discussion about the picture.

CHART DEVELOPMENT
Phase I—Single Words: The students volunteer words to label the picture, and the teacher writes the words on the chart. Most of the labels will be single words. Students draw lines to connect parts of the picture to the words.

COMPREHENSION FOCUS
The teacher develops comprehension of the picture by asking questions, many of which will begin with *why*.
   The chart is displayed in the classroom.

Storytime

READ ALOUD
Swimmy
by Leo Lionni
or _____

DISCUSSION FOCUS
Discuss how color helped disguise the school of fish. How does natural coloring protect animals?

Writing

Five-Day Theme: All About Me
or _____

INTRODUCTION
The teacher and the students have a conversation related to the theme.

WRITING ACTIVITIES
While the students are writing or drawing, the teacher meets with individuals or small groups to discuss the theme. The student's independent work may or may not relate to the theme. Each student's work is kept in a folder.

SHARING
The students share with another person or the group something they have written or drawn.

Alphabet

Letters: *F f* or _____

INTRODUCTION—STUDENT PROJECTS LESSON
The teacher reviews the letters and letter formation. The class discusses making a fish from construction paper.

STUDENT ACTIVITY
The students make their own version of a fish.

SHARING
The students take their projects home.

Lesson 10

Pictures and Words

INTRODUCTION
Picture: Houses or _____
   The teacher leads a brief discussion about the picture.

CHART DEVELOPMENT
Phase I—Single Words: The students volunteer words to label the picture, and the teacher writes the words on the chart. Most of the labels will be single words. Students draw lines to connect parts of the picture to the words.

COMPREHENSION FOCUS
The teacher develops comprehension of the picture by asking questions, many of which will begin with *what*.
   The chart is displayed in the classroom.

Storytime

READ ALOUD
Don't Forget The Bacon!
by Pat Hutchins
or _____

DISCUSSION FOCUS
The class tries to list the items on the boy's shopping list.

Writing

Five-Day Theme: All About Me
or _____

INTRODUCTION
The teacher leads a class discussion about points of interest generated during the first four days of the theme and introduces the student activity.

STUDENT ACTIVITY
The students make a picture of themselves.

SHARING
The teacher mounts the pictures and combines them into a whole class mobile.

Alphabet

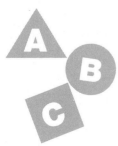

Letters: *H h* or _____

INTRODUCTION—BRAINSTORMING LESSON
The teacher introduces the letters and demonstrates letter formation. On the chalkboard, the teacher writes student-volunteered words and illustrations of words containing the letters.

STUDENT ACTIVITY
On their papers, students write
■ examples of the letters

■ their favorite words or illustrations from the chalkboard
■ other words or drawings

SHARING
The students share with another person or the group something they have written or drawn.
   Papers are dated and filed.

Lesson 11

Pictures and Words

INTRODUCTION
Picture: Family or _____
The teacher leads a brief discussion about the picture.

CHART DEVELOPMENT
Phase I—Single Words: The students volunteer words to label the picture, and the teacher writes the words on the chart. Most of the labels will be single words. Students draw lines to connect parts of the picture to the words.

COMPREHENSION FOCUS
The teacher develops comprehension of the picture by asking questions, many of which will begin with *who*.
The chart is displayed in the classroom.

Storytime

READ ALOUD
Jennie's Hat
by Ezra Jack Keats
or _____

DISCUSSION FOCUS
What interesting words did you hear in this story? Could you use different words to tell about the hat?

Writing

Five-Day Theme: My Family
or _____

INTRODUCTION
The teacher and the students have a conversation related to the theme. The conversation might include a reference to the Pictures and Words chart made earlier in the day.

WRITING ACTIVITIES
While the students are writing or drawing, the teacher meets with individuals or small groups to discuss the theme. The student's independent work may or may not relate to the theme. Each student's work is kept in a folder.

SHARING
The students share with another person or the group something they have written or drawn.

Alphabet

Letters: *H h* or _____

INTRODUCTION—STUDENT PROJECTS LESSON
The teacher reviews the letters and letter formation. The class constructs hats from newspapers or construction paper.

STUDENT ACTIVITY
The students make their own version of a hat.

SHARING
The students take their projects home.

Pictures and Words

INTRODUCTION
Picture: Firefighters or _____

The teacher leads a brief discussion about the picture.

CHART DEVELOPMENT
Phase I—Single Words: The students volunteer words to label the picture, and the teacher writes the words on the chart. Most of the labels will be single words. Students draw lines to connect parts of the picture to the words.

COMPREHENSION FOCUS
The teacher develops comprehension of the picture by asking questions, many of which will begin with *where*.

The chart is displayed in the classroom.

Storytime

READ ALOUD
Harry the Dirty Dog
by Gene Zion
Clifford the Big Red Dog
by Norman Bridwell
or _____

DISCUSSION FOCUS
Discuss the dogs and their human friends in one or both of these stories.

Writing

Five-Day Theme: My Family
or _____

INTRODUCTION
The teacher and the students have a conversation related to the theme.

WRITING ACTIVITIES
While the students are writing or drawing, the teacher meets with individuals or small groups to discuss the theme. The student's independent work may or may not relate to the theme. Each student's work is kept in a folder.

SHARING
The students share with another person or the group something they have written or drawn.

Alphabet

Letters: *H h* or _____

INTRODUCTION—RESEARCH LESSON—Magazines
The teacher reviews the letters and letter formation. The teacher leads a discussion about words for objects that may be found in magazines which contain the designated letters.

STUDENT ACTIVITY
The students cut or tear the letters or related objects from magazines and glue them on individual papers or the class chart. Some of the objects may be labeled.

SHARING
The teacher and students discuss items on the class chart. The chart is displayed in the classroom.

Lesson 13

Pictures and Words

INTRODUCTION
Picture: Bubble Gum or _____
The teacher leads a brief discussion about the picture.

CHART DEVELOPMENT
Phase I—Single Words: The students volunteer words to label the picture, and the teacher writes the words on the chart. Most of the labels will be single words. Students draw lines to connect parts of the picture to the words.

COMPREHENSION FOCUS
The teacher develops comprehension of the picture by asking questions, many of which will begin with *when*.
The chart is displayed in the classroom.

Storytime

READ ALOUD
The Tale of Benjamin Bunny
by Beatrix Potter
or _____

DISCUSSION FOCUS
What family members are mentioned in this story?

Writing

Five-Day Theme: My Family
or _____

INTRODUCTION
The teacher and the students have a conversation related to the theme.

WRITING ACTIVITIES
While the students are writing or drawing, the teacher meets with individuals or small groups to discuss the theme. The student's independent work may or may not relate to the theme. Each student's work is kept in a folder.

SHARING
The students share with another person or the group something they have written or drawn.

Alphabet

Letters: *D d* or _____

INTRODUCTION—BRAINSTORMING LESSON
The teacher introduces the letters and demonstrates letter formation. On the chalkboard, the teacher writes student-volunteered words and illustrations of words containing the letters.

STUDENT ACTIVITY
On their papers, students write
■ examples of the letters
■ their favorite words or illustrations from the chalkboard
■ other words or drawings

SHARING
The students share with another person or the group something they have written or drawn.
Papers are dated and filed.

Lesson 14

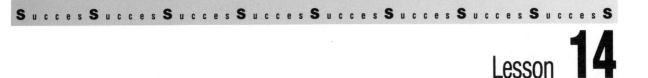

Pictures and Words

INTRODUCTION
Picture: Rain or _____
   The teacher leads a brief discussion about the picture.

CHART DEVELOPMENT
Phase I—Single Words: The students volunteer words to label the picture, and the teacher writes the words on the chart. Most of the labels will be single words. Students draw lines to connect parts of the picture to the words.

COMPREHENSION FOCUS
The teacher develops comprehension of the picture by asking questions, many of which will begin with *where*.
   The chart is displayed in the classroom.

Storytime

READ ALOUD
Rain, Rain, Rivers
by Uri Shulevitz
or _____

DISCUSSION FOCUS
Do the colors make you think of rainy weather? Discuss other colors that go with types of weather.

Writing

Five-Day Theme: My Family
or _____

INTRODUCTION
The teacher and the students have a conversation related to the theme.

WRITING ACTIVITIES
While the students are writing or drawing, the teacher meets with individuals or small groups to discuss the theme. The student's independent work may or may not relate to the theme. Each student's work is kept in a folder.

SHARING
The students share with another person or the group something they have written or drawn.

Alphabet

Letters: *D d* or _____

INTRODUCTION—STUDENT PROJECTS LESSON
The teacher reviews the letters and letter formation. The class discusses making a duck from paper plates and construction paper.

STUDENT ACTIVITY
The students make their own version of a duck.

SHARING
The students take their projects home.

Lesson 15

Pictures and Words

INTRODUCTION
Picture: Dentist or _____
The teacher leads a brief discussion about the picture.

CHART DEVELOPMENT
Phase I—Single Words: The students volunteer words to label the picture, and the teacher writes the words

on the chart. Most of the labels will be single words. Students draw lines to connect parts of the picture to the words.

COMPREHENSION FOCUS
The teacher develops comprehension of the picture by asking questions, many of which will begin with *when*.
The chart is displayed in the classroom.

Storytime

READ ALOUD
Be Nice to Spiders
by Margaret Bloy Graham
or _____

DISCUSSION FOCUS
What was funny about this story? Discuss words that made it funny.

Writing

Five-Day Theme: My Family
or _____

INTRODUCTION
The teacher leads a class discussion about points of interest generated during the first four days of the theme and introduces the student activity.

STUDENT ACTIVITY
The students illustrate and name the members of their own family. Make a class book.

SHARING
Read the class book and place it in the classroom book collection.

Alphabet

Letters: *D d* or _____

INTRODUCTION—RESEARCH LESSON—Magazines
The teacher reviews the letters and letter formation. The teacher leads a discussion about words for objects that may be found in magazines which contain the designated letters.

STUDENT ACTIVITY
The students cut or tear the letters or related objects from magazines and glue

them on individual papers or the class chart. Some of the objects may be labeled.

SHARING
The teacher and students discuss items on the class chart. The chart is displayed in the classroom.

Lesson **16**

Pictures and Words

INTRODUCTION
Picture: Fall or _____
   The teacher leads a brief discussion about the picture.

CHART DEVELOPMENT
Phase I—Single Words: The students volunteer words to label the picture, and the teacher writes the words on the chart. Most of the labels will be single words. Students draw lines to connect parts of the picture to the words.

COMPREHENSION FOCUS
The teacher develops comprehension of the picture by asking questions, many of which will begin with *why*.
   The chart is displayed in the classroom.

Storytime

READ ALOUD
Apples and Pumpkins
by Anne Rockwell
or _____

DISCUSSION FOCUS
Talk about words and pictures which show changes over a period of time.

Writing

Five-Day Theme: Fall
or _____

INTRODUCTION
The teacher and the students have a conversation related to the theme. Conversations might include a reference to the Pictures and Words chart made earlier in the day.

WRITING ACTIVITIES
While the students are writing or drawing, the teacher meets with individuals or small groups to discuss the theme. The student's independent work may or may not relate to the theme. Each student's work is kept in a folder.

SHARING
The students share with another person or the group something they have written or drawn.

Alphabet

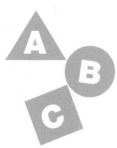

Letters: *I i* or _____

INTRODUCTION— BRAINSTORMING LESSON
The teacher introduces the letters and demonstrates letter formation. On the chalkboard, the teacher writes student-volunteered words and illustrations of words containing the letters.

STUDENT ACTIVITY
On their papers, students write
■ examples of the letters
■ their favorite words or illustrations from the chalkboard
■ other words or drawings

SHARING
The students share with another person or the group something they have written or drawn.
   Papers are dated and filed.

Lesson 17

Pictures and Words

INTRODUCTION
Picture: Circles or _____
    The teacher leads a brief discussion about the picture.

CHART DEVELOPMENT
Phase I—Single Words: The students volunteer words to label the picture, and the teacher writes the words on the chart. Most of the labels will be single words. Students draw lines to connect parts of the picture to the words.

COMPREHENSION FOCUS
The teacher develops comprehension of the picture by asking questions, many of which will begin with *where*.
    The chart is displayed in the classroom.

Storytime

READ ALOUD
Inch by Inch
by Leo Lionni
or _____

DISCUSSION FOCUS
Make a list of the places the inchworm was (measured) in the story.

Writing

Five-Day Theme: Fall
or _____

INTRODUCTION
The teacher and the students have a conversation related to the theme.

WRITING ACTIVITIES
While the students are writing or drawing, the teacher meets with individuals or small groups to discuss the theme. The student's independent work may or may not relate to the theme. Each student's work is kept in a folder.

SHARING
The students share with another person or the group something they have written or drawn.

Alphabet

Letters: *I i* or _____

INTRODUCTION—STUDENT PROJECTS LESSON
The teacher reviews the letters and letter formation. The class discusses making an inchworm from construction paper circles.

STUDENT ACTIVITY
The students make their own version of an inchworm.

SHARING
The students take their projects home.

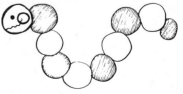

Lesson 18

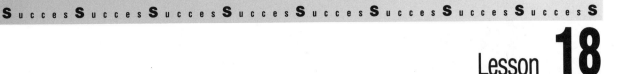

Pictures and Words

INTRODUCTION
Picture: Bears or _____
  The teacher leads a brief discussion about the picture.

CHART DEVELOPMENT
Phase I—Single Words: The students volunteer words to label the picture, and the teacher writes the words on the chart. Most of the labels will be single words. Students draw lines to connect parts of the picture to the words.

COMPREHENSION FOCUS
The teacher develops comprehension of the picture by asking questions, many of which will begin with *how*.
  The chart is displayed in the classroom.

Storytime

READ ALOUD
Jessie Bear, What Will You Wear? by Nancy White Carlstrom
or _____

DISCUSSION FOCUS
Talk about the words that rhyme. Is there a repeated pattern?

Writing

Five-Day Theme: Fall
or _____

INTRODUCTION
The teacher and the students have a conversation related to the theme.

WRITING ACTIVITIES
While the students are writing or drawing, the teacher meets with individuals or small groups to discuss the theme. The student's independent work may or may not relate to the theme. Each student's work is kept in a folder.

SHARING
The students share with another person or the group something they have written or drawn.

Alphabet

Letters: *I i* or _____

INTRODUCTION—RESEARCH LESSON—Newspapers
The teacher reviews the letters and letter formation.

STUDENT ACTIVITY
The students use highlighter pens or crayons to mark the letters in newspapers.

SHARING
The students share something they have marked on their paper with another person or the group.

Lesson 19

Pictures and Words

INTRODUCTION
Picture: Ponds or _____
   The teacher leads a brief discussion about the picture.

CHART DEVELOPMENT
Phase I—Single Words: The students volunteer words to label the picture, and the teacher writes the words on the chart. Most of the labels will be single words. Students draw lines to connect parts of the picture to the words.

COMPREHENSION FOCUS
The teacher develops comprehension of the picture by asking questions, many of which will begin with *who*.
   The chart is displayed in the classroom.

Storytime

READ ALOUD
Jam
by Margaret Mahy
or _____

DISCUSSION FOCUS
Discuss the procedures for making jam. What is needed to make jam?

Writing

Five-Day Theme: Fall
or _____

INTRODUCTION
The teacher and the students have a conversation related to the theme.

WRITING ACTIVITIES
While the students are writing or drawing, the teacher meets with individuals or small groups to discuss the theme. The student's independent work may or may not relate to the theme. Each student's work is kept in a folder.

SHARING
The students share with another person or the group something they have written or drawn.

Alphabet

Letters: *J j* or _____

INTRODUCTION—BRAINSTORMING LESSON
The teacher introduces the letters and demonstrates letter formation. On the chalkboard, the teacher writes student-volunteered words and illustrations of words containing the letters.

STUDENT ACTIVITY
On their papers, students write
■ examples of the letters
■ their favorite words or illustrations from the chalkboard
■ other words or drawings

SHARING
The students share with another person or the group something they have written or drawn.
   Papers are dated and filed.

Lesson 20

Pictures and Words

INTRODUCTION
Picture: Football Player or _____
   The teacher leads a brief discussion about the picture.

CHART DEVELOPMENT
Phase I—Single Words: The students volunteer words to label the picture, and the teacher writes the words on the chart. Most of the labels will be single words. Students draw lines to connect parts of the picture to the words.

COMPREHENSION FOCUS
The teacher develops comprehension of the picture by asking questions, many of which will begin with *what*.
   The chart is displayed in the classroom.

Storytime

READ ALOUD
Frederick
by Leo Lionni
or _____

DISCUSSION FOCUS
How do the illustrations show that time is passing?

Writing

Five-Day Theme: Fall
or _____

INTRODUCTION
The teacher leads a class discussion about points of interest generated during the first four days of the theme and introduces the student activity.

STUDENT ACTIVITY
The students bring or gather leaves with interesting veining and shape. The class does crayon leaf rubbings. Try using different weights and textures of paper.

SHARING
Display the leaf rubbings.

Alphabet

Letters: *J j* or _____

INTRODUCTION—RESEARCH LESSON—Magazines
The teacher reviews the letters and letter formation. The teacher leads a discussion about words for objects that may be found in magazines which contain the designated letters.

STUDENT ACTIVITY
The students cut or tear the letters or related objects from magazines and glue them on individual papers or the class chart. Some of the objects may be labeled.

SHARING
The teacher and students discuss items on the class chart. The chart is displayed in the classroom.

Lesson 21

Pictures and Words

INTRODUCTION
Picture: Birds or _____
 The teacher leads a brief discussion about the picture.

CHART DEVELOPMENT
Phase II—Word Clusters and Title: The students volunteer words to label the picture, and the teacher writes the words on the chart. Most of the labels will be word clusters. Students draw lines to connect parts of the picture to the words. The teacher writes a student-chosen title on the chart.

COMPREHENSION FOCUS
The teacher develops comprehension of the picture by asking questions, many of which will begin with *how*.
 The chart is displayed in the classroom.

Storytime

READ ALOUD
The Little House
by Virginia Lee Burton
or _____

DISCUSSION FOCUS
Discuss the words that tell about time passing.

Writing

Five-Day Theme: Birds
or _____

INTRODUCTION
The teacher and the students have a conversation related to the theme. Conversations might include a reference to the Pictures and Words chart made earlier in the day.

WRITING ACTIVITIES
While the students are writing or drawing, the teacher meets with individuals or small groups to discuss the theme. The student's independent work may or may not relate to the theme. Each student's work is kept in a folder.

SHARING
The students share with another person or the group something they have written or drawn.

Alphabet

Letters: *J j* or _____

INTRODUCTION—STUDENT PROJECTS LESSON
The teacher reviews the letters and letter formation. The class discusses making a jack-in-the-box from milk cartons or construction paper. A lid could be connected with a brad.

STUDENT ACTIVITY
The students make their own version of a jack-in-the-box.

SHARING
The students take their projects home.

Pictures and Words

INTRODUCTION
Picture: Boats or _____
    The teacher leads a brief discussion about the picture.

CHART DEVELOPMENT
Phase II—Word Clusters and Title: The students volunteer words to label the picture, and the teacher writes the words on the chart. Most of the labels will be word clusters. Students draw lines to connect parts of the picture to the words. The teacher writes a student-chosen title on the chart.

COMPREHENSION FOCUS
The teacher develops comprehension of the picture by asking questions, many of which will begin with *why*.
    The chart is displayed in the classroom.

Storytime

READ ALOUD
Feathers for Lunch
by Lois Ehlert
or _____

DISCUSSION FOCUS
Discuss bright and pale colors. Which colors are bright in the story?

Writing

Five-Day Theme: Birds
or _____

INTRODUCTION
The teacher and the students have a conversation related to the theme.

WRITING ACTIVITIES
While the students are writing or drawing, the teacher meets with individuals or small groups to discuss the theme. The student's independent work may or may not relate to the theme. Each student's work is kept in a folder.

SHARING
The students share with another person or the group something they have written or drawn.

Alphabet

Letters: *A a* or _____

INTRODUCTION—BRAINSTORMING LESSON
The teacher introduces the letters and demonstrates letter formation. On the chalkboard, the teacher writes student-volunteered words and illustrations of words containing the letters.

STUDENT ACTIVITY
On their papers, students write
- examples of the letters
- their favorite words or illustrations from the chalkboard
- other words or drawings

SHARING
The students share with another person or the group something they have written or drawn.
    Papers are dated and filed.

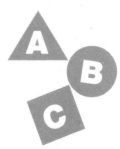

Lesson **23**

Pictures and Words

INTRODUCTION
Picture: Kitchens or _____
   The teacher leads a brief discussion about the picture.

CHART DEVELOPMENT
Phase II—Word Clusters and Title: The students volunteer words to label the picture, and the teacher writes the words on the chart. Most of the labels will be word clusters. Students draw lines to connect parts of the picture to the words. The teacher writes a student-chosen title on the chart.

COMPREHENSION FOCUS
The teacher develops comprehension of the picture by asking questions, many of which will begin with *who*.
   The chart is displayed in the classroom.

Storytime

READ ALOUD
Alligators All Around
by Maurice Sendak
Pierre
by Maurice Sendak
or _____

DISCUSSION FOCUS
What funny things can you see in the illustrations? Do you know of any other books illustrated by Maurice Sendak?

Writing

Five-Day Theme: Birds
or _____

INTRODUCTION
The teacher and the students have a conversation related to the theme.

WRITING ACTIVITIES
While the students are writing or drawing, the teacher meets with individuals or small groups to discuss the theme. The student's independent work may or may not relate to the theme. Each student's work is kept in a folder.

SHARING
The students share with another person or the group something they have written or drawn.

Alphabet

Letters: *A a* or _____

INTRODUCTION—STUDENT PROJECTS LESSON
The teacher reviews the letters and letter formation. The class discusses making a construction paper alligator. A brad might be used to add a movable jaw.

STUDENT ACTIVITY
The students make their own version of an alligator.

SHARING
The students take their projects home.

122

Lesson 24

Pictures and Words

INTRODUCTION
Picture: Airplanes or _____
   The teacher leads a brief discussion about the picture.

CHART DEVELOPMENT
Phase II—Word Clusters and Title: The students volunteer words to label the picture, and the teacher writes the words on the chart. Most of the labels will be word clusters. Students draw lines to connect parts of the picture to the words. The teacher writes a student-chosen title on the chart.

COMPREHENSION FOCUS
The teacher develops comprehension of the picture by asking questions, many of which will begin with *where*.
   The chart is displayed in the classroom.

Storytime

READ ALOUD
Ten, Nine, Eight
by Molly Bang
or _____

DISCUSSION FOCUS
Would your countdown to bedtime be the same as the child in the story?

Writing

Five-Day Theme: Birds
or _____

INTRODUCTION
The teacher and the students have a conversation related to the theme.

WRITING ACTIVITIES
While the students are writing or drawing, the teacher meets with individuals or small groups to discuss the theme. The student's independent work may or may not relate to the theme. Each student's work is kept in a folder.

SHARING
The students share with another person or the group something they have written or drawn.

Alphabet

Letters: *A a* or _____

INTRODUCTION—RESEARCH LESSON—Magazines
The teacher reviews the letters and letter formation. The teacher leads a discussion about words for objects that may be found in magazines which contain the designated letters.

STUDENT ACTIVITY
The students cut or tear the letters or related objects from magazines and glue them on individual papers or the class chart. Some of the objects may be labeled.

SHARING
The teacher and students discuss items on the class chart. The chart is displayed in the classroom.

Lesson **25**

Pictures and Words

INTRODUCTION
Picture: Hearing or _____
  The teacher leads a brief discussion about the picture.

CHART DEVELOPMENT
Phase II—Word Clusters and Title: The students volunteer words to label the picture, and the teacher writes the words on the chart. Most of the labels will be word clusters. Students draw lines to connect parts of the picture to the words. The teacher writes a student-chosen title on the chart.

COMPREHENSION FOCUS
The teacher develops comprehension of the picture by asking questions, many of which will begin with *what*.
  The chart is displayed in the classroom.

Storytime

READ ALOUD
What Is a Bird?
by Ron Hirschi
or _____

DISCUSSION FOCUS
Discuss how the illustrations help you know that this is a true book.

Writing

Five-Day Theme: Birds
or _____

INTRODUCTION
The teacher leads a class discussion about points of interest generated during the first four days of the theme and introduces the student activity.

STUDENT ACTIVITY
The class dramatizes the book *Feathers for Lunch* or *Are You My Mother?*

SHARING
Videotape or present "the play" to another classroom.

Alphabet

Letters: *P p* or _____

INTRODUCTION—BRAINSTORMING LESSON
The teacher introduces the letters and demonstrates letter formation. On the chalkboard, the teacher writes student-volunteered words and illustrations of words containing the letters.

STUDENT ACTIVITY
On their papers, students write
■ examples of the letters
■ their favorite words or illustrations from the chalkboard
■ other words or drawings

SHARING
The students share with another person or the group something they have written or drawn.
  Papers are dated and filed.

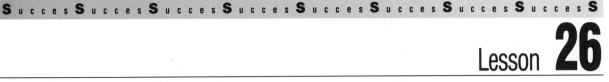
Lesson 26

Pictures and Words

INTRODUCTION
Picture: Transportation or _____
   The teacher leads a brief discussion about the picture.

CHART DEVELOPMENT
Phase II—Word Clusters and Title: The students volunteer words to label the picture, and the teacher writes the words on the chart. Most of the labels will be word clusters. Students draw lines to connect parts of the picture to the words. The teacher writes a student-chosen title on the chart.

COMPREHENSION FOCUS
The teacher develops comprehension of the picture by asking questions, many of which will begin with *why*.
   The chart is displayed in the classroom.

Storytime

READ ALOUD
Little Bear
by Else Holmelund Minarik
Flossie and the Fox
by Patricia McKissack
or _____

DISCUSSION FOCUS
How many characters are in the story? How do they feel about each other?

Writing

Five-Day Theme: Transportation or _____

INTRODUCTION
The teacher and the students have a conversation related to the theme. Conversations might include a reference to the Pictures and Words chart made earlier in the day.

WRITING ACTIVITIES
While the students are writing or drawing, the teacher meets with individuals or small groups to discuss the theme. The student's independent work may or may not relate to the theme. Each student's work is kept in a folder.

SHARING
The students share with another person or the group something they have written or drawn.

Alphabet

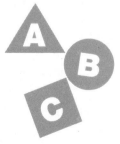

Letters: *P p* or _____

INTRODUCTION—STUDENT PROJECTS LESSON
The teacher reviews the letters and letter formation. The class discusses making a puppet from paper bags.

STUDENT ACTIVITY
The students make their own version of a puppet.

SHARING
The students take their projects home.

Lesson 27

Pictures and Words

INTRODUCTION
Picture: Police Officer or _____
The teacher leads a brief discussion about the picture.

CHART DEVELOPMENT
Phase II—Word Clusters and Title: The students volunteer words to label the picture, and the teacher writes the words on the chart. Most of the labels will be word clusters. Students draw lines to connect parts of the picture to the words. The teacher writes a student-chosen title on the chart.

COMPREHENSION FOCUS
The teacher develops comprehension of the picture by asking questions, many of which will begin with *how*.
The chart is displayed in the classroom.

Storytime

READ ALOUD
Tomie dePaola's Mother Goose
by Tomie dePaola
or _____

DISCUSSION FOCUS
Compare two or three different selections and talk about how rhyming words are used.

Writing

Five-Day Theme: Transportation
or _____

INTRODUCTION
The teacher and the students have a conversation related to the theme.

WRITING ACTIVITIES
While the students are writing or drawing, the teacher meets with individuals or small groups to discuss the theme. The student's independent work may or may not relate to the theme. Each student's work is kept in a folder.

SHARING
The students share with another person or the group something they have written or drawn.

Alphabet

Letters: *P p* or _____

INTRODUCTION—RESEARCH LESSON—Newspapers
The teacher reviews the letters and letter formation.

STUDENT ACTIVITY
The students use highlighter pens or crayons to mark the letters in newspapers.

SHARING
The students share something they have marked on their paper with another person or the group.

Lesson 28

Pictures and Words

INTRODUCTION
Picture: Eyes or _____
The teacher leads a brief discussion about the picture.

CHART DEVELOPMENT
Phase II—Word Clusters and Title: The students volunteer words to label the picture, and the teacher writes the words on the chart. Most of the labels will be word clusters. Students draw lines to connect parts of the picture to the words. The teacher writes a student-chosen title on the chart.

COMPREHENSION FOCUS
The teacher develops comprehension of the picture by asking questions, many of which will begin with *who*.
The chart is displayed in the classroom.

Storytime

READ ALOUD
The Bears Bicycle
by David McPhail
or _____

DISCUSSION FOCUS
Is this story real? Could this happen with a real child and a bike?

Writing

Five-Day Theme: Transportation
or _____

INTRODUCTION
The teacher and the students have a conversation related to the theme.

WRITING ACTIVITIES
While the students are writing or drawing, the teacher meets with individuals or small groups to discuss the theme. The student's independent work may or may not relate to the theme. Each student's work is kept in a folder.

SHARING
The students share with another person or the group something they have written or drawn.

Alphabet

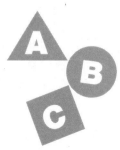

Letters: *B b* or _____

INTRODUCTION—
BRAINSTORMING LESSON
The teacher introduces the letters and demonstrates letter formation. On the chalkboard, the teacher writes student-volunteered words and illustrations of words containing the letters.

STUDENT ACTIVITY
On their papers, students write
■ examples of the letters
■ their favorite words or illustrations from the chalkboard
■ other words or drawings

SHARING
The students share with another person or the group something they have written or drawn.
Papers are dated and filed.

Lesson 29

Pictures and Words

INTRODUCTION
Picture: Chairs or _____
The teacher leads a brief discussion about the picture.

CHART DEVELOPMENT
Phase II—Word Clusters and Title: The students volunteer words to label the picture, and the teacher writes the words on the chart. Most of the labels will be word clusters. Students draw lines to connect parts of the picture to the words. The teacher writes a student-chosen title on the chart.

COMPREHENSION FOCUS
The teacher develops comprehension of the picture by asking questions, many of which will begin with *what*.
The chart is displayed in the classroom.

Storytime

READ ALOUD
Brown Bear, Brown Bear
by Bill Martin, Jr.
or _____

DISCUSSION FOCUS
Why are the color words important in this story?

Writing

Five-Day Theme: Transportation
or _____

INTRODUCTION
The teacher and the students have a conversation related to the theme.

WRITING ACTIVITIES
While the students are writing or drawing, the teacher meets with individuals or small groups to discuss the theme. The student's independent work may or may not relate to the theme. Each student's work is kept in a folder.

SHARING
The students share with another person or the group something they have written or drawn.

Alphabet

Letters: *B b* or _____

INTRODUCTION—STUDENT PROJECTS LESSON
The teacher reviews the letters and letter formation. The class discusses making a brown bear with circles of brown construction paper.

STUDENT ACTIVITY
The students make their own version of a brown bear.

SHARING
The students take their projects home.

Lesson **30**

Pictures and Words

INTRODUCTION
Picture: Desert or _____
   The teacher leads a brief discussion about the picture.

CHART DEVELOPMENT
Phase II—Word Clusters and Title: The students volunteer words to label the picture, and the teacher writes the words on the chart. Most of the labels will be word clusters. Students draw lines to connect parts of the picture to the words. The teacher writes a student-chosen title on the chart.

COMPREHENSION FOCUS
The teacher develops comprehension of the picture by asking questions, many of which will begin with *why*.
   The chart is displayed in the classroom.

Storytime

READ ALOUD
Trucks
by Byron Barton
Trucks
by Gail Gibbons
or _____

DISCUSSION FOCUS
How are cars and trucks alike and how are they different?

Writing

Five-Day Theme: Transportation
or _____

INTRODUCTION
The teacher leads a class discussion about points of interest generated during the first four days of the theme and introduces the student activity.

STUDENT ACTIVITY
Each child illustrates a vehicle or cuts one out of a magazine.

SHARING
The vehicles are placed on a large drawing of a highway for a classroom bulletin board.

Alphabet

Letters: *B b* or _____

INTRODUCTION—RESEARCH LESSON—Magazines
The teacher reviews the letters and letter formation. The teacher leads a discussion about words for objects that may be found in magazines which contain the designated letters.

STUDENT ACTIVITY
The students cut or tear the letters or related objects from magazines and glue them on individual papers or the class chart. Some of the objects may be labeled.

SHARING
The teacher and students discuss items on the class chart. The chart is displayed in the classroom.

Lesson 31

Pictures and Words

INTRODUCTION
Picture: Bedtime or _____
The teacher leads a brief discussion about the picture.

CHART DEVELOPMENT
Phase II—Word Clusters and Title: The students volunteer words to label the picture, and the teacher writes the words on the chart. Most of the labels will be word clusters. Students draw lines to connect parts of the picture to the words. The teacher writes a student-chosen title on the chart.

COMPREHENSION FOCUS
The teacher develops comprehension of the picture by asking questions, many of which will begin with *how*.
The chart is displayed in the classroom.

Storytime

READ ALOUD
Roll Over
by Merle Peek
or _____

DISCUSSION FOCUS
What happened each time they said "Roll over"?

Writing

Five-Day Theme: Bedtime
or _____

INTRODUCTION
The teacher and the students have a conversation related to the theme. Conversations might contain a reference to the Pictures and Words chart made earlier in the day.

WRITING ACTIVITIES
While the students are writing or drawing, the teacher meets with individuals or small groups to discuss the theme. The student's independent work may or may not relate to the theme. Each student's work is kept in a folder.

SHARING
The students share with another person or the group something they have written or drawn.

Alphabet

Letters: *V v* or _____

INTRODUCTION— BRAINSTORMING LESSON
The teacher introduces the letters and demonstrates letter formation. On the chalkboard, the teacher writes student-volunteered words and illustrations of words containing the letters.

STUDENT ACTIVITY
On their papers, students write
- examples of the letters
- their favorite words or illustrations from the chalkboard
- other words or drawings

SHARING
The students share with another person or the group something they have written or drawn.
Papers are dated and filed.

Lesson **32**

Pictures and Words

INTRODUCTION
Picture: Water or _____
The teacher leads a brief discussion about the picture.

CHART DEVELOPMENT
Phase II—Word Clusters and Title: The students volunteer words to label the picture, and the teacher writes the words on the chart. Most of the labels will be word clusters. Students draw lines to connect parts of the picture to the words. The teacher writes a student-chosen title on the chart.

COMPREHENSION FOCUS
The teacher develops comprehension of the picture by asking questions, many of which will begin with *where*.
The chart is displayed in the classroom.

Storytime

READ ALOUD
Arthur's Valentine
by Marc Brown
or _____

DISCUSSION FOCUS
What did each character do?

Writing

Five-Day Theme: Bedtime
or _____

INTRODUCTION
The teacher and the students have a conversation related to the theme.

WRITING ACTIVITIES
While the students are writing or drawing, the teacher meets with individuals or small groups to discuss the theme. The student's independent work may or may not relate to the theme. Each student's work is kept in a folder.

SHARING
The students share with another person or the group something they have written or drawn.

Alphabet

Letters: *V v* or _____

INTRODUCTION—STUDENT PROJECTS LESSON
The teacher reviews the letters and letter formation. The class discusses making a valentine with construction paper and lace.

STUDENT ACTIVITY
The students make their own version of a valentine.

SHARING
The students take their projects home.

131

Lesson 33

Pictures and Words

INTRODUCTION
Picture: Astronauts or _____
   The teacher leads a brief discussion about the picture.

CHART DEVELOPMENT
Phase II—Word Clusters and Title: The students volunteer words to label the picture, and the teacher writes the words on the chart. Most of the labels will be word clusters. Students draw lines to connect parts of the picture to the words. The teacher writes a student-chosen title on the chart.

COMPREHENSION FOCUS
The teacher develops comprehension of the picture by asking questions, many of which will begin with *what*.
   The chart is displayed in the classroom.

Storytime

READ ALOUD
I Want to Be an Astronaut
by Byron Barton
or _____

DISCUSSION FOCUS
Is this story about a real event?

Writing

Five-Day Theme: Bedtime
or _____

INTRODUCTION
The teacher and the students have a conversation related to the theme.

WRITING ACTIVITIES
While the students are writing or drawing, the teacher meets with individuals or small groups to discuss the theme. The student's independent work may or may not relate to the theme. Each student's work is kept in a folder.

SHARING
The students share with another person or the group something they have written or drawn.

Alphabet

Letters: *V v* or _____

INTRODUCTION—RESEARCH LESSON—Magazines
The teacher reviews the letters and letter formation. The teacher leads a discussion about words for objects that may be found in magazines which contain the designated letters.

STUDENT ACTIVITY
The students cut or tear the letters or related objects from magazines and glue them on individual papers or the class chart. Some of the objects may be labeled.

SHARING
The teacher and students discuss items on the class chart. The chart is displayed in the classroom.

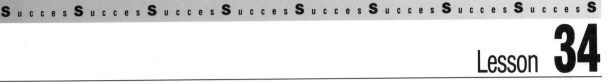

Lesson 34

Pictures and Words

INTRODUCTION
Picture: Pirate or _____
The teacher leads a brief discussion about the picture.

CHART DEVELOPMENT
Phase II—Word Clusters and Title: The students volunteer words to label the picture, and the teacher writes the words on the chart. Most of the labels will be word clusters. Students draw lines to connect parts of the picture to the words. The teacher writes a student-chosen title on the chart.

COMPREHENSION FOCUS
The teacher develops comprehension of the picture by asking questions, many of which will begin with *what*.
The chart is displayed in the classroom.

Storytime

READ ALOUD
Beneath a Blue Umbrella
by Jack Prelutsky
or _____

DISCUSSION FOCUS
Talk about the rhyming words in the short poem "Jennifer Juniper."

Writing

Five-Day Theme: Bedtime
or _____

INTRODUCTION
The teacher and the students have a conversation related to the theme.

WRITING ACTIVITIES
While the students are writing or drawing, the teacher meets with individuals or small groups to discuss the theme. The student's independent work may or may not relate to the theme. Each student's work is kept in a folder.

SHARING
The students share with another person or the group something they have written or drawn.

Alphabet

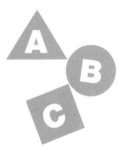

Letters: *X x* or _____

INTRODUCTION—BRAINSTORMING LESSON
The teacher introduces the letters and demonstrates letter formation. On the chalkboard, the teacher writes student-volunteered words and illustrations of words containing the letters.

STUDENT ACTIVITY
On their papers, students write
■ examples of the letters
■ their favorite words or illustrations from the chalkboard
■ other words or drawings

SHARING
The students share with another person or the group something they have written or drawn.
Papers are dated and filed.

Lesson **35**

Pictures and Words

INTRODUCTION
Picture: Tennis shoes or _____
   The teacher leads a brief discussion about the picture.

CHART DEVELOPMENT
Phase II—Word Clusters and Title: The students volunteer words to label the picture, and the teacher writes the words on the chart. Most of the labels will be word clusters. Students draw lines to connect parts of the picture to the words. The teacher writes a student-chosen title on the chart.

COMPREHENSION FOCUS
The teacher develops comprehension of the picture by asking questions, many of which will begin with *why*.
   The chart is displayed in the classroom.

Storytime

READ ALOUD
Ira Sleeps Over
by Bernard Waber
or _____

DISCUSSION FOCUS
How did the boy's feelings change during the story?

Writing

Five-Day Theme: Bedtime
or _____

INTRODUCTION
The teacher leads a class discussion about points of interest generated during the first four days of the theme and introduces the student activity.

STUDENT ACTIVITY
Make a class book about individual bedtime rituals.

SHARING
Read the bound class book and place it with the classroom book collection.

Alphabet

Letters: *X x* or _____

INTRODUCTION—RESEARCH LESSON—Newspapers
The teacher reviews the letters and letter formation.

STUDENT ACTIVITY
The students use highlighter pens or crayons to mark the letters in newspapers.

SHARING
The students share something they have marked on their paper with another person or the group.

Lesson 36

Pictures and Words

INTRODUCTION
Picture: Safety or _____
The teacher leads a brief discussion about the picture.

CHART DEVELOPMENT
Phase II—Word Clusters and Title: The students volunteer words to label the picture, and the teacher writes the words on the chart. Most of the labels will be word clusters. Students draw lines to connect parts of the picture to the words. The teacher writes a student-chosen title on the chart.

COMPREHENSION FOCUS
The teacher develops comprehension of the picture by asking questions, many of which will begin with *how*.
The chart is displayed in the classroom.

Storytime

READ ALOUD
Funnybones
by Allan Ahlberg
or _____

DISCUSSION FOCUS
Make a list of the many different kinds of skeletons in the story.

Writing

Five-Day Theme: Safety
or _____

INTRODUCTION
The teacher and the students have a conversation related to the theme. Conversations might include a reference to the Pictures and Words chart made earlier in the day.

WRITING ACTIVITIES
While the students are writing or drawing, the teacher meets with individuals or small groups to discuss the theme. The student's independent work may or may not relate to the theme. Each student's work is kept in a folder.

SHARING
The students share with another person or the group something they have written or drawn.

Alphabet

Letters: *X x* or _____

INTRODUCTION—STUDENT PROJECTS LESSON
The teacher reviews the letters and letter formation. The class discusses making an X-ray by drawing on black construction paper with white chalk.

STUDENT ACTIVITY
The students make their own version of an X-ray.

SHARING
The students take their projects home.

Lesson 37

Pictures and Words

INTRODUCTION
Picture: Rectangles or _____
The teacher leads a brief discussion about the picture.

CHART DEVELOPMENT
Phase II—Word Clusters and Title: The students volunteer words to label the picture, and the teacher writes the words on the chart. Most of the labels will be word clusters. Students draw lines to connect parts of the picture to the words. The teacher writes a student-chosen title on the chart.

COMPREHENSION FOCUS
The teacher develops comprehension of the picture by asking questions, many of which will begin with *where*.
The chart is displayed in the classroom.

Storytime

READ ALOUD
Willy the Wimp
by Anthony Browne
or _____

DISCUSSION FOCUS
Discuss or make a list of the things Willy did. Talk about the results of these actions.

Writing

Five-Day Theme: Safety
or _____

INTRODUCTION
The teacher and the students have a conversation related to the theme.

WRITING ACTIVITIES
While the students are writing or drawing, the teacher meets with individuals or small groups to discuss the theme. The student's independent work may or may not relate to the theme. Each student's work is kept in a folder.

SHARING
The students share with another person or the group something they have written or drawn.

Alphabet

Letters: *W w* or _____

INTRODUCTION—BRAINSTORMING LESSON
The teacher introduces the letters and demonstrates letter formation. On the chalkboard, the teacher writes student-volunteered words and illustrations of words containing the letters.

STUDENT ACTIVITY
On their papers, students write
■ examples of the letters
■ their favorite words or illustrations from the chalkboard
■ other words or drawings

SHARING
The students share with another person or the group something they have written or drawn.
Papers are dated and filed.

Pictures and Words

INTRODUCTION
Picture: Wizard or _____
   The teacher leads a brief discussion about the picture.

CHART DEVELOPMENT
Phase II—Word Clusters and Title: The students volunteer words to label the picture, and the teacher writes the words on the chart. Most of the labels will be word clusters. Students draw lines to connect parts of the picture to the words. The teacher writes a student-chosen title on the chart.

COMPREHENSION FOCUS
The teacher develops comprehension of the picture by asking questions, many of which will begin with *what*.
   The chart is displayed in the classroom.

Storytime

READ ALOUD
Caps for Sale
by Esphyr Slobodkina
or _____

DISCUSSION FOCUS
What did the man do? Talk about the monkeys. Were they good or bad?

Writing

Five-Day Theme: Safety
or _____

INTRODUCTION
The teacher and the students have a conversation related to the theme.

WRITING ACTIVITIES
While the students are writing or drawing, the teacher meets with individuals or small groups to discuss the theme. The student's independent work may or may not relate to the theme. Each student's work is kept in a folder.

SHARING
The students share with another person or the group something they have written or drawn.

Alphabet

Letters: *W w* or _____

INTRODUCTION—STUDENT PROJECTS LESSON
The teacher reviews the letters and letter formation. The class discusses construction of a wishing wand made from straws, paper stars, and glitter.

STUDENT ACTIVITY
The students make their own version of a wishing wand.

SHARING
The students take their projects home.

137

Lesson 39

Pictures and Words

INTRODUCTION
Picture: Gorilla or _____
The teacher leads a brief discussion about the picture.

CHART DEVELOPMENT
Phase II—Word Clusters and Title: The students volunteer words to label the picture, and the teacher writes the words on the chart. Most of the labels will be word clusters. Students draw lines to connect parts of the picture to the words. The teacher writes a student-chosen title on the chart.

COMPREHENSION FOCUS
The teacher develops comprehension of the picture by asking questions, many of which will begin with *where*.
The chart is displayed in the classroom.

Storytime

READ ALOUD
The Gorilla Did It
by Barbara Hazen
or _____

DISCUSSION FOCUS
Make a chart with the headings: Who did it? What was it? What happened? Use examples students recall from the story to complete the chart.

Writing

Five-Day Theme: Safety
or _____

INTRODUCTION
The teacher and the students have a conversation related to the theme.

WRITING ACTIVITIES
While the students are writing or drawing, the teacher meets with individuals or small groups to discuss the theme. The student's independent work may or may not relate to the theme. Each student's work is kept in a folder.

SHARING
The students share with another person or the group something they have written or drawn.

Alphabet

Letters: W w or _____

INTRODUCTION—RESEARCH LESSON—Magazines
The teacher reviews the letters and letter formation. The teacher leads a discussion about words for objects that may be found in magazines which contain the designated letters.

STUDENT ACTIVITY
The students cut or tear the letters or related objects from magazines and glue them on individual papers or the class chart. Some of the objects may be labeled.

SHARING
The teacher and students discuss items on the class chart. The chart is displayed in the classroom.

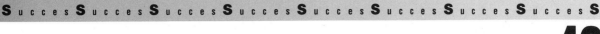

Pictures and Words

INTRODUCTION
Picture: Dessert or _____
   The teacher leads a brief discussion about the picture.

CHART DEVELOPMENT
Phase II—Word Clusters and Title: The students volunteer words to label the picture, and the teacher writes the words on the chart. Most of the labels will be word clusters. Students draw lines to connect parts of the picture to the words. The teacher writes a student-chosen title on the chart.

COMPREHENSION FOCUS
The teacher develops comprehension of the picture by asking questions, many of which will begin with *when*.
   The chart is displayed in the classroom.

Storytime

READ ALOUD
Yummers!
by James Marshall
or _____

DISCUSSION FOCUS
What makes this story funny?

Writing

Five-Day Theme: Safety
or _____

INTRODUCTION
The teacher leads a class discussion about points of interest generated during the first four days of the theme and introduces the student activity.

STUDENT ACTIVITY
Share Tana Hoban's book *I Read Signs* or take a walk in the school neighborhood to look at real signs. Discuss and make safety-related signs.

SHARING
Display the signs in the school hallway.

Alphabet

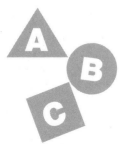

Letters: *Y y* or _____

INTRODUCTION— BRAINSTORMING LESSON
The teacher introduces the letters and demonstrates letter formation. On the chalkboard, the teacher writes student-volunteered words and illustrations of words containing the letters.

STUDENT ACTIVITY
On their papers, students write
- examples of the letters
- their favorite words or illustrations from the chalkboard
- other words or drawings

SHARING
The students share with another person or the group something they have written or drawn.
   Papers are dated and filed.

Lesson **41**

Pictures and Words

INTRODUCTION
Picture: Monsters or _____
   The teacher leads a brief discussion about the picture.

CHART DEVELOPMENT
Phase III—Sentences: The students volunteer words to label the picture, and the teacher writes the words on the chart. Students draw lines to connect parts of the picture to the words. The teacher writes a student-chosen title and at least one sentence on the chart.

COMPREHENSION FOCUS
The teacher develops comprehension of the picture by asking questions, many of which will begin with *where*.
   The chart is displayed in the classroom.

Storytime

READ ALOUD
Where the Wild Things Are
by Maurice Sendak
or _____

DISCUSSION FOCUS
Tell about the monsters. Can you tell if they are mean by their facial expressions?

Writing

Five-Day Theme: Scary Things
or _____

INTRODUCTION
The teacher and the students have a conversation related to the theme. Conversations might include a reference to the Pictures and Words chart made earlier in the day.

WRITING ACTIVITIES
While the students are writing or drawing, the teacher meets with individuals or small groups to discuss the theme. The student's independent work may or may not relate to the theme. Each student's work is kept in a folder.

SHARING
The students share with another person or the group something they have written or drawn.

Alphabet

Letters: *Y y* or _____

INTRODUCTION—STUDENT PROJECTS LESSON
The teacher reviews the letters and letter formation. The class discusses construction of a yellow yarn design out of assorted lengths and kinds of yellow yarn.

STUDENT ACTIVITY
The students make their own version of a yellow yarn design.

SHARING
The students take their projects home.

Lesson 42

Pictures and Words

INTRODUCTION
Picture: Yo-yos or _____
   The teacher leads a brief discussion about the picture.

CHART DEVELOPMENT
Phase III—Sentences: The students volunteer words to label the picture, and the teacher writes the words on the chart. Students draw lines to connect parts of the picture to the words. The teacher writes a student-chosen title and at least one sentence on the chart.

COMPREHENSION FOCUS
The teacher develops comprehension of the picture by asking questions, many of which will begin with *how*.
   The chart is displayed in the classroom.

Storytime

READ ALOUD
Napping House
by Don and Audrey Wood
or _____

DISCUSSION FOCUS
Discuss first, last, and middle parts of this story.

Writing

Five-Day Theme: Scary Things
or _____

INTRODUCTION
The teacher and the students have a conversation related to the theme.

WRITING ACTIVITIES
While the students are writing or drawing, the teacher meets with individuals or small groups to discuss the theme. The student's independent work may or may not relate to the theme. Each student's work is kept in a folder.

SHARING
The students share with another person or the group something they have written or drawn.

Alphabet

Letters: *Y y* or _____

INTRODUCTION—RESEARCH LESSON—Magazines
The teacher reviews the letters and letter formation. The teacher leads a discussion about words for objects that may be found in magazines which contain the designated letters.

STUDENT ACTIVITY
The students cut or tear the letters or related objects from magazines and glue them on individual papers or the class chart. Some of the objects may be labeled.

SHARING
The teacher and students discuss items on the class chart. The chart is displayed in the classroom.

141

Lesson **43**

Pictures and Words

INTRODUCTION
Picture: Cooking or _____
   The teacher leads a brief discussion about the picture.

CHART DEVELOPMENT
Phase III—Sentences: The students volunteer words to label the picture, and the teacher writes the words on the chart. Lines are drawn to connect parts of the picture to the words. The teacher writes a student-chosen title and at least one sentence on the chart.

COMPREHENSION FOCUS
The teacher develops comprehension of the picture by asking questions, many of which will begin with *why*.
   The chart is displayed in the classroom.

Storytime

READ ALOUD
Blueberries for Sal
by Robert McCloskey
or _____

DISCUSSION FOCUS
Compare the two mothers in the story.

Writing

Five-Day Theme: Scary Things
or _____

INTRODUCTION
The teacher and the students have a conversation related to the theme.

WRITING ACTIVITIES
While the students are writing or drawing, the teacher meets with individuals or small groups to discuss the theme. The student's independent work may or may not relate to the theme. Each student's work is kept in a folder.

SHARING
The students share with another person or the group something they have written or drawn.

Alphabet

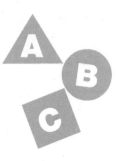

Letters: *U u* or _____

INTRODUCTION— BRAINSTORMING LESSON
The teacher introduces the letters and demonstrates letter formation. On the chalkboard, the teacher writes student-volunteered words and illustrations of words containing the letters.

STUDENT ACTIVITY
On their papers, students write
■ examples of the letters
■ their favorite words or illustrations from the chalkboard
■ other words or drawings

SHARING
The students share with another person or the group something they have written or drawn.
   Papers are dated and filed.

Lesson **44**

Pictures and Words

INTRODUCTION
Picture: Umbrella or _____
   The teacher leads a brief discussion about the picture.

CHART DEVELOPMENT
Phase III—Sentences: The students volunteer words to label the picture, and the teacher writes the words on the chart. Students draw lines to connect parts of the picture to the words. The teacher writes a student-chosen title and at least one sentence on the chart.

COMPREHENSION FOCUS
The teacher develops comprehension of the picture by asking questions, many of which will begin with *when*.
   The chart is displayed in the classroom.

Storytime

READ ALOUD
I Hear a Noise
by Diane Goode
or _____

DISCUSSION FOCUS
Discuss ways that the characters in this story are real. Discuss words or pictures that you think show that the characters are not real.

Writing

Five-Day Theme: Scary Things
or _____

INTRODUCTION
The teacher and the students have a conversation related to the theme.

WRITING ACTIVITIES
While the students are writing or drawing, the teacher meets with individuals or small groups to discuss the theme. The student's independent work may or may not relate to the theme. Each student's work is kept in a folder.

SHARING
The students share with another person or the group something they have written or drawn.

Alphabet

Letters: *U u* or _____

INTRODUCTION—STUDENT PROJECTS LESSON
The teacher reviews the letters and letter formation. The class discusses construction of an umbrella made from wallpaper, fabric scraps, or construction paper.

STUDENT ACTIVITY
The students make their own version of an umbrella.

SHARING
The students take their projects home.

143

Lesson **45**

Pictures and Words

INTRODUCTION
Picture: Sky or _____
   The teacher leads a brief discussion about the picture.

CHART DEVELOPMENT
Phase III—Sentences: The students volunteer words to label the picture, and the teacher writes the words on the chart. Students draw lines to connect parts of the picture to the words. The teacher writes a student-chosen title and at least one sentence on the chart.

COMPREHENSION FOCUS
The teacher develops comprehension of the picture by asking questions, many of which will begin with *what*.
   The chart is displayed in the classroom.

Storytime

READ ALOUD
Teeny Tiny
by Jill Bennett
A Dark, Dark Tale
by Ruth Brown
or _____

DISCUSSION FOCUS
Compare these two stories. How are they alike and different?

Writing

Five-Day Theme: Scary Things
or _____

INTRODUCTION
The teacher leads a class discussion about points of interest generated during the first four days of the theme and introduces the student activity.

STUDENT ACTIVITY
The students make a Monster ABC book of monsters that speak in "UGGH"

language. This could contain a monster for each letter. For example, monsters could be named Ack! or Blem! or Cork!

SHARING
The students share with another person or the group something they have written or drawn.

Alphabet

Letters: *U u* or _____

INTRODUCTION—RESEARCH LESSON—Newspapers
The teacher reviews the letters and letter formation.

STUDENT ACTIVITY
The students use highlighter pens or crayons to mark the letters in newspapers.

SHARING
The students share something they have marked on their paper with another person or the group.

Lesson 46

Pictures and Words

INTRODUCTION
Picture: Nursery Rhymes or
_____

The teacher leads a brief discussion about the picture.

CHART DEVELOPMENT
Phase III—Sentences: The students volunteer words to label the picture, and the teacher writes the words on the chart.

Lines are drawn to connect parts of the picture to the words. The teacher writes a student-chosen title and at least one sentence on the chart.

COMPREHENSION FOCUS
The teacher develops comprehension of the picture by asking questions, many of which will begin with *who*.

The chart is displayed in the classroom.

Storytime

READ ALOUD
If You Give a Mouse a Cookie
by L. J. Numeroff
or _____

DISCUSSION FOCUS
Reread this story and have children raise their hands each time they hear the pattern.

Writing

Five-Day Theme: Nursery Rhymes
or _____

INTRODUCTION
The teacher and the students have a conversation related to the theme. Conversations might include a reference to the Pictures and Words chart made earlier in the day.

WRITING ACTIVITIES
While the students are writing or drawing, the teacher meets with

individuals or small groups to discuss the theme. The student's independent work may or may not relate to the theme. Each student's work is kept in a folder.

SHARING
The students share with another person or the group something they have written or drawn.

Alphabet

Letters: *Z z* or _____

**INTRODUCTION—
BRAINSTORMING LESSON**
The teacher introduces the letters and demonstrates letter formation. On the chalkboard, the teacher writes student-volunteered words and illustrations of words containing the letters.

STUDENT ACTIVITY
On their papers, students write
■ examples of the letters

■ their favorite words or illustrations from the chalkboard
■ other words or drawings

SHARING
The students share with another person or the group something they have written or drawn.

Papers are dated and filed.

145

Lesson 47

Pictures and Words

INTRODUCTION
Picture: Zebra or _____
  The teacher leads a brief discussion about the picture.

CHART DEVELOPMENT
Phase III—Sentences: The students volunteer words to label the picture, and the teacher writes the words on the chart. Students draw lines to connect parts of the picture to the words. The teacher writes a student-chosen title and at least one sentence on the chart.

COMPREHENSION FOCUS
The teacher develops comprehension of the picture by asking questions, many of which will begin with *where*.
  The chart is displayed in the classroom.

Storytime

READ ALOUD
Millions of Cats
by Wanda Gàg
or _____

DISCUSSION FOCUS
What happens when you have too many pets?

Writing

Five-Day Theme: Nursery Rhymes
or _____

INTRODUCTION
The teacher and the students have a conversation related to the theme.

WRITING ACTIVITIES
While the students are writing or drawing, the teacher meets with individuals or small groups to discuss the theme. The student's independent work may or may not relate to the theme. Each student's work is kept in a folder.

SHARING
The students share with another person or the group something they have written or drawn.

Alphabet

Letters: *Z z* or _____

INTRODUCTION—STUDENT PROJECTS LESSON
The teacher reviews the letters and letter formation. The class discusses construction of a paper zebra.

STUDENT ACTIVITY
The students make their own version of a zebra.

SHARING
The students take their projects home.

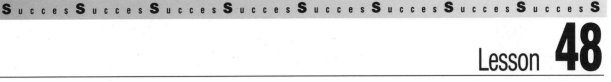

Pictures and Words

INTRODUCTION
Picture: Plants or _____
   The teacher leads a brief discussion about the picture.

CHART DEVELOPMENT
Phase III—Sentences: The students volunteer words to label the picture, and the teacher writes the words on the chart. Students draw lines to connect parts of the picture to the words. The teacher writes a student-chosen title and at least one sentence on the chart.

COMPREHENSION FOCUS
The teacher develops comprehension of the picture by asking questions, many of which will begin with *why*.
   The chart is displayed in the classroom.

Storytime

READ ALOUD
Zella, Zack and Zodiak
by Bill Peet
or _____

DISCUSSION FOCUS
Did you hear rhyming words? Were there any rhyming words with *Z*?

Writing

Five-Day Theme: Nursery Rhymes
or _____

INTRODUCTION
The teacher and the students have a conversation related to the theme.

WRITING ACTIVITIES
While the students are writing or drawing, the teacher meets with individuals or small groups to discuss the theme. The student's independent work may or may not relate to the theme. Each student's work is kept in a folder.

SHARING
The students share with another person or the group something they have written or drawn.

Alphabet

Letters: *Z z* or _____

INTRODUCTION—RESEARCH LESSON—Magazines
The teacher reviews the letters and letter formation. The teacher leads a discussion about words for objects that may be found in magazines which contain the designated letters.

STUDENT ACTIVITY
The students cut or tear the letters or related objects from magazines and glue them on individual papers or the class chart. Some of the objects may be labeled.

SHARING
The teacher and students discuss items on the class chart. The chart is displayed in the classroom.

Lesson **49**

Pictures and Words

INTRODUCTION
Picture: Hands or _____

The teacher leads a brief discussion about the picture.

CHART DEVELOPMENT
Phase III—Sentences: The students volunteer words to label the picture, and the teacher writes the words on the chart. Students draw lines to connect parts of the picture to the words. The teacher writes a student-chosen title and at least one sentence on the chart.

COMPREHENSION FOCUS
The teacher develops comprehension of the picture by asking questions, many of which will begin with *what*.

The chart is displayed in the classroom.

Storytime

READ ALOUD
Here Are My Hands
by Bill Martin, Jr., and John Archambault
or _____

DISCUSSION FOCUS
Before reading this book, make a list of things hands can do.

Writing

Five-Day Theme: Nursery Rhymes
or _____

INTRODUCTION
The teacher and the students have a conversation related to the theme.

WRITING ACTIVITIES
While the students are writing or drawing, the teacher meets with individuals or small groups to discuss the theme. The student's independent work may or may not relate to the theme. Each student's work is kept in a folder.

SHARING
The students share with another person or the group something they have written or drawn.

Alphabet

Letters: *M m* or _____

INTRODUCTION— BRAINSTORMING LESSON
The teacher introduces the letters and demonstrates letter formation. On the chalkboard, the teacher writes student-volunteered words and illustrations of words containing the letters.

STUDENT ACTIVITY
On their papers, students write
■ examples of the letters
■ their favorite words or illustrations from the chalkboard
■ other words or drawings

SHARING
The students share with another person or the group something they have written or drawn.

Papers are dated and filed.

Lesson **50**

Pictures and Words

INTRODUCTION
Picture: Mother Goose or _____
   The teacher leads a brief discussion about the picture.

CHART DEVELOPMENT
Phase III—Sentences: The students volunteer words to label the picture, and the teacher writes the words on the chart. Students draw lines to connect parts of the picture to the words. The teacher writes a student-chosen title and at least one sentence on the chart.

COMPREHENSION FOCUS
The teacher develops comprehension of the picture by asking questions, many of which will begin with *who*.
   The chart is displayed in the classroom.

Storytime

READ ALOUD
Whistle for Willie
by Ezra Jack Keats
or _____

DISCUSSION FOCUS
Discuss how the children felt about Willie. How do you think Willie felt?

Writing

Five-Day Theme: Nursery Rhymes
or _____

INTRODUCTION
The teacher leads a class discussion about points of interest generated during the first four days of the theme and introduces the student activity.

STUDENT ACTIVITY
Small groups or individuals plan how to act out nursery rhymes.

SHARING
The nursery rhymes are acted out for the class or visitors. The audience tries to guess which rhyme is being dramatized.

Alphabet

Letters: *M m* or _____

INTRODUCTION—RESEARCH LESSON—Magazines
The teacher reviews the letters and letter formation. The teacher leads a discussion about words for objects that may be found in magazines which contain the designated letters.

STUDENT ACTIVITY
The students cut or tear the letters or related objects from magazines and glue them on individual papers or the class chart. Some of the objects may be labeled.

SHARING
The teacher and students discuss items on the class chart. The chart is displayed in the classroom.

Lesson 51

Pictures and Words

INTRODUCTION
Picture: Weather or _____
The teacher leads a brief discussion about the picture.

CHART DEVELOPMENT
Phase III—Sentences: The students volunteer words to label the picture, and the teacher writes the words on the chart. Students draw lines to connect parts of the picture to the words. The teacher writes a student-chosen title and at least one sentence on the chart.

COMPREHENSION FOCUS
The teacher develops comprehension of the picture by asking questions, many of which will begin with *what*.
The chart is displayed in the classroom.

Storytime

READ ALOUD
Three Billy Goats Gruff
(any two versions)
or _____

DISCUSSION FOCUS
Look at two versions of *Three Billy Goats Gruff*. Compare how the illustrations and words show and describe the sizes of the goats.

Writing

Five-Day Theme: Weather
or _____

INTRODUCTION
The teacher and the students have a conversation related to the theme. Conversations might include a reference to the Pictures and Words chart made earlier in the day.

WRITING ACTIVITIES
While the students are writing or drawing, the teacher meets with individuals or small groups to discuss the theme. The student's independent work may or may not relate to the theme. Each student's work is kept in a folder.

SHARING
The students share with another person or the group something they have written or drawn.

Alphabet

Letters: *M m* or _____

INTRODUCTION—STUDENT PROJECTS LESSON
The teacher reviews the letters and letter formation. The class discusses construction of a monster made from assorted scraps of paper, yarn, and paper tubes or other materials.

STUDENT ACTIVITY
The students make their own version of a monster.

SHARING
The students take their projects home.

Lesson **52**

Pictures and Words

INTRODUCTION
Picture: Radio or _____
   The teacher leads a brief discussion about the picture.

CHART DEVELOPMENT
Phase III—Sentences: The students volunteer words to label the picture, and the teacher writes the words on the chart. Students draw lines to connect parts of the picture to the words. The teacher writes a student-chosen title and at least one sentence on the chart.

COMPREHENSION FOCUS
The teacher develops comprehension of the picture by asking questions, many of which will begin with *how*.
   The chart is displayed in the classroom.

Storytime

READ ALOUD
Cloudy with a Chance of Meatballs by Judi Barrett
or _____

DISCUSSION FOCUS
Make and share funny pictures to show the weather described in this book.

Writing

Five-Day Theme: Weather
or _____

INTRODUCTION
The teacher and the students have a conversation related to the theme.

WRITING ACTIVITIES
While the students are writing or drawing, the teacher meets with individuals or small groups to discuss the theme. The student's independent work may or may not relate to the theme. Each student's work is kept in a folder.

SHARING
The students share with another person or the group something they have written or drawn.

Alphabet

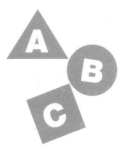

Letters: *N n* or _____

INTRODUCTION—BRAINSTORMING LESSON
The teacher introduces the letters and demonstrates letter formation. On the chalkboard, the teacher writes student-volunteered words and illustrations of words containing the letters.

STUDENT ACTIVITY
On their papers, students write
■ examples of the letters
■ their favorite words or illustrations from the chalkboard
■ other words or drawings

SHARING
The students share with another person or the group something they have written or drawn.
   Papers are dated and filed.

Lesson 53

Pictures and Words

INTRODUCTION
Picture: Nickel or _____

The teacher leads a brief discussion about the picture.

CHART DEVELOPMENT
Phase III—Sentences: The students volunteer words to label the picture, and the teacher writes the words on the chart. Students draw lines to connect parts of the picture to the words. The teacher writes a student-chosen title and at least one sentence on the chart.

COMPREHENSION FOCUS
The teacher develops comprehension of the picture by asking questions, many of which will begin with *what*.

The chart is displayed in the classroom.

Storytime

READ ALOUD
Where Do Horses Live?
by Ron Hirschi
Animal Homes
by Brian Wildsmith
or _____

DISCUSSION FOCUS
Talk about places where animals live.

Writing

Five-Day Theme: Weather
or _____

INTRODUCTION
The teacher and the students have a conversation related to the theme.

WRITING ACTIVITIES
While the students are writing or drawing, the teacher meets with individuals or small groups to discuss the theme. The student's independent work may or may not relate to the theme. Each student's work is kept in a folder.

SHARING
The students share with another person or the group something they have written or drawn.

Alphabet

Letters: *N n* or _____

INTRODUCTION—STUDENT PROJECTS LESSON
The teacher reviews the letters and letter formation. The class discusses construction of a noodle necklace by stringing a variety of pasta on yarn.

STUDENT ACTIVITY
The students make their own version of a noodle necklace.

SHARING
The students take their projects home.

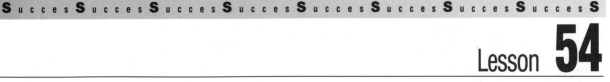

Lesson 54

Pictures and Words

INTRODUCTION
Picture: Mice or _____
   The teacher leads a brief discussion about the picture.

CHART DEVELOPMENT
Phase III—Sentences: The students volunteer words to label the picture, and the teacher writes the words on the chart. Students draw lines to connect parts of the picture to the words. The teacher writes a student-chosen title and at least one sentence on the chart.

COMPREHENSION FOCUS
The teacher develops comprehension of the picture by asking questions, many of which will begin with *where*.
   The chart is displayed in the classroom.

Storytime

READ ALOUD
Whose Mouse Are You?
by Robert Kraus
or _____

DISCUSSION FOCUS
Discuss the characters and what Mouse said about them.

Writing

Five-Day Theme: Weather
or _____

INTRODUCTION
The teacher and the students have a conversation related to the theme.

WRITING ACTIVITIES
While the students are writing or drawing, the teacher meets with individuals or small groups to discuss the theme. The student's independent work may or may not relate to the theme. Each student's work is kept in a folder.

SHARING
The students share with another person or the group something they have written or drawn.

Alphabet

Letters: *N n* or _____

INTRODUCTION—RESEARCH LESSON—Newspapers
The teacher reviews the letters and letter formation.

STUDENT ACTIVITY
The students use highlighter pens or crayons to mark the letters in newspapers.

SHARING
The students share something they have marked on their paper with another person or the group.

Lesson 55

Pictures and Words

INTRODUCTION
Picture: Rainbow or _____
   The teacher leads a brief discussion about the picture.

CHART DEVELOPMENT
Phase III—Sentences: The students volunteer words to label the picture, and the teacher writes the words on the chart. Students draw lines to connect parts of the picture to the words. The teacher writes a student-chosen title and at least one sentence on the chart.

COMPREHENSION FOCUS
The teacher develops comprehension of the picture by asking questions, many of which will begin with *why*.
   The chart is displayed in the classroom.

Storytime

READ ALOUD
A Rainbow of My Own
by Don Freeman
or _____

DISCUSSION FOCUS
Talk about what the rainbow looks like and what colors we see in it.

Writing

Five-Day Theme: Weather
or _____

INTRODUCTION
The teacher leads a class discussion about points of interest generated during the first four days of the theme and introduces the student activity.

STUDENT ACTIVITY
Reread the weather Pictures and Words chart from Lesson 46. Choose five weather words that could be illustrated. Divide the class into five groups to make a poster about a weather word. Groups could pick their topic word from a rain hat.

SHARING
The groups explain their poster to the whole class. The posters are displayed in the classroom.

Alphabet

Letters: *R r* or _____

INTRODUCTION— BRAINSTORMING LESSON
The teacher introduces the letters and demonstrates letter formation. On the chalkboard, the teacher writes student-volunteered words and illustrations of words containing the letters.

STUDENT ACTIVITY
On their papers, students write
■ examples of the letters
■ their favorite words or illustrations from the chalkboard
■ other words or drawings

SHARING
The students share with another person or the group something they have written or drawn.
   Papers are dated and filed.

Pictures and Words

INTRODUCTION
Picture: Space or _____
   The teacher leads a brief discussion about the picture.

CHART DEVELOPMENT
Phase III—Sentences: The students volunteer words to label the picture, and the teacher writes the words on the chart. Students draw lines to connect parts of the picture to the words. The teacher writes a student-chosen title and at least one sentence on the chart.

COMPREHENSION FOCUS
The teacher develops comprehension of the picture by asking questions, many of which will begin with *who*.
   The chart is displayed in the classroom.

Storytime

READ ALOUD
New Kid on the Block
by Jack Prelutsky
or _____

DISCUSSION FOCUS
Can we find some poems with rhyming words? Discuss.

Writing

Five-Day Theme: Space
or _____

INTRODUCTION
The teacher and the students have a conversation related to the theme. Conversations might include a reference to the Pictures and Words chart made earlier in the day.

WRITING ACTIVITIES
While the students are writing or drawing, the teacher meets with individuals or small groups to discuss the theme. The student's independent work may or may not relate to the theme. Each student's work is kept in a folder.

SHARING
The students share with another person or the group something they have written or drawn.

Alphabet

Letters: *R r* or _____

INTRODUCTION—STUDENT PROJECTS LESSON
The teacher reviews the letters and letter formation. The class discusses making a rainbow with tempera or watercolor paints.

STUDENT ACTIVITY
The students make their own version of a rainbow.

SHARING
The students take their projects home.

Lesson 57

Pictures and Words

INTRODUCTION
Picture: Hats or _____

The teacher leads a brief discussion about the picture.

CHART DEVELOPMENT
Phase III—Sentences: The students volunteer words to label the picture, and the teacher writes the words on the chart. Students draw lines to connect parts of the picture to the words. The teacher writes a student-chosen title and at least one sentence on the chart.

COMPREHENSION FOCUS
The teacher develops comprehension of the picture by asking questions, many of which will begin with *what*.

The chart is displayed in the classroom.

Storytime

READ ALOUD
Earthlets
by Jeanne Willis
or _____

DISCUSSION FOCUS
Why is this book funny? Is the ending funny?

Writing

Five-Day Theme: Space
or _____

INTRODUCTION
The teacher and the students have a conversation related to the theme.

WRITING ACTIVITIES
While the students are writing or drawing, the teacher meets with individuals or small groups to discuss the theme. The student's independent work may or may not relate to the theme. Each student's work is kept in a folder.

SHARING
The students share with another person or the group something they have written or drawn.

Alphabet

Letters: *R r* or _____

INTRODUCTION—RESEARCH LESSON—Magazines
The teacher reviews the letters and letter formation. The teacher leads a discussion about words for objects that may be found in magazines which contain the designated letters.

STUDENT ACTIVITY
The students cut or tear the letters or related objects from magazines and glue them on individual papers or the class chart. Some of the objects may be labeled.

SHARING
The teacher and students discuss items on the class chart. The chart is displayed in the classroom.

Pictures and Words

INTRODUCTION
Picture: Cats or _____
    The teacher leads a brief discussion about the picture.

CHART DEVELOPMENT
Phase III—Sentences: The students volunteer words to label the picture, and the teacher writes the words on the chart. Students draw lines to connect parts of the picture to the words. The teacher writes a student-chosen title and at least one sentence on the chart.

COMPREHENSION FOCUS
The teacher develops comprehension of the picture by asking questions, many of which will begin with *what*.
    The chart is displayed in the classroom.

Storytime

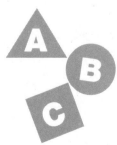

READ ALOUD
Rotten Ralph
by Jack Gantos
or _____

DISCUSSION FOCUS
Help Rotten Ralph think of ways he can stay out of trouble.

Writing

Five-Day Theme: Space
or _____

INTRODUCTION
The teacher and the students have a conversation related to the theme.

WRITING ACTIVITIES
While the students are writing or drawing, the teacher meets with individuals or small groups to discuss the theme. The student's independent work may or may not relate to the theme. Each student's work is kept in a folder.

SHARING
The students share with another person or the group something they have written or drawn.

Alphabet

Letters: *C c* or _____

INTRODUCTION—BRAINSTORMING LESSON
The teacher introduces the letters and demonstrates letter formation. On the chalkboard, the teacher writes student-volunteered words and illustrations of words containing the letters.

STUDENT ACTIVITY
On their papers, students write
■ examples of the letters
■ their favorite words or illustrations from the chalkboard
■ other words or drawings

SHARING
The students share with another person or the group something they have written or drawn.
    Papers are dated and filed.

Lesson **59**

Pictures and Words

INTRODUCTION
Picture: Ice Cream or _____
The teacher leads a brief discussion about the picture.

CHART DEVELOPMENT
Phase III—Sentences: The students volunteer words to label the picture, and the teacher writes the words on the chart. Students draw lines to connect parts of the picture to the words. The teacher writes a student-chosen title and at least one sentence on the chart.

COMPREHENSION FOCUS
The teacher develops comprehension of the picture by asking questions, many of which will begin with *who*.
The chart is displayed in the classroom.

Storytime

READ ALOUD
The Caterpillar and the Polliwog
by Jack Kent
or _____

DISCUSSION FOCUS
Compare the changes that occur in the book.

Writing

Five-Day Theme: Space
or _____

INTRODUCTION
The teacher and the students have a conversation related to the theme.

WRITING ACTIVITIES
While the students are writing or drawing, the teacher meets with individuals or small groups to discuss the theme. The student's independent work may or may not relate to the theme. Each student's work is kept in a folder.

SHARING
The students share with another person or the group something they have written or drawn.

Alphabet

Letters: *C c* or _____

INTRODUCTION—STUDENT PROJECTS LESSON
The teacher reviews the letters and letter formation. The class discusses construction of a caterpillar from egg cartons and pipe cleaners.

STUDENT ACTIVITY
The students make their own version of a caterpillar.

SHARING
The students take their projects home.

158

Lesson **60**

Pictures and Words

INTRODUCTION
Picture: Crying or _____
   The teacher leads a brief discussion about the picture.

CHART DEVELOPMENT
Phase III—Sentences: The students volunteer words to label the picture, and the teacher writes the words on the chart. Students draw lines to connect parts of the picture to the words. The teacher writes a student-chosen title and at least one sentence on the chart.

COMPREHENSION FOCUS
The teacher develops comprehension of the picture by asking questions, many of which will begin with *why*.
   The chart is displayed in the classroom.

Storytime

READ ALOUD
Rocket in My Pocket
by Carl Withers
or _____

DISCUSSION FOCUS
Can we find some poems that do not rhyme?

Writing

Five-Day Theme: Space
or _____

INTRODUCTION
The teacher leads a class discussion about points of interest generated during the first four days of the theme and introduces the student activity.

STUDENT ACTIVITY
The students use "junk" materials to build spaceships. This project could be done by individuals, small groups, or by the whole class.

SHARING
Display the spaceship.

Alphabet

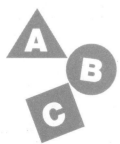

Letters: *C c* or _____

INTRODUCTION—RESEARCH LESSON—Magazines
The teacher reviews the letters and letter formation. The teacher leads a discussion about words for objects that may be found in magazines which contain the designated letters.

STUDENT ACTIVITY
The students cut or tear the letters or related objects from magazines and glue them on individual papers or the class chart. Some of the objects may be labeled.

SHARING
The teacher and students discuss items on the class chart. The chart is displayed in the classroom.

Lesson **61**

Pictures and Words

INTRODUCTION
Picture: Grandparents or _____
   The teacher leads a brief discussion about the picture.

CHART DEVELOPMENT
Phase III—Sentences: The students volunteer words to label the picture, and the teacher writes the words on the chart. Students draw lines to connect parts of the picture to the words. The teacher writes a student-chosen title and at least one sentence on the chart.

COMPREHENSION FOCUS
The teacher develops comprehension of the picture by asking questions, many of which will begin with *where*.
   The chart is displayed in the classroom.

Storytime

READ ALOUD
The Chick and the Duckling
by Mirra Ginsburg
or _____

DISCUSSION FOCUS
Talk about what happens when the chick copies everything the duckling does.

Writing

Five-Day Theme: Grandparents
or _____

INTRODUCTION
The teacher and the students have a conversation related to the theme. Conversations might include a reference to the Pictures and Words chart made earlier in the day.

WRITING ACTIVITIES
While the students are writing or drawing, the teacher meets with individuals or small groups to discuss the theme. The student's independent work may or may not relate to the theme. Each student's work is kept in a folder.

SHARING
The students share with another person or the group something they have written or drawn.

Alphabet

Letters: *E e* or _____

INTRODUCTION— BRAINSTORMING LESSON
The teacher introduces the letters and demonstrates letter formation. On the chalkboard, the teacher writes student-volunteered words and illustrations of words containing the letters.

STUDENT ACTIVITY
On their papers, students write
■ examples of the letters
■ their favorite words or illustrations from the chalkboard
■ other words or drawings

SHARING
The students share with another person or the group something they have written or drawn.
   Papers are dated and filed.

Lesson 62

Pictures and Words

INTRODUCTION
Picture: Elephants or _____
   The teacher leads a brief discussion about the picture.

CHART DEVELOPMENT
Phase III—Sentences: The students volunteer words to label the picture, and the teacher writes the words on the chart. Students draw lines to connect parts of the picture to the words. The teacher writes a student-chosen title and at least one sentence on the chart.

COMPREHENSION FOCUS
The teacher develops comprehension of the picture by asking questions, many of which will begin with *how*.
   The chart is displayed in the classroom.

Storytime

READ ALOUD
Too Much Noise
by Ann McGovern
or _____

DISCUSSION FOCUS
Make the animal noises all at once. Talk about the problem in the story.

Writing

Five-Day Theme: Grandparents
or _____

INTRODUCTION
The teacher and the students have a conversation related to the theme.

WRITING ACTIVITIES
While the students are writing or drawing, the teacher meets with individuals or small groups to discuss the theme. The student's independent work may or may not relate to the theme. Each student's work is kept in a folder.

SHARING
The students share with another person or the group something they have written or drawn.

Alphabet

Letters: *E e* or _____

INTRODUCTION—STUDENT PROJECTS LESSON
The teacher reviews the letters and letter formation. The class discusses construction of an elephant.

STUDENT ACTIVITY
The students make their own version of an elephant.

SHARING
The students take their projects home.

Lesson **63**

Pictures and Words

INTRODUCTION
Picture: Crops or _____
  The teacher leads a brief discussion about the picture.

CHART DEVELOPMENT
Phase III—Sentences: The students volunteer words to label the picture, and the teacher writes the words on the chart. Students draw lines to connect parts of the picture to the words. The teacher writes a student-chosen title and at least one sentence on the chart.

COMPREHENSION FOCUS
The teacher develops comprehension of the picture by asking questions, many of which will begin with _what_.
  The chart is displayed in the classroom.

Storytime

READ ALOUD
Wilfrid Gordon McDonald Partridge by Mem Fox
or _____

DISCUSSION FOCUS
Discuss Wilfrid Gordon's gifts. Was this a happy story or a sad story?

Writing

Five-Day Theme: Grandparents
or _____

INTRODUCTION
The teacher and the students have a conversation related to the theme.

WRITING ACTIVITIES
While the students are writing or drawing, the teacher meets with individuals or small groups to discuss the theme. The student's independent work may or may not relate to the theme. Each student's work is kept in a folder.

SHARING
The students share with another person or the group something they have written or drawn.

Alphabet

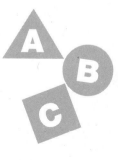

Letters: _E e_ or _____

INTRODUCTION—RESEARCH LESSON—Newspapers
The teacher reviews the letters and letter formation.

STUDENT ACTIVITY
The students use highlighter pens or crayons to mark the letters in newspapers.

SHARING
The students share something they have marked on their paper with another person or the group.

Lesson **64**

Pictures and Words

INTRODUCTION
Picture: Ocean or _____
The teacher leads a brief discussion about the picture.

CHART DEVELOPMENT
Phase III—Sentences: The students volunteer words to label the picture, and the teacher writes the words on the chart. Students draw lines to connect parts of the picture to the words. The teacher writes a student-chosen title and at least one sentence on the chart.

COMPREHENSION FOCUS
The teacher develops comprehension of the picture by asking questions, many of which will begin with *who*.
The chart is displayed in the classroom.

Storytime

READ ALOUD
George and Martha
by James Marshall
One Fine Day
by Nonny Hogrogian
or _____

DISCUSSION FOCUS
What was an important event in this story?

Writing

Five-Day Theme: Grandparents
or _____

INTRODUCTION
The teacher and the students have a conversation related to the theme.

WRITING ACTIVITIES
While the students are writing or drawing, the teacher meets with individuals or small groups to discuss the theme. The student's independent work may or may not relate to the theme. Each student's work is kept in a folder.

SHARING
The students share with another person or the group something they have written or drawn.

Alphabet

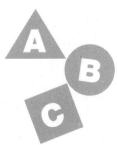

Letters: *O o* or _____

INTRODUCTION—BRAINSTORMING LESSON
The teacher introduces the letters and demonstrates letter formation. On the chalkboard, the teacher writes student-volunteered words and illustrations of words containing the letters.

STUDENT ACTIVITY
On their papers, students write
■ examples of the letters
■ their favorite words or illustrations from the chalkboard
■ other words or drawings

SHARING
The students share with another person or the group something they have written or drawn.
Papers are dated and filed.

Lesson **65**

Pictures and Words

INTRODUCTION
Picture: Octopus or _____
The teacher leads a brief discussion about the picture.

CHART DEVELOPMENT
Phase III—Sentences: The students volunteer words to label the picture, and the teacher writes the words on the chart. Students draw lines to connect parts of the picture to the words. The teacher writes a student-chosen title and at least one sentence on the chart.

COMPREHENSION FOCUS
The teacher develops comprehension of the picture by asking questions, many of which will begin with *how*.
The chart is displayed in the classroom.

Storytime

READ ALOUD
Color Zoo
by Lois Ehlert
or _____

DISCUSSION FOCUS
How many shapes can we find? How many colors can we find?

Writing

Five-Day Theme: Grandparents
or _____

INTRODUCTION
The teacher leads a class discussion about points of interest generated during the first four days of the theme and introduces the student activity.

STUDENT ACTIVITY
The students illustrate an occasion they remember sharing with a grandparent or a senior friend.

SHARING
Display illustrations or make into a class book.

Alphabet

Letters: *O o* or _____

INTRODUCTION—STUDENT PROJECTS LESSON
The teacher reviews the letters and letter formation. The class discusses construction of an oval octopus. They might use oval paper shapes with rug yarn legs.

STUDENT ACTIVITY
The students make their own version of an oval octopus.

SHARING
The students take their projects home.

Lesson 66

Pictures and Words

INTRODUCTION
Picture: Rocks or _____
   The teacher leads a brief discussion about the picture.

CHART DEVELOPMENT
Phase III—Sentences: The students volunteer words to label the picture, and the teacher writes the words on the chart. Students draw lines to connect parts of the picture to the words. The teacher writes a student-chosen title and at least one sentence on the chart.

COMPREHENSION FOCUS
The teacher develops comprehension of the picture by asking questions, many of which will begin with *what*.
   The chart is displayed in the classroom.

Storytime

READ ALOUD
Play with Me
by Marie Hall Ets
or _____

DISCUSSION FOCUS
Imagine yourself as the character in this story. How would you tell what you did?

Writing

Five-Day Theme: Rocks
or _____

INTRODUCTION
The teacher and the students have a conversation related to the theme. Conversations might include a reference to the Pictures and Words chart made earlier in the day.

WRITING ACTIVITIES
While the students are writing or drawing, the teacher meets with individuals or small groups to discuss the theme. The student's independent work may or may not relate to the theme. Each student's work is kept in a folder.

SHARING
The students share with another person or the group something they have written or drawn.

Alphabet

Letters: *O o* or _____

INTRODUCTION—RESEARCH LESSON—Magazines
The teacher reviews the letters and letter formation. The teacher leads a discussion about words for objects that may be found in magazines which contain the designated letters.

STUDENT ACTIVITY
The students cut or tear the letters or related objects from magazines and glue them on individual papers or the class chart. Some of the objects may be labeled.

SHARING
The teacher and students discuss items on the class chart. The chart is displayed in the classroom.

Lesson 67

Pictures and Words

INTRODUCTION
Picture: Cartoon Characters or _____

The teacher leads a brief discussion about the picture.

CHART DEVELOPMENT
Phase III—Sentences: The students volunteer words to label the picture, and the teacher writes the words on the chart.

Students draw lines to connect parts of the picture to the words. The teacher writes a student-chosen title and at least one sentence on the chart.

COMPREHENSION FOCUS
The teacher develops comprehension of the picture by asking questions, many of which will begin with _why_.

The chart is displayed in the classroom.

Storytime

READ ALOUD
Everybody Needs A Rock
by Byrd Baylor
or _____

DISCUSSION FOCUS
How are rocks alike and different?

Writing

Five-Day Theme: Rocks
or _____

INTRODUCTION
The teacher and the students have a conversation related to the theme.

WRITING ACTIVITIES
While the students are writing or drawing, the teacher meets with

individuals or small groups to discuss the theme. The student's independent work may or may not relate to the theme. Each student's work is kept in a folder.

SHARING
The students share with another person or the group something they have written or drawn.

Alphabet

Letters: _K k_ or _____

INTRODUCTION—BRAINSTORMING LESSON
The teacher introduces the letters and demonstrates letter formation. On the chalkboard, the teacher writes student-volunteered words and illustrations of words containing the letters.

STUDENT ACTIVITY
On their papers, students write
■ examples of the letters

■ their favorite words or illustrations from the chalkboard
■ other words or drawings

SHARING
The students share with another person or the group something they have written or drawn.

Papers are dated and filed.

Lesson 68

Pictures and Words

INTRODUCTION
Picture: Vegetables or _____
   The teacher leads a brief discussion about the picture.

CHART DEVELOPMENT
Phase III—Sentences: The students volunteer words to label the picture, and the teacher writes the words on the chart. Students draw lines to connect parts of the picture to the words. The teacher writes a student-chosen title and at least one sentence on the chart.

COMPREHENSION FOCUS
The teacher develops comprehension of the picture by asking questions, many of which will begin with *who.*
   The chart is displayed in the classroom.

Storytime

READ ALOUD
Growing Vegetable Soup
by Lois Ehlert
or _____

DISCUSSION FOCUS
Talk about all the steps in making vegetable soup.

Writing

Five-Day Theme: Rocks
or _____

INTRODUCTION
The teacher and the students have a conversation related to the theme.

WRITING ACTIVITIES
While the students are writing or drawing, the teacher meets with individuals or small groups to discuss the theme. The student's independent work may or may not relate to the theme. Each student's work is kept in a folder.

SHARING
The students share with another person or the group something they have written or drawn.

Alphabet

Letters: *K k* or _____

INTRODUCTION—RESEARCH LESSON—Magazines
The teacher reviews the letters and letter formation. The teacher leads a discussion about words for objects that may be found in magazines which contain the designated letters.

STUDENT ACTIVITY
The students cut or tear the letters or related objects from magazines and glue them on individual papers or the class chart. Some of the objects may be labeled.

SHARING
The teacher and students discuss items on the class chart. The chart is displayed in the classroom.

Lesson 69

Pictures and Words

INTRODUCTION
Picture: Kites or _____
The teacher leads a brief discussion about the picture.

CHART DEVELOPMENT
Phase III—Sentences: The students volunteer words to label the picture, and the teacher writes the words on the chart. Students draw lines to connect parts of the picture to the words. The teacher writes a student-chosen title and at least one sentence on the chart.

COMPREHENSION FOCUS
The teacher develops comprehension of the picture by asking questions, many of which will begin with *where*.
The chart is displayed in the classroom.

Storytime

READ ALOUD
Anno's Counting Book
by Mitsumasa Anno
or _____

DISCUSSION FOCUS
What objects are counted in this book? Talk about the ways the author placed the objects on the pages.

Writing

Five-Day Theme: Rocks
or _____

INTRODUCTION
The teacher and the students have a conversation related to the theme.

WRITING ACTIVITIES
While the students are writing or drawing, the teacher meets with individuals or small groups to discuss the theme. The student's independent work may or may not relate to the theme. Each student's work is kept in a folder.

SHARING
The students share with another person or the group something they have written or drawn.

Alphabet

Letters: *K k* or _____

INTRODUCTION—STUDENT PROJECTS LESSON
The teacher reviews the letters and letter formation. The class discusses making a kite from construction paper, yarn, and tissue paper.

STUDENT ACTIVITY
The students make their own version of a kite.

SHARING
The students take their projects home.

Pictures and Words

INTRODUCTION
Picture: Doctors or _____
   The teacher leads a brief discussion about the picture.

CHART DEVELOPMENT
Phase III—Sentences: The students volunteer words to label the picture, and the teacher writes the words on the chart. Students draw lines to connect parts of the picture to the words. The teacher writes a student-chosen title and at least one sentence on the chart.

COMPREHENSION FOCUS
The teacher develops comprehension of the picture by asking questions, many of which will begin with *when*.
   The chart is displayed in the classroom.

Storytime

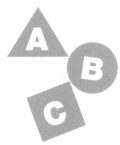

READ ALOUD
Rock Collecting
by Roma Gans
or _____

DISCUSSION FOCUS
Where can you find interesting rocks?

Writing

Five-Day Theme: Rocks
or _____

INTRODUCTION
The teacher leads a class discussion about points of interest generated during the first four days of the theme and introduces the student activity.

STUDENT ACTIVITY
Make a collections bag or box and begin a rock collection.

SHARING
The students could bring or find rocks on a "rock hunt" and trade them with classmates.

Alphabet

Letters: *G g* or _____

INTRODUCTION— BRAINSTORMING LESSON
The teacher introduces the letters and demonstrates letter formation. On the chalkboard, the teacher writes student-volunteered words and illustrations of words containing the letters.

STUDENT ACTIVITY
On their papers, students write
■ examples of the letters
■ their favorite words or illustrations from the chalkboard
■ other words or drawings

SHARING
The students share with another person or the group something they have written or drawn.
   Papers are dated and filed.

Lesson 71

Pictures and Words

INTRODUCTION
Picture: The five senses or _____
   The teacher leads a brief discussion about the picture.

CHART DEVELOPMENT
Phase III—Sentences: The students volunteer words to label the picture, and the teacher writes the words on the chart. Students draw lines to connect parts of the picture to the words. The teacher writes a student-chosen title and at least one sentence on the chart.

COMPREHENSION FOCUS
The teacher develops comprehension of the picture by asking questions, many of which will begin with *what*.
   The chart is displayed in the classroom.

Storytime

READ ALOUD
Goggles
by Ezra Jack Keats
or _____

DISCUSSION FOCUS
Write a "chain of events" for this story on the chalkboard or chart paper.

Writing

Five-Day Theme: The Five Senses
or _____

INTRODUCTION
The teacher and the students have a conversation related to the theme. Conversations might include a reference to the Pictures and Words chart made earlier in the day.

WRITING ACTIVITIES
While the students are writing or drawing, the teacher meets with individuals or small groups to discuss the theme. The student's independent work may or may not relate to the theme. Each student's work is kept in a folder.

SHARING
The students share with another person or the group something they have written or drawn.

Alphabet

Letters: *G g* or _____

INTRODUCTION—STUDENT PROJECTS LESSON
The teacher reviews the letters and letter formation. The class discusses construction of green goggles by cutting the letter shape on the fold of green construction paper as shown in the illustration.

STUDENT ACTIVITY
The students make their own version of green goggles.

SHARING
The students take their projects home.

170

Lesson 72

Pictures and Words

INTRODUCTION
Picture: Sweaters or _____

The teacher leads a brief discussion about the picture.

CHART DEVELOPMENT
Phase III—Sentences: The students volunteer words to label the picture, and the teacher writes the words on the chart. Students draw lines to connect parts of the picture to the words. The teacher writes a student-chosen title and at least one sentence on the chart.

COMPREHENSION FOCUS
The teacher develops comprehension of the picture by asking questions, many of which will begin with *when*.

The chart is displayed in the classroom.

Storytime

READ ALOUD
No Roses for Harry
by Gene Zion
or _____

DISCUSSION FOCUS
Talk about receiving a present that you don't like. What can you do?

Writing

Five-Day Theme: The Five Senses
or _____

INTRODUCTION
The teacher and the students have a conversation related to the theme.

WRITING ACTIVITIES
While the students are writing or drawing, the teacher meets with individuals or small groups to discuss the theme. The student's independent work may or may not relate to the theme. Each student's work is kept in a folder.

SHARING
The students share with another person or the group something they have written or drawn.

Alphabet

Letters: *G g* or _____

INTRODUCTION—RESEARCH LESSON—Newspapers
The teacher reviews the letters and letter formation.

STUDENT ACTIVITY
The students use highlighter pens or crayons to mark the letters in newspapers.

SHARING
The students share something they have marked on their paper with another person or the group.

Lesson 73

Pictures and Words

INTRODUCTION
Picture: Squares or _____
   The teacher leads a brief discussion about the picture.

CHART DEVELOPMENT
Phase III—Sentences: The students volunteer words to label the picture, and the teacher writes the words on the chart. Students draw lines to connect parts of the picture to the words. The teacher writes a student-chosen title and at least one sentence on the chart.

COMPREHENSION FOCUS
The teacher develops comprehension of the picture by asking questions, many of which will begin with *where*.
   The chart is displayed in the classroom.

Storytime

READ ALOUD
Shapes, Shapes, Shapes
by Tana Hoban
or _____

DISCUSSION FOCUS
Find shapes in these photographic illustrations.

Writing

Five-Day Theme: The Five Senses
or _____

INTRODUCTION
The teacher and the students have a conversation related to the theme.

WRITING ACTIVITIES
While the students are writing or drawing, the teacher meets with individuals or small groups to discuss the theme. The student's independent work may or may not relate to the theme. Each student's work is kept in a folder.

SHARING
The students share with another person or the group something they have written or drawn.

Alphabet

Letters: *S s* or _____

INTRODUCTION— BRAINSTORMING LESSON
The teacher introduces the letters and demonstrates letter formation. On the chalkboard, the teacher writes student-volunteered words and illustrations of words containing the letters.

STUDENT ACTIVITY
On their papers, students write
■ examples of the letters
■ their favorite words or illustrations from the chalkboard
■ other words or drawings

SHARING
The students share with another person or the group something they have written or drawn.
   Papers are dated and filed.

Pictures and Words

INTRODUCTION
Picture: Mountains or _____
  The teacher leads a brief discussion about the picture.

CHART DEVELOPMENT
Phase III—Sentences: The students volunteer words to label the picture, and the teacher writes the words on the chart. Students draw lines to connect parts of the picture to the words. The teacher writes a student-chosen title and at least one sentence on the chart.

COMPREHENSION FOCUS
The teacher develops comprehension of the picture by asking questions, many of which will begin with *who*.
  The chart is displayed in the classroom.

Storytime

READ ALOUD
Salty Dog by Gloria Rand
or _____

DISCUSSION FOCUS
Can a pet be a helper and a friend?

Writing

Five-Day Theme: The Five Senses
or _____

INTRODUCTION
The teacher and the students have a conversation related to the theme.

WRITING ACTIVITIES
While the students are writing or drawing, the teacher meets with individuals or small groups to discuss the theme. The student's independent work may or may not relate to the theme. Each student's work is kept in a folder.

SHARING
The students share with another person or the group something they have written or drawn.

Alphabet

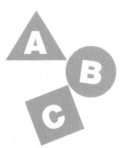

Letters: *S s* or _____

INTRODUCTION—STUDENT PROJECTS LESSON
The teacher reviews the letters and letter formation. The class discusses construction of a sailboat. They might use the bottom of milk cartons with a straw and a paper sail.

STUDENT ACTIVITY
The students make their own version of a sailboat.

SHARING
The students take their projects home.

Lesson 75

Pictures and Words

INTRODUCTION
Picture: Elves or _____
   The teacher leads a brief discussion about the picture.

CHART DEVELOPMENT
Phase III—Sentences: The students volunteer words to label the picture, and the teacher writes the words on the chart. Students draw lines to connect parts of the picture to the words. The teacher writes a student-chosen title and at least one sentence on the chart.

COMPREHENSION FOCUS
The teacher develops comprehension of the picture by asking questions, many of which will begin with *who*.
   The chart is displayed in the classroom.

Storytime

READ ALOUD
My Five Senses
by Aliki
or _____

DISCUSSION FOCUS
What does the phrase "the five senses" mean?

Writing

Five-Day Theme: The Five Senses
or _____

INTRODUCTION
The teacher leads a class discussion about points of interest generated during the first four days of the theme and introduces the student activity.

STUDENT ACTIVITY
Make an individual booklet about the five senses.

SHARING
The students read their booklets to each other or the entire class.

Alphabet

Letters: *S s* or _____

INTRODUCTION—RESEARCH LESSON—Magazines
The teacher reviews the letters and letter formation. The teacher leads a discussion about words for objects that may be found in magazines which contain the designated letters.

STUDENT ACTIVITY
The students cut or tear the letters or related objects from magazines and glue them on individual papers or the class chart. Some of the objects may be labeled.

SHARING
The teacher and students discuss items on the class chart. The chart is displayed in the classroom.

Pictures and Words

INTRODUCTION
Picture: Toys or _____
  The teacher leads a brief discussion about the picture.

CHART DEVELOPMENT
Phase III—Sentences: The students volunteer words to label the picture, and the teacher writes the words on the chart. Students draw lines to connect parts of the picture to the words. The teacher writes a student-chosen title and at least one sentence on the chart.

COMPREHENSION FOCUS
The teacher develops comprehension of the picture by asking questions, many of which will begin with *how*.
  The chart is displayed in the classroom.

Storytime

READ ALOUD
Sing a Song of Popcorn: Every Child's Book of Poems
edited by Beatrice Schenk deRegniers
or _____

DISCUSSION FOCUS
Choose two poems about objects. Compare and discuss the way the author described the objects.

Writing

Five-Day Theme: Toys
or _____

INTRODUCTION
The teacher and the students have a conversation related to the theme. Conversations might include a reference to the Pictures and Words chart made earlier in the day.

WRITING ACTIVITIES
While the students are writing or drawing, the teacher meets with individuals or small groups to discuss the theme. The student's independent work may or may not relate to the theme. Each student's work is kept in a folder.

SHARING
The students share with another person or the group something they have written or drawn.

Alphabet

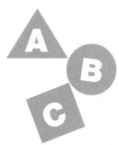

Letters: *Q q* or _____

INTRODUCTION— BRAINSTORMING LESSON
The teacher introduces the letters and demonstrates letter formation. On the chalkboard, the teacher writes student-volunteered words and illustrations of words containing the letters.

STUDENT ACTIVITY
On their papers, students write
■ examples of the letters
■ their favorite words or illustrations from the chalkboard
■ other words or drawings

SHARING
The students share with another person or the group something they have written or drawn.
  Papers are dated and filed.

175

Lesson 77

Pictures and Words

INTRODUCTION
Picture: Teachers or _____
The teacher leads a brief discussion about the picture.

CHART DEVELOPMENT
Phase III—Sentences: The students volunteer words to label the picture, and the teacher writes the words on the chart. Students draw lines to connect parts of the picture to the words. The teacher writes a student-chosen title and at least one sentence on the chart.

COMPREHENSION FOCUS
The teacher develops comprehension of the picture by asking questions, many of which will begin with *who*.
The chart is displayed in the classroom.

Storytime

READ ALOUD
The Patchwork Quilt
by Valerie Flournoy
The Quilt
by Ann Jonas
or _____

DISCUSSION FOCUS
Discuss quilts and patterns in fabric. Why do people make quilts? What do they use?

Writing

Five-Day Theme: Toys
or _____

INTRODUCTION
The teacher and the students have a conversation related to the theme.

WRITING ACTIVITIES
While the students are writing or drawing, the teacher meets with individuals or small groups to discuss the theme. The student's independent work may or may not relate to the theme. Each student's work is kept in a folder.

SHARING
The students share with another person or the group something they have written or drawn.

Alphabet

Letters: *Q q* or _____

INTRODUCTION—STUDENT PROJECTS LESSON
The teacher reviews the letters and letter formation. The class discusses construction of quilts out of scraps of fabric or wall paper glued to construction paper. Stitching lines can be drawn with crayon.

STUDENT ACTIVITY
The students make their own version of a quilt.

SHARING
The students take their projects home.

S u c c e s **S** u c c e s **S** u c c e s **S** u c c e s **S** u c c e s **S** u c c e s **S** u c c e s **S** u c c e s **S**

Lesson **78**

Pictures and Words

INTRODUCTION
Picture: Bedroom or _____
   The teacher leads a brief discussion about the picture.

CHART DEVELOPMENT
Phase III—Sentences: The students volunteer words to label the picture, and the teacher writes the words on the chart. Students draw lines to connect parts of the picture to the words. The teacher writes a student-chosen title and at least one sentence on the chart.

COMPREHENSION FOCUS
The teacher develops comprehension of the picture by asking questions, many of which will begin with *what*.
   The chart is displayed in the classroom.

Storytime

READ ALOUD
Alexander and the Wind-Up Mouse by Leo Lionni
or _____

DISCUSSION FOCUS
Talk about real and make-believe. What feelings did the wind-up mouse seem to have?

Writing

Five-Day Theme: Toys
or _____

INTRODUCTION
The teacher and the students have a conversation related to the theme.

WRITING ACTIVITIES
While the students are writing or drawing, the teacher meets with individuals or small groups to discuss the theme. The student's independent work may or may not relate to the theme. Each student's work is kept in a folder.

SHARING
The students share with another person or the group something they have written or drawn.

Alphabet

Letters: *Q q* or _____

INTRODUCTION—RESEARCH LESSON—Magazines
The teacher reviews the letters and letter formation. The teacher leads a discussion about words for objects that may be found in magazines which contain the designated letters.

STUDENT ACTIVITY
The students cut or tear the letters or related objects from magazine and glue them on individual papers or the class chart. Some of the objects may be labeled.

SHARING
The teacher and students discuss items on the class chart. The chart is displayed in the classroom.

177

Lesson 79

Pictures and Words

INTRODUCTION
Picture: Shopping or _____
   The teacher leads a brief discussion about the picture.

CHART DEVELOPMENT
Phase III—Sentences: The students volunteer words to label the picture, and the teacher writes the words on the chart. Students draw lines to connect parts of the picture to the words. The teacher writes a student-chosen title and at least one sentence on the chart.

COMPREHENSION FOCUS
The teacher develops comprehension of the picture by asking questions, many of which will begin with *where*.
   The chart is displayed in the classroom.

Storytime

READ ALOUD
Corduroy
by Don Freeman
or _____

DISCUSSION FOCUS
Did the author give Corduroy human feelings? How did the little girl show the way she felt?

Writing

Five-Day Theme: Toys
or _____

INTRODUCTION
The teacher and the students have a conversation related to the theme.

WRITING ACTIVITIES
While the students are writing or drawing, the teacher meets with individuals or small groups to discuss the theme. The student's independent work may or may not relate to the theme. Each student's work is kept in a folder.

SHARING
The students share with another person or the group something they have written or drawn.

Alphabet

Rhyming Word: Mat or _____

INTRODUCTION— BRAINSTORMING LESSON
The teacher introduces the rhyming word and writes student-volunteered words and illustrations of other rhyming words.

STUDENT ACTIVITY
On their papers, students write
■ their favorite words or illustrations from the chalkboard

■ other words or drawings

SHARING
The students share with another person or the group something they have written or drawn.
   Papers are dated and filed.

Lesson 80

Pictures and Words

INTRODUCTION
Picture: Candy or _____
The teacher leads a brief discussion about the picture.

CHART DEVELOPMENT
Phase III—Sentences: The students volunteer words to label the picture, and the teacher writes the words on the chart. Students draw lines to connect parts of the picture to the words. The teacher writes a student-chosen title and at least one sentence on the chart.

COMPREHENSION FOCUS
The teacher develops comprehension of the picture by asking questions, many of which will begin with *what*.
The chart is displayed in the classroom.

Storytime

READ ALOUD
Hi Cat!
by Ezra Jack Keats
or _____

DISCUSSION FOCUS
Look at the illustrations. Would you make a cat the way Ezra Jack Keats did? How would you do it?

Writing

Five-Day Theme: Toys
or _____

INTRODUCTION
The teacher leads a class discussion about points of interest generated during the first four days of the theme and introduces the student activity.

STUDENT ACTIVITY
The students make a toy.

SHARING
The students tell their classmates or the whole class about their toy.

Alphabet

Rhyming Word: Mat or _____

INTRODUCTION—STUDENT PROJECTS LESSON
The teacher reviews the rhyming word. The class discusses construction of a cat out of construction paper (as shown in the illustration).

STUDENT ACTIVITY
The students make their own version of a cat.

SHARING
The students take their projects home.

Lesson 81

Pictures and Words

INTRODUCTION
Picture: Money or _____
The teacher leads a brief discussion about the picture.

CHART DEVELOPMENT
Phase III—Sentences: The students volunteer words to label the picture, and the teacher writes the words on the chart. Students draw lines to connect parts of the picture to the words. The teacher writes a student-chosen title and at least one sentence on the chart.

COMPREHENSION FOCUS
The teacher develops comprehension of the picture by asking questions, many of which will begin with *when*.
The chart is displayed in the classroom.

Storytime

READ ALOUD
Fast-Slow High-Low
by Peter Spier
Dry or Wet
by Bruce McMillan
or _____

DISCUSSION FOCUS
Use the illustrations to talk about or write a list of opposites.

Writing

Five-Day Theme: Money
or _____

INTRODUCTION
The teacher and the students have a conversation related to the theme. Conversations might include a reference to the Pictures and Words chart made earlier in the day.

WRITING ACTIVITIES
While the students are writing or drawing, the teacher meets with individuals or small groups to discuss the theme. The student's independent work may or may not relate to the theme. Each student's work is kept in a folder.

SHARING
The students share with another person or the group something they have written or drawn.

Alphabet

Rhyming Word: Bed or _____

INTRODUCTION—
BRAINSTORMING LESSON
The teacher introduces the rhyming word and writes student-volunteered words and illustrations of other rhyming words.

STUDENT ACTIVITY
On their papers, students write
■ their favorite words or illustrations from the chalkboard

■ other words or drawings

SHARING
The students share with another person or the group something they have written or drawn.
Papers are dated and filed.

Lesson 82

Pictures and Words

INTRODUCTION
Picture: Rabbits or _____
  The teacher leads a brief discussion about the picture.

CHART DEVELOPMENT
Phase III—Sentences: The students volunteer words to label the picture, and the teacher writes the words on the chart. Students draw lines to connect parts of the picture to the words. The teacher writes a student-chosen title and at least one sentence on the chart.

COMPREHENSION FOCUS
The teacher develops comprehension of the picture by asking questions, many of which will begin with *where*.
  The chart is displayed in the classroom.

Storytime

READ ALOUD
Who Said Red?
by Mary Serfozo
or _____

DISCUSSION FOCUS
Play a verbal game after reading the book aloud. One child says a color. Another child answers with the first thing he/she thinks of. For example, for "blue," answer "my sweater."

Writing

Five-Day Theme: Money
or _____

INTRODUCTION
The teacher and the students have a conversation related to the theme.

WRITING ACTIVITIES
While the students are writing or drawing, the teacher meets with individuals or small groups to discuss the theme. The student's independent work may or may not relate to the theme. Each student's work is kept in a folder.

SHARING
The students share with another person or the group something they have written or drawn.

Alphabet

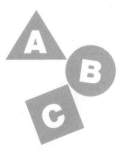

Rhyming Word: Bed or _____

INTRODUCTION—RESEARCH LESSON—Magazines
The teacher reviews the rhyming word. The teacher leads a discussion about words for objects that may be found in magazines that relate to the color red or
_____

STUDENT ACTIVITY
The students cut or tear related objects from magazines and glue them on individual papers or the class chart. Some of the objects may be labeled.

SHARING
The teacher and students discuss items on the class chart. The chart is displayed in the classroom.

Lesson 83

Pictures and Words

INTRODUCTION
Picture: Fox or _____
The teacher leads a brief discussion about the picture.

CHART DEVELOPMENT
Phase III—Sentences: The students volunteer words to label the picture, and the teacher writes the words on the chart. Students draw lines to connect parts of the picture to the words. The teacher writes a student-chosen title and at least one sentence on the chart.

COMPREHENSION FOCUS
The teacher develops comprehension of the picture by asking questions, many of which will begin with *how*.
The chart is displayed in the classroom.

Storytime

READ ALOUD
Mike Mulligan and His Steam Shovel by Virginia Lee Burton
or _____

DISCUSSION FOCUS
How did Mike Mulligan solve his problem? Is there a part of the book that tells what made Mike and Maryanne work faster and better?

Writing

Five-Day Theme: Money
or _____

INTRODUCTION
The teacher and the students have a conversation related to the theme.

WRITING ACTIVITIES
While the students are writing or drawing, the teacher meets with individuals or small groups to discuss the theme. The student's independent work may or may not relate to the theme. Each student's work is kept in a folder.

SHARING
The students share with another person or the group something they have written or drawn.

Alphabet

Rhyming Word: Fox or _____

INTRODUCTION—BRAINSTORMING LESSON
The teacher introduces the rhyming word and writes student-volunteered words and illustrations of other rhyming words.

STUDENT ACTIVITY
On their papers, students write
■ their favorite words or illustrations from the chalkboard

■ other words or drawings

SHARING
The students share with another person or the group something they have written or drawn.
Papers are dated and filed.

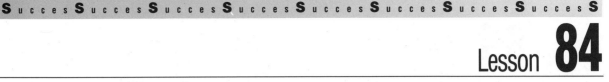

Pictures and Words

INTRODUCTION
Picture: Girls or _____
The teacher leads a brief discussion about the picture.

CHART DEVELOPMENT
Phase III—Sentences: The students volunteer words to label the picture, and the teacher writes the words on the chart. Students draw lines to connect parts of the picture to the words. The teacher writes a student-chosen title and at least one sentence on the chart.

COMPREHENSION FOCUS
The teacher develops comprehension of the picture by asking questions, many of which will begin with *who*.
The chart is displayed in the classroom.

Storytime

READ ALOUD
Madeline
by Ludwig Bemelmans
or _____

DISCUSSION FOCUS
Discuss and list some events that the class thinks were important.

Writing

Five-Day Theme: Money
or _____

INTRODUCTION
The teacher and the students have a conversation related to the theme.

WRITING ACTIVITIES
While the students are writing or drawing, the teacher meets with individuals or small groups to discuss the theme. The student's independent work may or may not relate to the theme. Each student's work is kept in a folder.

SHARING
The students share with another person or the group something they have written or drawn.

Alphabet

Rhyming Word: Fox or _____

INTRODUCTION—STUDENT PROJECTS LESSON
The teacher reviews the rhyming word. The class discusses construction of a decorated box. The students use assorted scrap art materials to decorate a small box.

STUDENT ACTIVITY
The students make their own version of a decorated box.

SHARING
The students take their projects home.

Lesson 85

Pictures and Words

INTRODUCTION
Picture: Mother or _____
    The teacher leads a brief discussion about the picture.

CHART DEVELOPMENT
Phase III—Sentences: The students volunteer words to label the picture, and the teacher writes the words on the chart. Students draw lines to connect parts of the picture to the words. The teacher writes a student-chosen title and at least one sentence on the chart.

COMPREHENSION FOCUS
The teacher develops comprehension of the picture by asking questions, many of which will begin with *what*.
    The chart is displayed in the classroom.

Storytime

READ ALOUD
A Chair for My Mother
by Vera B. Williams
or _____

DISCUSSION FOCUS
Brainstorm things that happened in the story. Record some of them in order on a simple time-line.

Writing

Five-Day Theme: Money
or _____

INTRODUCTION
The teacher leads a class discussion about points of interest generated during the first four days of the theme and introduces the student activity.

STUDENT ACTIVITY
Reread part of *A Chair for My Mother*. Make a class book on the theme, "If I had a big jar of money . . ."

SHARING
Read the class book and place it with the classroom book collection.

Alphabet

Rhyming Word: Drill or _____

INTRODUCTION—
BRAINSTORMING LESSON
The teacher introduces the rhyming word and writes student-volunteered words and illustrations of other rhyming words.

STUDENT ACTIVITY
On their papers, students write
■ their favorite words or illustrations from the chalkboard

■ other words or drawings

SHARING
The students share with another person or the group something they have written or drawn.
    Papers are dated and filed.

Pictures and Words

INTRODUCTION
Picture: Cartoons or _____
The teacher leads a brief discussion about the picture.

CHART DEVELOPMENT
Phase III—Sentences: The students volunteer words to label the picture, and the teacher writes the words on the chart. Students draw lines to connect parts of the picture to the words. The teacher writes a student-chosen title and at least one sentence on the chart.

COMPREHENSION FOCUS
The teacher develops comprehension of the picture by asking questions, many of which will begin with *who*.
The chart is displayed in the classroom.

Storytime

READ ALOUD
Curious George
by H. A. Rey
or _____

DISCUSSION FOCUS
Who are the main characters in the story?

Writing

Five-Day Theme: Cartoons
or _____

INTRODUCTION
The teacher and the students have a conversation related to the theme. Conversations might include a reference to the Pictures and Words chart made earlier in the day.

WRITING ACTIVITIES
While the students are writing or drawing, the teacher meets with individuals or small groups to discuss the theme. The student's independent work may or may not relate to the theme. Each student's work is kept in a folder.

SHARING
The students share with another person or the group something they have written or drawn.

Alphabet

Rhyming Word: Drill or _____

INTRODUCTION—RESEARCH LESSON—Magazines
The teacher reviews the rhyming word. The teacher leads a discussion about words for objects that may be found in magazines that relate to things that can spill or _____

STUDENT ACTIVITY
The students cut or tear related objects from magazines and glue them on individual papers or the class chart. Some of the objects may be labeled.

SHARING
The teacher and students discuss items on the class chart. The chart is displayed in the classroom.

Lesson 87

Pictures and Words

INTRODUCTION
Picture: Playground or _____
   The teacher leads a brief discussion about the picture.

CHART DEVELOPMENT
Phase III—Sentences: The students volunteer words to label the picture, and the teacher writes the words on the chart. Students draw lines to connect parts of the picture to the words. The teacher writes a student-chosen title and at least one sentence on the chart.

COMPREHENSION FOCUS
The teacher develops comprehension of the picture by asking questions, many of which will begin with *when*.
   The chart is displayed in the classroom.

Storytime

READ ALOUD
It's Mine, It's Mine
by Leo Lionni
or _____

DISCUSSION FOCUS
What happened when no one was willing to share?

Writing

Five-Day Theme: Cartoons
or _____

INTRODUCTION
The teacher and the students have a conversation related to the theme.

WRITING ACTIVITIES
While the students are writing or drawing, the teacher meets with individuals or small groups to discuss the theme. The student's independent work may or may not relate to the theme. Each student's work is kept in a folder.

SHARING
The students share with another person or the group something they have written or drawn.

Alphabet

Rhyming Word: Fun or _____

INTRODUCTION—BRAINSTORMING LESSON
The teacher introduces the rhyming word and writes student-volunteered words and illustrations of other rhyming words.

STUDENT ACTIVITY
On their papers, students write
■ their favorite words or illustrations from the chalkboard
■ other words or drawings

SHARING
The students share with another person or the group something they have written or drawn.
   Papers are dated and filed.

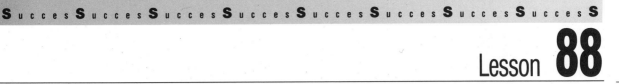
Lesson 88

Pictures and Words

INTRODUCTION
Picture: Basketball Player or
_____

The teacher leads a brief discussion about the picture.

CHART DEVELOPMENT
Phase III—Sentences: The students volunteer words to label the picture, and the teacher writes the words on the chart.

Students draw lines to connect parts of the picture to the words. The teacher writes a student-chosen title and at least one sentence on the chart.

COMPREHENSION FOCUS
The teacher develops comprehension of the picture by asking questions, many of which will begin with _how_.

The chart is displayed in the classroom.

Storytime

READ ALOUD
Sun Up, Sun Down
by Gail Gibbons
or _____

DISCUSSION FOCUS
How does the sun affect our daily life?

Writing

Five-Day Theme: Cartoons
or _____

INTRODUCTION
The teacher and the students have a conversation related to the theme.

WRITING ACTIVITIES
While the students are writing or drawing, the teacher meets with

individuals or small groups to discuss the theme. The student's independent work may or may not relate to the theme. Each student's work is kept in a folder.

SHARING
The students share with another person or the group something they have written or drawn.

Alphabet

Rhyming Word: Fun or _____

INTRODUCTION—STUDENT PROJECTS LESSON
The teacher reviews the rhyming word. The class discusses construction of a sun. A crayon-resist method could be used.

STUDENT ACTIVITY
The students make their own version of a sun.

SHARING
The students take their projects home.

Lesson 89

Pictures and Words

INTRODUCTION
Picture: Donald Duck or _____
The teacher leads a brief discussion about the picture.

CHART DEVELOPMENT
Phase III—Sentences: The students volunteer words to label the picture, and the teacher writes the words on the chart. Students draw lines to connect parts of the picture to the words. The teacher writes a student-chosen title and at least one sentence on the chart.

COMPREHENSION FOCUS
The teacher develops comprehension of the picture by asking questions, many of which will begin with *what*.
The chart is displayed in the classroom.

Storytime

READ ALOUD
Jack and the Beanstalk
(any version)
or _____

DISCUSSION FOCUS
What were the objects that Jack took from the Giant?

Writing

Five-Day Theme: Cartoons
or _____

INTRODUCTION
The teacher and the students have a conversation related to the theme.

WRITING ACTIVITIES
While the students are writing or drawing, the teacher meets with individuals or small groups to discuss the theme. The student's independent work may or may not relate to the theme. Each student's work is kept in a folder.

SHARING
The students share with another person or the group something they have written or drawn.

Alphabet

Rhyming Word: Quack or _____

INTRODUCTION—BRAINSTORMING LESSON
The teacher introduces the rhyming word and writes student-volunteered words and illustrations of other rhyming words.

STUDENT ACTIVITY
On their papers, students write
■ their favorite words or illustrations from the chalkboard

■ other words or drawings

SHARING
The students share with another person or the group something they have written or drawn.
Papers are dated and filed.

188

Lesson 90

Pictures and Words

INTRODUCTION
Picture: House or _____
  The teacher leads a brief discussion about the picture.

CHART DEVELOPMENT
Phase III—Sentences: The students volunteer words to label the picture, and the teacher writes the words on the chart. Students draw lines to connect parts of the picture to the words. The teacher writes a student-chosen title and at least one sentence on the chart.

COMPREHENSION FOCUS
The teacher develops comprehension of the picture by asking questions, many of which will begin with *where*.
  The chart is displayed in the classroom.

Storytime

READ ALOUD
How a House Is Built
by Gail Gibbons
or _____

DISCUSSION FOCUS
What steps are there in building a house? Discuss the order of these steps.

Writing

Five-Day Theme: Cartoons
or _____

INTRODUCTION
The teacher leads a class discussion about points of interest generated during the first four days of the theme and introduces the student activity.

STUDENT ACTIVITY
Have a cartoon festival. Make Mickey Mouse ears or masks of favorite cartoon characters.

SHARING
The students model their masks for their classmates or have a parade.

Alphabet

Rhyming Word: Quack or _____

INTRODUCTION—RESEARCH LESSON—Magazines
The teacher reviews the rhyming word. The teacher leads a discussion about words for objects that may be found in magazines that relate to the color black or _____

STUDENT ACTIVITY
The students cut or tear related objects from magazines and glue them on individual papers or the class chart. Some of the objects may be labeled.

SHARING
The teacher and students discuss items on the class chart. The chart is displayed in the classroom.

Lesson 91

Pictures and Words

INTRODUCTION
Picture: Winter or _____
   The teacher leads a brief discussion about the picture.

CHART DEVELOPMENT
Phase III—Sentences: The students volunteer words to label the picture, and the teacher writes the words on the chart. Students draw lines to connect parts of the picture to the words. The teacher writes a student-chosen title and at least one sentence on the chart.

COMPREHENSION FOCUS
The teacher develops comprehension of the picture by asking questions, many of which will begin with *why*.
   The chart is displayed in the classroom.

Storytime

READ ALOUD
Happy Birthday, Moon
by Frank Asch
or _____

DISCUSSION FOCUS
Discuss the main character. How do we know who the most important character is?

Writing

Five-Day Theme: Winter
or _____

INTRODUCTION
The teacher and the students have a conversation related to the theme. Conversations might include a reference to the Pictures and Words chart made earlier in the day.

WRITING ACTIVITIES
While the students are writing or drawing, the teacher meets with individuals or small groups to discuss the theme. The student's independent work may or may not relate to the theme. Each student's work is kept in a folder.

SHARING
The students share with another person or the group something they have written or drawn.

Alphabet

Rhyming Word: Well or _____

**INTRODUCTION—
BRAINSTORMING LESSON**
The teacher introduces the rhyming word and writes student-volunteered words and illustrations of other rhyming words on the chalkboard.

STUDENT ACTIVITY
On their papers, students write
■ their favorite words or illustrations from the chalkboard

■ other words or drawings

SHARING
The students share with another person or the group something they have written or drawn.
   Papers are dated and filed.

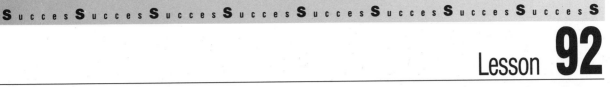
Lesson 92

Pictures and Words

INTRODUCTION
Picture: Forest or _____
   The teacher leads a brief discussion about the picture.

CHART DEVELOPMENT
Phase III—Sentences: The students volunteer words to label the picture, and the teacher writes the words on the chart. Students draw lines to connect parts of the picture to the words. The teacher writes a student-chosen title and at least one sentence on the chart.

COMPREHENSION FOCUS
The teacher develops comprehension of the picture by asking questions, many of which will begin with *what*.
   The chart is displayed in the classroom.

Storytime

READ ALOUD
The Mitten
by Jan Brett
The Mitten
by Alvin Tresselt
or _____

DISCUSSION FOCUS
Talk about the animals who visited the mitten. Did the order of their arrival and their size affect the story?

Writing

Five-Day Theme: Winter
or _____

INTRODUCTION
The teacher and the students have a conversation related to the theme.

WRITING ACTIVITIES
While the students are writing or drawing, the teacher meets with individuals or small groups to discuss the theme. The student's independent work may or may not relate to the theme. Each student's work is kept in a folder.

SHARING
The students share with another person or the group something they have written or drawn.

Alphabet

Rhyming Word: Well or _____

INTRODUCTION—STUDENT PROJECTS LESSON
The teacher reviews the rhyming word. The class discusses construction of a bell. Egg carton sections could be used.

STUDENT ACTIVITY
The students make their own versions of a bell.

SHARING
The students take their projects home.

191

Lesson 93

Pictures and Words

INTRODUCTION
Picture: Pigs or _____

The teacher leads a brief discussion about the picture.

CHART DEVELOPMENT
Phase III—Sentences: The students volunteer words to label the picture, and the teacher writes the words on the chart. Students draw lines to connect parts of the picture to the words. The teacher writes a student-chosen title and at least one sentence on the chart.

COMPREHENSION FOCUS
The teacher develops comprehension of the picture by asking questions, many of which will begin with *where*.

The chart is displayed in the classroom.

Storytime

READ ALOUD
Small Pig
by Arnold Lobel
or _____

DISCUSSION FOCUS
Think of some things that happened in this story. Discuss and vote to decide the most important event.

Writing

Five-Day Theme: Winter
or _____

INTRODUCTION
The teacher and the students have a conversation related to the theme.

WRITING ACTIVITIES
While the students are writing or drawing, the teacher meets with individuals or small groups to discuss the theme. The student's independent work may or may not relate to the theme. Each student's work is kept in a folder.

SHARING
The students share with another person or the group something they have written or drawn.

Alphabet

Rhyming Word: Trick or _____

INTRODUCTION—BRAINSTORMING LESSON
The teacher introduces the rhyming word and writes student-volunteered words and illustrations of other rhyming words on the chalkboard.

STUDENT ACTIVITY
On their papers, students write
■ their favorite words or illustrations from the chalkboard
■ other words or drawings

SHARING
The students share with another person or the group something they have written or drawn.

Papers are dated and filed.

Pictures and Words

INTRODUCTION
Picture: Lollipops or _____
   The teacher leads a brief discussion about the picture.

CHART DEVELOPMENT
Phase III—Sentences: The students volunteer words to label the picture, and the teacher writes the words on the chart. Students draw lines to connect parts of the picture to the words. The teacher writes a student-chosen title and at least one sentence on the chart.

COMPREHENSION FOCUS
The teacher develops comprehension of the picture by asking questions, many of which will begin with *how*.
   The chart is displayed in the classroom.

Storytime

READ ALOUD
Amelia Bedelia
by Peggy Parish
or _____

DISCUSSION FOCUS
Talk about why Amelia Bedelia makes people laugh.

Writing

Five-Day Theme: Winter
or _____

INTRODUCTION
The teacher and the students have a conversation related to the theme.

WRITING ACTIVITIES
While the students are writing or drawing, the teacher meets with individuals or small groups to discuss the theme. The student's independent work may or may not relate to the theme. Each student's work is kept in a folder.

SHARING
The students share with another person or the group something they have written or drawn.

Alphabet

Rhyming Word: Trick or _____

INTRODUCTION—RESEARCH LESSON—Magazines
The teacher reviews the rhyming word. The teacher leads a discussion about objects that may be found in magazines that relate to things that are quick.

STUDENT ACTIVITY
The students cut or tear related objects from magazines and glue them on individual papers or the class chart. Some of the objects may be labeled.

SHARING
The teacher and students discuss items on the class chart. The chart is displayed in the classroom.

Lesson 95

Pictures and Words

INTRODUCTION
Picture: Dogs or _____
The teacher leads a brief discussion about the picture.

CHART DEVELOPMENT
Phase III—Sentences: The students volunteer words to label the picture, and the teacher writes the words on the chart. Students draw lines to connect parts of the picture to the words. The teacher writes a student-chosen title and at least one sentence on the chart.

COMPREHENSION FOCUS
The teacher develops comprehension of the picture by asking questions, many of which will begin with *what*.
The chart is displayed in the classroom.

Storytime

READ ALOUD
The Snowy Day
by Ezra Jack Keats
or _____

DISCUSSION FOCUS
This whole story happens on one winter day. Can you tell about this season?

Writing

Five-Day Theme: Winter
or _____

INTRODUCTION
The teacher leads a class discussion about points of interest generated during the first four days of the theme and introduces the student activity.

STUDENT ACTIVITY
The students make torn-paper snow pictures.

SHARING
Display the pictures or bind them into a class book.

Alphabet

Rhyming Word: Dog or _____

INTRODUCTION—BRAINSTORMING LESSON
The teacher introduces the rhyming word and writes student-volunteered words and illustrations of other rhyming words on the chalkboard.

STUDENT ACTIVITY
On their papers, students write
■ their favorite words or illustrations from the chalkboard
■ other words or drawings

SHARING
The students share with another person or the group something they have written or drawn.
Papers are dated and filed.

Lesson 96

Pictures and Words

INTRODUCTION
Picture: Dinosaurs or _____
   The teacher leads a brief discussion about the picture.

CHART DEVELOPMENT
Phase III—Sentences: The students volunteer words to label the picture, and the teacher writes the words on the chart. Students draw lines to connect parts of the picture to the words. The teacher writes a student-chosen title and at least one sentence on the chart.

COMPREHENSION FOCUS
The teacher develops comprehension of the picture by asking questions, many of which will begin with *when*.
   The chart is displayed in the classroom.

Storytime

READ ALOUD
Chicken Soup with Rice
by Maurice Sendak
or _____

DISCUSSION FOCUS
Children with December birthdays name things they heard in the December verse. Repeat with several other months (at least one from each season).

Writing

Five-Day Theme: Dinosaurs
or _____

INTRODUCTION
The teacher and the students have a conversation related to the theme. Conversations might include a reference to the Pictures and Words chart made earlier in the day.

WRITING ACTIVITIES
While the students are writing or drawing, the teacher meets with individuals or small groups to discuss the theme. The student's independent work may or may not relate to the theme. Each student's work is kept in a folder.

SHARING
The students share with another person or the group something they have written or drawn.

Alphabet

Rhyming Word: Dog or _____

INTRODUCTION—STUDENT PROJECTS LESSON
The teacher reviews the rhyming word. The class discusses painting a crayon-resist picture with a thin gray wash.

STUDENT ACTIVITY
The students make their own version of a picture of fog.

SHARING
The students take their projects home.

195

Lesson 97

Pictures and Words

INTRODUCTION
Picture: Fish or _____
The teacher leads a brief discussion about the picture.

CHART DEVELOPMENT
Phase III—Sentences: The students volunteer words to label the picture, and the teacher writes the words on the chart. Students draw lines to connect parts of the picture to the words. The teacher writes a student-chosen title and at least one sentence on the chart.

COMPREHENSION FOCUS
The teacher develops comprehension of the picture by asking questions, many of which will begin with *where*.
The chart is displayed in the classroom.

Storytime

READ ALOUD
Fish Eyes
by Lois Ehlert
or _____

DISCUSSION FOCUS
Discuss how colors make the fish show up on these dark background pages.

Writing

Five-Day Theme: Dinosaurs
or _____

INTRODUCTION
The teacher and the students have a conversation related to the theme.

WRITING ACTIVITIES
While the students are writing or drawing, the teacher meets with individuals or small groups to discuss the theme. The student's independent work may or may not relate to the theme. Each student's work is kept in a folder.

SHARING
The students share with another person or the group something they have written or drawn.

Alphabet

Rhyming Word: Rug or _____

INTRODUCTION— BRAINSTORMING LESSON
The teacher introduces the rhyming word and writes student-volunteered words and illustrations of other rhyming words on the chalkboard.

STUDENT ACTIVITY
On their papers, students write
■ their favorite words or illustrations from the chalkboard

■ other words or drawings

SHARING
The students share with another person or the group something they have written or drawn.
Papers are dated and filed.

Pictures and Words

INTRODUCTION
Picture: Hot dogs or _____
  The teacher leads a brief discussion about the picture.

CHART DEVELOPMENT
Phase III—Sentences: The students volunteer words to label the picture, and the teacher writes the words on the chart. Students draw lines to connect parts of the picture to the words. The teacher writes a student-chosen title and at least one sentence on the chart.

COMPREHENSION FOCUS
The teacher develops comprehension of the picture by asking questions, many of which will begin with *how*.
  The chart is displayed in the classroom.

Storytime

READ ALOUD
Dinosaurs, Dinosaurs
by Byron Barton
Dinosaurs
by Gail Gibbons
or _____

DISCUSSION FOCUS
Did the author know what color the dinosaurs were? Does anyone know?

Writing

Five-Day Theme: Dinosaurs
or _____

INTRODUCTION
The teacher and the students have a conversation related to the theme.

WRITING ACTIVITIES
While the students are writing or drawing, the teacher meets with individuals or small groups to discuss the theme. The student's independent work may or may not relate to the theme. Each student's work is kept in a folder.

SHARING
The students share with another person or the group something they have written or drawn.

Alphabet

Rhyming Word: Rug or _____

INTRODUCTION—RESEARCH LESSON—Magazines
The teacher reviews the rhyming word. The teacher leads a discussion about objects that may be found in magazines that relate to bugs or _____

STUDENT ACTIVITY
The students cut or tear related objects from magazines and glue them on individual papers or the class chart. Some of the objects may be labeled.

SHARING
The teacher and students discuss items on the class chart. The chart is displayed in the classroom.

Lesson **99**

Pictures and Words

INTRODUCTION
Picture: Man or _____
   The teacher leads a brief discussion about the picture.

CHART DEVELOPMENT
Phase III—Sentences: The students volunteer words to label the picture, and the teacher writes the words on the chart. Students draw lines to connect parts of the picture to the words. The teacher writes a student-chosen title and at least one sentence on the chart.

COMPREHENSION FOCUS
The teacher develops comprehension of the picture by asking questions, many of which will begin with *who*.
   The chart is displayed in the classroom.

Storytime

READ ALOUD
The Mixed-Up Chameleon
by Eric Carle
or _____

DISCUSSION FOCUS
Can we find real animals in this book?

Writing

Five-Day Theme: Dinosaurs
or _____

INTRODUCTION
The teacher and the students have a conversation related to the theme.

WRITING ACTIVITIES
While the students are writing or drawing, the teacher meets with individuals or small groups to discuss the theme. The student's independent work may or may not relate to the theme. Each student's work is kept in a folder.

SHARING
The students share with another person or the group something they have written or drawn.

Alphabet

Rhyming Word: Man or _____

**INTRODUCTION—
BRAINSTORMING LESSON**
The teacher introduces the rhyming word and writes student-volunteered words and illustrations of other rhyming words on the chalkboard.

STUDENT ACTIVITY
On their papers, students write
■ their favorite words or illustrations from the chalkboard

■ other words or drawings

SHARING
The students share with another person or the group something they have written or drawn.
   Papers are dated and filed.

Pictures and Words

INTRODUCTION
Picture: Swamp or _____
The teacher leads a brief discussion about the picture.

CHART DEVELOPMENT
Phase III—Sentences: The students volunteer words to label the picture, and the teacher writes the words on the chart. Students draw lines to connect parts of the picture to the words. The teacher writes a student-chosen title and at least one sentence on the chart.

COMPREHENSION FOCUS
The teacher develops comprehension of the picture by asking questions, many of which will begin with *what*.
The chart is displayed in the classroom.

Storytime

READ ALOUD
Bones, Bones, Dinosaur Bones
by Byron Barton
or _____

DISCUSSION FOCUS
Compare present-day animal sizes to dinosaur sizes. How do we know how big dinosaurs probably were?

Writing

Five-Day Theme: Dinosaurs
or _____

INTRODUCTION
The teacher leads a class discussion about points of interest generated during the first four days of the theme and introduces the student activity.

STUDENT ACTIVITY
The students build their own dinosaurs from "bones." Bones could be paper, painted doggy treats, pipe cleaners, or even real washed-and-dried chicken bones.

SHARING
The students share and display their dinosaur creations.

Alphabet

Rhyming Word: Fans or _____

INTRODUCTION—STUDENT PROJECTS LESSON
The teacher reviews the rhyming word. The class discusses construction of fans made from folded paper.

STUDENT ACTIVITY
The students make their own versions of fans.

SHARING
The students take their projects home.

Lesson 101

Pictures and Words

INTRODUCTION
Picture: Meal or _____

The teacher leads a brief discussion about the picture.

CHART DEVELOPMENT
Phase III—Sentences: The students volunteer words to label the picture, and the teacher writes the words on the chart. Students draw lines to connect parts of the picture to the words. The teacher writes a student-chosen title and at least one sentence on the chart.

COMPREHENSION FOCUS
The teacher develops comprehension of the picture by asking questions, many of which will begin with *what*.

The chart is displayed in the classroom.

Storytime

READ ALOUD
The Planets in Our Solar System by Franklyn Branley
or _____

DISCUSSION FOCUS
Before reading the book, brainstorm ideas the class has about planets. *After* reading the book, briefly discuss those same ideas.

Writing

Five-Day Theme: Food Groups
or _____

INTRODUCTION
The teacher and the students have a conversation related to the theme. Conversations might include a reference to the Pictures and Words chart made earlier in the day.

WRITING ACTIVITIES
While the students are writing or drawing, the teacher meets with individuals or small groups to discuss the theme. The student's independent work may or may not relate to the theme. Each student's work is kept in a folder.

SHARING
The students share with another person or the group something they have written or drawn.

Alphabet

Rhyming Word: Jet or _____

INTRODUCTION—BRAINSTORMING LESSON
The teacher introduces the rhyming word and writes student-volunteered words and illustrations of other rhyming words on the chalkboard.

STUDENT ACTIVITY
On their papers, students write
■ their favorite words or illustrations from the chalkboard
■ other words or drawings

SHARING
The students share with another person or the group something they have written or drawn.

Papers are dated and filed.

Pictures and Words

INTRODUCTION
Picture: Horses or _____
    The teacher leads a brief discussion about the picture.

CHART DEVELOPMENT
Phase III—Sentences: The students volunteer words to label the picture, and the teacher writes the words on the chart. Students draw lines to connect parts of the picture to the words. The teacher writes a student-chosen title and at least one sentence on the chart.

COMPREHENSION FOCUS
The teacher develops comprehension of the picture by asking questions, many of which will begin with *where*.
    The chart is displayed in the classroom.

Storytime

READ ALOUD
Flying
by Donald Crews
Flying
by Gail Gibbons
or _____

DISCUSSION FOCUS
Has anyone been on an airplane? Discuss where people go on planes. Why do we go on airplanes?

Writing

Five-Day Theme: Food Groups
or _____

INTRODUCTION
The teacher and the students have a conversation related to the theme.

WRITING ACTIVITIES
While the students are writing or drawing, the teacher meets with individuals or small groups to discuss the theme. The student's independent work may or may not relate to the theme. Each student's work is kept in a folder.

SHARING
The students share with another person or the group something they have written or drawn.

Alphabet

Rhyming Word: Jet or _____

INTRODUCTION—RESEARCH LESSON—Magazines
The teacher reviews the rhyming word. The teacher leads a discussion about objects that may be found in magazines that relate to things you can catch in a net or _____

STUDENT ACTIVITY
The students cut or tear related objects from magazines and glue them on individual papers or the class chart. Some of the objects may be labeled.

SHARING
The teacher and students discuss items on the class chart. The chart is displayed in the classroom.

Lesson 103

Pictures and Words

INTRODUCTION
Picture: Stars or _____

The teacher leads a brief discussion about the picture.

CHART DEVELOPMENT
Phase III—Sentences: The students volunteer words to label the picture, and the teacher writes the words on the chart. Students draw lines to connect parts of the picture to the words. The teacher writes a student-chosen title and at least one sentence on the chart.

COMPREHENSION FOCUS
The teacher develops comprehension of the picture by asking questions, many of which will begin with *when*.

The chart is displayed in the classroom.

Storytime

READ ALOUD
Will's Mammoth
by Rafe Martin
or _____

DISCUSSION FOCUS
What is a wooly mammoth? When did mammoths live? Did Will really play with mammoths? Can you tell what it might be like from the illustrations?

Writing

Five-Day Theme: Food Groups
or _____

INTRODUCTION
The teacher and the students have a conversation related to the theme.

WRITING ACTIVITIES
While the students are writing or drawing, the teacher meets with individuals or small groups to discuss the theme. The student's independent work may or may not relate to the theme. Each student's work is kept in a folder.

SHARING
The students share with another person or the group something they have written or drawn.

Alphabet

Rhyming Word: Star or _____

INTRODUCTION—BRAINSTORMING LESSON
The teacher introduces the rhyming word and writes student-volunteered words and illustrations of other rhyming words on the chalkboard.

STUDENT ACTIVITY
On their papers, students write
■ their favorite words or illustrations from the chalkboard

■ other words or drawings

SHARING
The students share with another person or the group something they have written or drawn.

Papers are dated and filed.

Pictures and Words

INTRODUCTION
Picture: Cows or _____
The teacher leads a brief discussion about the picture.

CHART DEVELOPMENT
Phase III—Sentences: The students volunteer words to label the picture, and the teacher writes the words on the chart. Students draw lines to connect parts of the picture to the words. The teacher writes a student-chosen title and at least one sentence on the chart.

COMPREHENSION FOCUS
The teacher develops comprehension of the picture by asking questions, many of which will begin with *how*.
The chart is displayed in the classroom.

Storytime

READ ALOUD
The Milk Makers
by Gail Gibbons
or _____

DISCUSSION FOCUS
Talk about where cows live.

Writing

Five-Day Theme: Food Groups
or _____

INTRODUCTION
The teacher and the students have a conversation related to the theme.

WRITING ACTIVITIES
While the students are writing or drawing the teacher meets with individuals or small groups to discuss the theme. The student's independent work may or may not relate to the theme. Each student's work is kept in a folder.

SHARING
The students share with another person or the group something they have written or drawn.

Alphabet

Rhyming Word: Star or _____

INTRODUCTION—STUDENT PROJECTS LESSON
The teacher reviews the rhyming word. The class discusses construction of a construction-paper car with wheels that turn on brads.

STUDENT ACTIVITY
The students make their own versions of a car.

SHARING
The students take their projects home.

Lesson 105

Pictures and Words

INTRODUCTION
Picture: Buildings or _____
The teacher leads a brief discussion about the picture.

CHART DEVELOPMENT
Phase III—Sentences: The students volunteer words to label the picture, and the teacher writes the words on the chart. Students draw lines to connect parts of the picture to the words. The teacher writes a student-chosen title and at least one sentence on the chart.

COMPREHENSION FOCUS
The teacher develops comprehension of the picture by asking questions, many of which will begin with *who*.
The chart is displayed in the classroom.

Storytime

READ ALOUD
Little Red Hen
(any version)
or _____

DISCUSSION FOCUS
Would you have shared the bread?

Writing

Five-Day Theme: Food Groups
or _____

INTRODUCTION
The teacher leads a class discussion about points of interest generated during the first four days of the theme and introduces the student activity.

STUDENT ACTIVITY
Make bread or have a "bread tasting" party.

SHARING
The students tell each other or the group their favorite kind of bread.

Alphabet

Rhyming Word: Rake or _____

**INTRODUCTION—
BRAINSTORMING LESSON**
The teacher introduces the rhyming word and writes student-volunteered words and illustrations of other rhyming words on the chalkboard.

STUDENT ACTIVITY
On their papers, students write
■ their favorite words or illustrations
  from the chalkboard

■ other words or drawings

SHARING
The students share with another person or the group something they have written or drawn.
Papers are dated and filed.

Pictures and Words

INTRODUCTION
Picture: Machines or _____
  The teacher leads a brief discussion about the picture.

CHART DEVELOPMENT
Phase III—Sentences: The students volunteer words to label the picture, and the teacher writes the words on the chart. Students draw lines to connect parts of the picture to the words. The teacher writes a student-chosen title and at least one sentence on the chart.

COMPREHENSION FOCUS
The teacher develops comprehension of the picture by asking questions, many of which will begin with *why*.
  The chart is displayed in the classroom.

Storytime

READ ALOUD
Q Is for Duck
by Mary Elting and Michael Folsom
or _____

DISCUSSION FOCUS
Discuss why *Q* could be for duck. Is this funny to you? Why?

Writing

Five-Day Theme: Machines
or _____

INTRODUCTION
The teacher and the students have a conversation related to the theme. Conversations might include a reference to the Pictures and Words chart made earlier in the day.

WRITING ACTIVITIES
While the students are writing or drawing, the teacher meets with individuals or small groups to discuss the theme. The student's independent work may or may not relate to the theme. Each student's work is kept in a folder.

SHARING
The students share with another person or the group something they have written or drawn.

Alphabet

Rhyming Word: Rake or _____

INTRODUCTION—RESEARCH LESSON—Magazines
The teacher reviews the rhyming word. The teacher leads a discussion about objects that may be found in magazines that relate to things you bake or _____

STUDENT ACTIVITY
The students cut or tear related objects from magazines and glue them on individual papers or the class chart. Some of the objects may be labeled.

SHARING
The teacher and students discuss items on the class chart. The chart is displayed in the classroom.

Lesson **107**

Pictures and Words

INTRODUCTION
Picture: Seeing or _____
   The teacher leads a brief discussion about the picture.

CHART DEVELOPMENT
Phase III—Sentences: The students volunteer words to label the picture, and the teacher writes the words on the chart. Students draw lines to connect parts of the picture to the words. The teacher writes a student-chosen title and at least one sentence on the chart.

COMPREHENSION FOCUS
The teacher develops comprehension of the picture by asking questions, many of which will begin with *what*.
   The chart is displayed in the classroom.

Storytime

READ ALOUD
Look! Look! Look!
by Tana Hoban
or _____

DISCUSSION FOCUS
This book is a game. Could we use magazine pictures to make a game like this?

Writing

Five-Day Theme: Machines
or _____

INTRODUCTION
The teacher and the students have a conversation related to the theme.

WRITING ACTIVITIES
While the students are writing or drawing, the teacher meets with individuals or small groups to discuss the theme. The student's independent work may or may not relate to the theme. Each student's work is kept in a folder.

SHARING
The students share with another person or the group something they have written or drawn.

Alphabet

Rhyming Word: Hook or _____

INTRODUCTION—BRAINSTORMING LESSON
The teacher introduces the rhyming word and writes student-volunteered words and illustrations of other rhyming words on the chalkboard.

STUDENT ACTIVITY
On their papers, students write
■ their favorite words or illustrations from the chalkboard
■ other words or drawings

SHARING
The students share with another person or the group something they have written or drawn.
   Papers are dated and filed.

Pictures and Words

INTRODUCTION
Picture: Desk or _____
   The teacher leads a brief discussion about the picture.

CHART DEVELOPMENT
Phase III—Sentences: The students volunteer words to label the picture, and the teacher writes the words on the chart. Students draw lines to connect parts of the picture to the words. The teacher writes a student-chosen title and at least one sentence on the chart.

COMPREHENSION FOCUS
The teacher develops comprehension of the picture by asking questions, many of which will begin with *where*.
   The chart is displayed in the classroom.

Storytime

READ ALOUD
Machines at Work
by Byron Barton
Machines
by Anne & Harlow Rockwell
Dig, Drill, Dump, Fill
by Tana Hoban
or _____

DISCUSSION FOCUS
After reading the book, have one child tell the class about one of the picture machines.

Writing

Five-Day Theme: Machines
or _____

INTRODUCTION
The teacher and the students have a conversation related to the theme.

WRITING ACTIVITIES
While the students are writing or drawing, the teacher meets with individuals or small groups to discuss the theme. The student's independent work may or may not relate to the theme. Each student's work is kept in a folder.

SHARING
The students share with another person or the group something they have written or drawn.

Alphabet

Rhyming Word: Hook or _____

INTRODUCTION—STUDENT PROJECTS LESSON
The teacher reviews the rhyming word. The class discusses construction of a miniature book.

STUDENT ACTIVITY
The students make their own versions of a miniature book.

SHARING
The students take their projects home.

Lesson 109

Pictures and Words

INTRODUCTION
Picture: T.V. star or _____
The teacher leads a brief discussion about the picture.

CHART DEVELOPMENT
Phase III—Sentences: The students volunteer words to label the picture, and the teacher writes the words on the chart. Students draw lines to connect parts of the picture to the words. The teacher writes a student-chosen title and at least one sentence on the chart.

COMPREHENSION FOCUS
The teacher develops comprehension of the picture by asking questions, many of which will begin with *who*.
The chart is displayed in the classroom.

Storytime

READ ALOUD
Sheep in a Jeep
by Nancy Shaw
or _____

DISCUSSION FOCUS
Which words rhyme? Is there a pattern?

Writing

Five-Day Theme: Machines
or _____

INTRODUCTION
The teacher and the students have a conversation related to the theme.

WRITING ACTIVITIES
While the students are writing or drawing, the teacher meets with individuals or small groups to discuss the theme. The student's independent work may or may not relate to the theme. Each student's work is kept in a folder.

SHARING
The students share with another person or the group something they have written or drawn.

Alphabet

Rhyming Word: Sheep or _____

INTRODUCTION—BRAINSTORMING LESSON
The teacher introduces the rhyming word and writes student-volunteered words and illustrations of other rhyming words on the chalkboard.

STUDENT ACTIVITY
On their papers, students write
■ their favorite words or illustrations from the chalkboard

■ other words or drawings

SHARING
The students share with another person or the group something they have written or drawn.
Papers are dated and filed.

Lesson 110

Pictures and Words

INTRODUCTION
Picture: Fire or _____
   The teacher leads a brief discussion about the picture.

CHART DEVELOPMENT
Phase III—Sentences: The students volunteer words to label the picture, and the teacher writes the words on the chart. Students draw lines to connect parts of the picture to the words. The teacher writes a student-chosen title and at least one sentence on the chart.

COMPREHENSION FOCUS
The teacher develops comprehension of the picture by asking questions, many of which will begin with *why*.
   The chart is displayed in the classroom.

Storytime

READ ALOUD
The Book of Foolish Machinery
by Donna Page
or _____

DISCUSSION FOCUS
Did this book have funny words? Can you think of something a funny machine could do?

Writing

Five-Day Theme: Machines
or _____

INTRODUCTION
The teacher leads a class discussion about points of interest generated during the first four days of the theme and introduces the student activity.

STUDENT ACTIVITY
Each student "invents" a machine. The inventions are drawn as "plans" and bound into a class book.

SHARING
The bound class book is read to the class and placed with the classroom book collection.

Alphabet

Rhyming Word: Sheep or _____

INTRODUCTION—RESEARCH LESSON—Magazines
The teacher reviews the rhyming word. The teacher leads a discussion about objects that may be found in magazines that relate to sleep or _____.

STUDENT ACTIVITY
The students cut or tear related objects from magazines and glue them on individual papers or the class chart. Some of the objects may be labeled.

SHARING
The teacher and students discuss items on the class chart. The chart is displayed in the classroom.

Lesson 111

Pictures and Words

INTRODUCTION
Picture: Community helpers or _____

   The teacher leads a brief discussion about the picture.

CHART DEVELOPMENT
Phase III—Sentences: The students volunteer words to label the picture, and the teacher writes the words on the chart.

Students draw lines to connect parts of the picture to the words. The teacher writes a student-chosen title and at least one sentence on the chart.

COMPREHENSION FOCUS
The teacher develops comprehension of the picture by asking questions, many of which will begin with *how*.
   The chart is displayed in the classroom.

Storytime

READ ALOUD
A Letter to Amy
by Ezra Jack Keats
or _____

DISCUSSION FOCUS
How can a letter give a message? Are there different kinds of letters?

Writing

Five-Day Theme: Community Helpers
or _____

INTRODUCTION
The teacher and the students have a conversation related to the theme. Conversations might include a reference to the Pictures and Words chart made earlier in the day.

WRITING ACTIVITIES
While the students are writing or drawing, the teacher meets with

individuals or small groups to discuss the theme. The student's independent work may or may not relate to the theme. Each student's work is kept in a folder.

SHARING
The students share with another person or the group something they have written or drawn.

Alphabet

Rhyming Word: Float or _____

**INTRODUCTION—
BRAINSTORMING LESSON**
The teacher introduces the rhyming word and writes student-volunteered words and illustrations of other rhyming words on the chalkboard.

STUDENT ACTIVITY
On their papers, students write
■ their favorite words or illustrations from the chalkboard

■ other words or drawings

SHARING
The students share with another person or the group something they have written or drawn.
   Papers are dated and filed.

Lesson 112

Pictures and Words

INTRODUCTION
Picture: Boats or _____
  The teacher leads a brief discussion about the picture.

CHART DEVELOPMENT
Phase III—Sentences: The students volunteer words to label the picture, and the teacher writes the words on the chart. Students draw lines to connect parts of the picture to the words. The teacher writes a student-chosen title and at least one sentence on the chart.

COMPREHENSION FOCUS
The teacher develops comprehension of the picture by asking questions, many of which will begin with *where*.
  The chart is displayed in the classroom.

Storytime

READ ALOUD
It's a Perfect Day
by Abigail Pizer
or _____

DISCUSSION FOCUS
Can we see a pattern in this book? Are the animals wild or tame?

Writing

Five-Day Theme: Community Helpers
or _____

INTRODUCTION
The teacher and the students have a conversation related to the theme.

WRITING ACTIVITIES
While the students are writing or drawing, the teacher meets with individuals or small groups to discuss the theme. The student's independent work may or may not relate to the theme. Each student's work is kept in a folder.

SHARING
The students share with another person or the group something they have written or drawn.

Alphabet

Rhyming Word: Float or _____

INTRODUCTION—STUDENT PROJECTS LESSON
The teacher reviews the rhyming word. The class discusses construction of boats out of jar lids, Styrofoam trays, or milk cartons.

STUDENT ACTIVITY
The students make their own versions of a boat.

SHARING
The students take their projects home.

211

Lesson 113

Pictures and Words

INTRODUCTION
Picture: Pebbles or _____
   The teacher leads a brief discussion about the picture.

CHART DEVELOPMENT
Phase III—Sentences: The students volunteer words to label the picture, and the teacher writes the words on the chart. Students draw lines to connect parts of the picture to the words. The teacher writes a student-chosen title and at least one sentence on the chart.

COMPREHENSION FOCUS
The teacher develops comprehension of the picture by asking questions, many of which will begin with *what*.
   The chart is displayed in the classroom.

Storytime

READ ALOUD
Sylvester and the Magic Pebble
by William Steig
or _____

DISCUSSION FOCUS
Reread the book. Listen and record some of the feelings words.

Writing

Five-Day Theme: Community Helpers
or _____

INTRODUCTION
The teacher and the students have a conversation related to the theme.

STUDENT ACTIVITIES
While the students are writing or drawing, the teacher meets with individuals or small groups to discuss the theme. The student's independent work may or may not relate to the theme. Each student's work is kept in a folder.

SHARING
The students share with another person or the group something they have written or drawn.

Alphabet

Rhyming Word: Right or _____

**INTRODUCTION—
BRAINSTORMING LESSON**
The teacher introduces the rhyming word and writes student-volunteered words and illustrations of other rhyming words on the chalkboard.

STUDENT ACTIVITY
On their papers, students write
■ their favorite words or illustrations from the chalkboard
■ other words or drawings

SHARING
The students share with another person or the group something they have written or drawn.
   Papers are dated and filed.

Pictures and Words

INTRODUCTION
Picture: Cereal or _____
   The teacher leads a brief discussion about the picture.

CHART DEVELOPMENT
Phase III—Sentences: The students volunteer words to label the picture, and the teacher writes the words on the chart. Students draw lines to connect parts of the picture to the words. The teacher writes a student-chosen title and at least one sentence on the chart.

COMPREHENSION FOCUS
The teacher develops comprehension of the picture by asking questions, many of which will begin with *when*.
   The chart is displayed in the classroom.

Storytime

READ ALOUD
Switch On, Switch Off
by Melvin Berger
or _____

DISCUSSION FOCUS
Discuss or make a list of the cause/effect situations, such as "turn off fan—fan stops, noise stops."

Writing

Five-Day Theme: Community Helpers
or _____

INTRODUCTION
The teacher and the students have a conversation related to the theme.

WRITING ACTIVITIES
While the students are writing or drawing, the teacher meets with individuals or small groups to discuss the theme. The student's independent work may or may not relate to the theme. Each student's work is kept in a folder.

SHARING
The students share with another person or the group something they have written or drawn.

Alphabet

Rhyming Word: Right or _____

INTRODUCTION—RESEARCH LESSON—Magazines
The teacher reviews the rhyming word. The teacher leads a discussion about objects that may be found in magazines that relate to things with lights or

_____

STUDENT ACTIVITY
The students cut or tear related objects from magazines and glue them on individual papers or the class chart. Some of the objects may be labeled.

SHARING
The teacher and students discuss items on the class chart. The chart is displayed in the classroom.

Lesson **115**

Pictures and Words

INTRODUCTION
Picture: Happy or _____

The teacher leads a brief discussion about the picture.

CHART DEVELOPMENT
Phase III—Sentences: The students volunteer words to label the picture, and the teacher writes the words on the chart. Students draw lines to connect parts of the picture to the words. The teacher writes a student-chosen title and at least one sentence on the chart.

COMPREHENSION FOCUS
The teacher develops comprehension of the picture by asking questions, many of which will begin with *why*.

The chart is displayed in the classroom.

Storytime

READ ALOUD
The Post Office Book
by Gail Gibbons
or _____

DISCUSSION FOCUS
Follow the steps a letter takes from being mailed to arriving at its destination.

Writing

Five-Day Theme: Community Helpers
or _____

INTRODUCTION
The teacher leads a class discussion about points of interest generated during the first four days of the theme and introduces the student activity.

STUDENT ACTIVITY
Have a dress-up day. The students dress as a favorite community helper. Hats made by the students could serve as alternative costumes. Have a parade!

SHARING
The students tell the class about their costumes and the importance of their jobs.

Alphabet

Rhyming Word: Play or _____

INTRODUCTION—BRAINSTORMING LESSON
The teacher introduces the rhyming word and writes student-volunteered words and illustrations of other rhyming words on the chalkboard.

STUDENT ACTIVITY
On their papers, students write
■ their favorite words or illustrations from the chalkboard

■ other words or drawings

SHARING
The students share with another person or the group something they have written or drawn.

Papers are dated and filed.

Pictures and Words

INTRODUCTION
Picture: Sports or _____
   The teacher leads a brief discussion about the picture.

CHART DEVELOPMENT
Phase III—Sentences: The students volunteer words to label the picture, and the teacher writes the words on the chart. Students draw lines to connect parts of the picture to the words. The teacher writes a student-chosen title and at least one sentence on the chart.

COMPREHENSION FOCUS
The teacher develops comprehension of the picture by asking questions, many of which will begin with *where*.
   The chart is displayed in the classroom.

Storytime

READ ALOUD
George Shrinks
by William Joyce
or _____

DISCUSSION FOCUS
Find and record words in the story that mean "large" or "small."

Writing

Five-Day Theme: Sports and Games or _____

INTRODUCTION
The teacher and the students have a conversation related to the theme. Conversations might include a reference to the Pictures and Words chart made earlier in the day.

WRITING ACTIVITIES
While the students are writing or drawing, the teacher meets with individuals or small groups to discuss the theme. The student's independent work may or may not relate to the theme. Each student's work is kept in a folder.

SHARING
The students share with another person or the group something they have written or drawn.

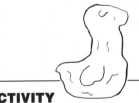

Alphabet

Rhyming Word: Play or _____

INTRODUCTION—STUDENT PROJECTS LESSON
The teacher reviews the rhyming word. The class discusses construction of clay sculptures.

STUDENT ACTIVITY
The students make their own clay sculptures.

SHARING
The students take their projects home.

Lesson 117

Pictures and Words

INTRODUCTION
Picture: A rose or _____
   The teacher leads a brief discussion about the picture.

CHART DEVELOPMENT
Phase III—Sentences: The students volunteer words to label the picture, and the teacher writes the words on the chart. Students draw lines to connect parts of the picture to the words. The teacher writes a student-chosen title and at least one sentence on the chart.

COMPREHENSION FOCUS
The teacher develops comprehension of the picture by asking questions, many of which will begin with *who*.
   The chart is displayed in the classroom.

Storytime

READ ALOUD
Each Peach Pear Plum
by Janet and Allan Ahlberg
The Missing Tarts
by B. G. Hennessy
or _____

DISCUSSION FOCUS
Reread and share the rhyming verses heard in the read-aloud book.

Writing

Five-Day Theme: Sports and Games
or _____

INTRODUCTION
The teacher and the students have a conversation related to the theme.

WRITING ACTIVITIES
While the students are writing or drawing, the teacher meets with individuals or small groups to discuss the theme. The student's independent work may or may not relate to the theme. Each student's work is kept in a folder.

SHARING
The students share with another person or the group something they have written or drawn.

Alphabet

Rhyming Word: Rose or _____

INTRODUCTION—
BRAINSTORMING LESSON
The teacher introduces the rhyming word and writes student-volunteered words and illustrations of other rhyming words on the chalkboard.

STUDENT ACTIVITY
On their papers, students write
■ their favorite words or illustrations from the chalkboard

■ other words or drawings

SHARING
The students share with another person or the group something they have written or drawn.
   Papers are dated and filed.

Pictures and Words

INTRODUCTION
Picture: Hearts or _____
The teacher leads a brief discussion about the picture.

CHART DEVELOPMENT
Phase III—Sentences: The students volunteer words to label the picture, and the teacher writes the words on the chart. Students draw lines to connect parts of the picture to the words. The teacher writes a student-chosen title and at least one sentence on the chart.

COMPREHENSION FOCUS
The teacher develops comprehension of the picture by asking questions, many of which will begin with *what*.
The chart is displayed in the classroom.

Storytime

READ ALOUD
Where Does the Brown Bear Go?
by Nicki Weiss
or _____

DISCUSSION FOCUS
Make a list of the characters.

Writing

Five-Day Theme: Sports and Games
or _____

INTRODUCTION
The teacher and the students have a conversation related to the theme.

WRITING ACTIVITIES
While the students are writing or drawing, the teacher meets with individuals or small groups to discuss the theme. The student's independent work may or may not relate to the theme. Each student's work is kept in a folder.

SHARING
The students share with another person or the group something they have written or drawn.

Alphabet

Rhyming Word: Rose or _____

INTRODUCTION—RESEARCH LESSON—Magazines
The teacher reviews the rhyming word. The teacher leads a discussion about objects that may be found in magazines that relate to things a nose smells or
_____

STUDENT ACTIVITY
The students cut or tear related objects from magazines and glue them on individual papers or the class chart. Some of the objects may be labeled.

SHARING
The teacher and students discuss items on the class chart. The chart is displayed in the classroom.

217

Lesson **119**

Pictures and Words

INTRODUCTION
Picture: Angus (enlarged from book) or _____

The teacher leads a brief discussion about the picture.

CHART DEVELOPMENT
Phase III—Sentences: The students volunteer words to label the picture, and the teacher writes the words on the chart.

Students draw lines to connect parts of the picture to the words. The teacher writes a student-chosen title and at least one sentence on the chart.

COMPREHENSION FOCUS
The teacher develops comprehension of the picture by asking questions, many of which will begin with _what_.

The chart is displayed in the classroom.

Storytime

READ ALOUD
Angus Lost
by Marjorie Flack
or _____

DISCUSSION FOCUS
Have you ever been lost? What did you do? What did Angus do?

Writing

Five-Day Theme: Sports and Games
or _____

INTRODUCTION
The teacher and the students have a conversation related to the theme.

WRITING ACTIVITIES
While the students are writing or drawing, the teacher meets with

individuals or small groups to discuss the theme. The student's independent work may or may not relate to the theme. Each student's work is kept in a folder.

SHARING
The students share with another person or the group something they have written or drawn.

Alphabet

Rhyming Word: Ring or _____

INTRODUCTION—BRAINSTORMING LESSON
The teacher introduces the rhyming word and writes student-volunteered words and illustrations of other rhyming words on the chalkboard.

STUDENT ACTIVITY
On their papers, students write
■ their favorite words or illustrations from the chalkboard

■ other words or drawings

SHARING
The students share with another person or the group something they have written or drawn.

Papers are dated and filed.

Lesson **120**

Pictures and Words

INTRODUCTION
Picture: Airport or _____
   The teacher leads a brief discussion about the picture.

CHART DEVELOPMENT
Phase III—Sentences: The students volunteer words to label the picture, and the teacher writes the words on the chart. Students draw lines to connect parts of the picture to the words. The teacher writes a student-chosen title and at least one sentence on the chart.

COMPREHENSION FOCUS
The teacher develops comprehension of the picture by asking questions, many of which will begin with *when*.
   The chart is displayed in the classroom.

Storytime

READ ALOUD
Dinosaur Bob
by William Joyce
or _____

DISCUSSION FOCUS
Was Dinosaur Bob's size helpful to the family? Discuss how.

Writing

Five-Day Theme: Sports and Games
or _____

INTRODUCTION
The teacher leads a class discussion about points of interest generated during the first four days of the theme and introduces the student activity.

STUDENT ACTIVITY
The students, as individuals or in groups, make games for the classroom or play area.

SHARING
Individuals or groups explain to the class how to play the games they made.

Alphabet

Rhyming Word: Ring or _____

INTRODUCTION—STUDENT PROJECTS LESSON
The teacher reviews the rhyming word. The class discusses the making of a string-art picture by pulling a piece of string coated with paint through folded paper.

STUDENT ACTIVITY
The students make their own versions of string art.

SHARING
The students take their projects home.

219

Lesson 121

Pictures and Words

INTRODUCTION
Picture: Map or _____
   The teacher leads a brief discussion about the picture.

CHART DEVELOPMENT
Phase III—Sentences: The students volunteer words to label the picture, and the teacher writes the words on the chart. Students draw lines to connect parts of the picture to the words. The teacher writes a student-chosen title and at least one sentence on the chart.

COMPREHENSION FOCUS
The teacher develops comprehension of the picture by asking questions, many of which will begin with *where*.
   The chart is displayed in the classroom.

Storytime

READ ALOUD
Have You Seen My Duckling?
by Nancy Tafuri
or _____

DISCUSSION FOCUS
How many ducklings do you see in each picture? Why did the artist try to make them hard to find?

Writing

Five-Day Theme: Maps and States
or _____

INTRODUCTION
The teacher and the students have a conversation related to the theme. Conversations might include a reference to the Pictures and Words chart made earlier in the day.

WRITING ACTIVITIES
While the students are writing or drawing, the teacher meets with individuals or small groups to discuss the theme. The student's independent work may or may not relate to the theme. Each student's work is kept in a folder.

SHARING
The students share with another person or the group something they have written or drawn.

Alphabet

Rhyming Word: Clock or _____

INTRODUCTION— BRAINSTORMING LESSON
The teacher introduces the rhyming word and writes student-volunteered words and illustrations of other rhyming words on the chalkboard.

STUDENT ACTIVITY
On their papers, students write
■ their favorite words or illustrations from the chalkboard
■ other words or drawings

SHARING
The students share with another person or the group something they have written or drawn.
   Papers are dated and filed.

Lesson 122

Pictures and Words

INTRODUCTION
Picture: Locks or _____
   The teacher leads a brief discussion about the picture.

CHART DEVELOPMENT
Phase III—Sentences: The students volunteer words to label the picture, and the teacher writes the words on the chart. Students draw lines to connect parts of the picture to the words. The teacher writes a student-chosen title and at least one sentence on the chart.

COMPREHENSION FOCUS
The teacher develops comprehension of the picture by asking questions, many of which will begin with *why*.
   The chart is displayed in the classroom.

Storytime

READ ALOUD
The Doorbell Rang
by Pat Hutchins
or _____

DISCUSSION FOCUS
Discuss the decreasing number of cookies per person as more guests arrive to share.

Writing

Five-Day Theme: Maps and States
or _____

INTRODUCTION
The teacher and the students have a conversation related to the theme.

WRITING ACTIVITIES
While the students are writing or drawing, the teacher meets with individuals or small groups to discuss the theme. The student's independent work may or may not relate to the theme. Each student's work is kept in a folder.

SHARING
The students share with another person or the group something they have written or drawn.

Alphabet

Rhyming Word: Clock or _____

INTRODUCTION—RESEARCH LESSON—Magazines
The teacher reviews the rhyming word. The teacher leads a discussion about objects that may be found in magazines that relate to things with locks or

_____

STUDENT ACTIVITY
The students cut or tear related objects from magazines and glue them on individual papers or the class chart. Some of the objects may be labeled.

SHARING
The teacher and students discuss items on the class chart. The chart is displayed in the classroom.

Lesson **123**

Pictures and Words

INTRODUCTION
Picture: Clouds or _____

The teacher leads a brief discussion about the picture.

CHART DEVELOPMENT
Phase III—Sentences: The students volunteer words to label the picture, and the teacher writes the words on the chart. Students draw lines to connect parts of the picture to the words. The teacher writes a student-chosen title and at least one sentence on the chart.

COMPREHENSION FOCUS
The teacher develops comprehension of the picture by asking questions, many of which will begin with *what*.

The chart is displayed in the classroom.

Storytime

READ ALOUD
It Looked Like Spilt Milk
by Charles G. Shaw
or _____

DISCUSSION FOCUS
Talk about different people seeing different things when they look at shapes.

Writing

Five-Day Theme: Maps and States
or _____

INTRODUCTION
The teacher and the students have a conversation related to the theme.

WRITING ACTIVITIES
While the students are writing or drawing, the teacher meets with individuals or small groups to discuss the theme. The student's independent work may or may not relate to the theme. Each student's work is kept in a folder.

SHARING
The students share with another person or the group something they have written or drawn.

Alphabet

Letters: *Bb, Nn,* or _____

INTRODUCTION—OBJECT LABELING
The teacher introduces the letters and writes on the chalkboard student-volunteered names of objects in the classroom that contain one or both of the letters.

STUDENT ACTIVITY
The students write their favorite words from the chalkboard or their own words on strips of paper. The words are displayed near the objects.

SHARING
The students share something they have written with another person or the group.

Pictures and Words

INTRODUCTION
Picture: State map or _____
   The teacher leads a brief discussion about the picture.

CHART DEVELOPMENT
Phase III—Sentences: The students volunteer words to label the picture, and the teacher writes the words on the chart. Students draw lines to connect parts of the picture to the words. The teacher writes a student-chosen title and at least one sentence on the chart.

COMPREHENSION FOCUS
The teacher develops comprehension of the picture by asking questions, many of which will begin with *where*.
   The chart is displayed in the classroom.

Storytime

READ ALOUD
Bread and Jam for Frances
by Russell Hoban
or _____

DISCUSSION FOCUS
Find some describing words. The students try to use these adjectives to tell about the story or any other situation.

Writing

Five-Day Theme: Maps and States
or _____

INTRODUCTION
The teacher and the students have a conversation related to the theme.

STUDENT ACTIVITY
While the students are writing or drawing, the teacher meets with individuals or small groups to discuss the theme. The student's independent work may or may not relate to the theme. Each student's work is kept in a folder.

SHARING
The students share with another person or the group something they have written or drawn.

Alphabet

Letters: *Cc, Ll*, or _____

INTRODUCTION—OBJECT LABELING
The teacher introduces the letters and writes on the chalkboard student-volunteered names of objects in the classroom that contain one or both of the letters.

STUDENT ACTIVITY
The students write their favorite words from the chalkboard or their own words on strips of paper. The words are displayed near the objects.

SHARING
The students share something they have written with another person or the group.

Lesson **125**

Pictures and Words

INTRODUCTION
Picture: Athletes or _____
   The teacher leads a brief discussion about the picture.

CHART DEVELOPMENT
Phase III—Sentences: The students volunteer words to label the picture, and the teacher writes the words on the chart. Students draw lines to connect parts of the picture to the words. The teacher writes a student-chosen title and at least one sentence on the chart.

COMPREHENSION FOCUS
The teacher develops comprehension of the picture by asking questions, many of which will begin with *who*.
   The chart is displayed in the classroom.

Storytime

READ ALOUD
Puzzle Maps U.S.A.
by Nancy Clouse
or _____

DISCUSSION FOCUS
Talk about how maps help people. What does a U.S. map show? What does our state look like?

Writing

Five-Day Theme: Maps and States
or _____

INTRODUCTION
The teacher leads a class discussion about points of interest generated during the first four days of the theme and introduces the student activity.

STUDENT ACTIVITY
The children make a large floor map puzzle, as suggested in the book *Puzzle Maps U.S.A.*

SHARING
The class assembles the puzzle and places it with the other games in the classroom for later use.

Alphabet

Letters: *Jj, Ss,* or _____

INTRODUCTION—OBJECT LABELING
The teacher introduces the letters and writes on the chalkboard student-volunteered names of objects in the classroom that contain one or both of the letters.

STUDENT ACTIVITY
The students write their favorite words from the chalkboard or their own words on strips of paper. The words are displayed near the objects.

SHARING
The students share something they have written with another person or the group.

Pictures and Words

INTRODUCTION
Picture: Plants or _____
   The teacher leads a brief discussion about the picture.

CHART DEVELOPMENT
Phase III—Sentences: The students volunteer words to label the picture, and the teacher writes the words on the chart. Students draw lines to connect parts of the picture to the words. The teacher writes a student-chosen title and at least one sentence on the chart.

COMPREHENSION FOCUS
The teacher develops comprehension of the picture by asking questions, many of which will begin with *what*.
   The chart is displayed in the classroom.

Storytime

READ ALOUD
The Carrot Seed
by Ruth Kraus
or _____

DISCUSSION FOCUS
Were all the characters helpful to the little boy?

Writing

Five-Day Theme: Plants
or _____

INTRODUCTION
The teacher and the students have a conversation related to the theme. Conversations might include a reference to the Pictures and Words chart made earlier in the day.

WRITING ACTIVITIES
While the students are writing or drawing, the teacher meets with individuals or small groups to discuss the theme. The student's independent work may or may not relate to the theme. Each student's work is kept in a folder.

SHARING
The students share with another person or the group something they have written or drawn.

Alphabet

Letters: *Rr, Kk,* or _____

INTRODUCTION—OBJECT LABELING
The teacher introduces the letters and writes on the chalkboard student-volunteered names of objects in the classroom that contain one or both of the letters.

STUDENT ACTIVITY
The students write their favorite words from the chalkboard or their own words on strips of paper. The words are displayed near the objects.

SHARING
The students share something they have written with another person or the group.

Lesson **127**

Pictures and Words

INTRODUCTION
Picture: Tractor or _____
    The teacher leads a brief discussion about the picture.

CHART DEVELOPMENT
Phase III—Sentences: The students volunteer words to label the picture, and the teacher writes the words on the chart. Students draw lines to connect parts of the picture to the words. The teacher writes a student-chosen title and at least one sentence on the chart.

COMPREHENSION FOCUS
The teacher develops comprehension of the picture by asking questions, many of which will begin with *how*.
    The chart is displayed in the classroom.

Storytime

READ ALOUD
Planting a Rainbow
by Lois Ehlert
or _____

DISCUSSION FOCUS
How did the artist use color? Discuss the growth from seed to flower.

Writing

Five-Day Theme: Plants
or _____

INTRODUCTION
The teacher and the students have a conversation related to the theme.

WRITING ACTIVITIES
While the students are writing or drawing, the teacher meets with individuals or small groups to discuss the theme. The student's independent work may or may not relate to the theme. Each student's work is kept in a folder.

SHARING
The students share with another person or the group something they have written or drawn.

Alphabet

Letters: *Ff, Vv,* or _____

INTRODUCTION—OBJECT LABELING
The teacher introduces the letters and writes on the chalkboard student-volunteered names of objects in the classroom that contain one or both of the letters.

STUDENT ACTIVITY
The students write their favorite words from the chalkboard or their own words on strips of paper. The words are displayed near the objects.

SHARING
The students share something they have written with another person or the group.

Pictures and Words

INTRODUCTION
Picture: Ants or _____
   The teacher leads a brief discussion about the picture.

CHART DEVELOPMENT
Phase III—Sentences: The students volunteer words to label the picture, and the teacher writes the words on the chart. Students draw lines to connect parts of the picture to the words. The teacher writes a student-chosen title and at least one sentence on the chart.

COMPREHENSION FOCUS
The teacher develops comprehension of the picture by asking questions, many of which will begin with *where*.
   The chart is displayed in the classroom.

Storytime

READ ALOUD
Ant Cities
by A. Dorros
or _____

DISCUSSION FOCUS
Talk about how an ant city is like a city where people live.

Writing

Five-Day Theme: Plants
or _____

INTRODUCTION
The teacher and the students have a conversation related to the theme.

WRITING ACTIVITIES
While the students are writing or drawing, the teacher meets with individuals or small groups to discuss the theme. The student's independent work may or may not relate to the theme. Each student's work is kept in a folder.

SHARING
The students share with another person or the group something they have written or drawn.

Alphabet

Letters: *Tt, Qq,* or _____

INTRODUCTION—OBJECT LABELING
The teacher introduces the letters and writes on the chalkboard student-volunteered names of objects in the classroom that contain one or both of the letters.

STUDENT ACTIVITY
The students write their favorite words from the chalkboard or their own words on strips of paper. The words are displayed near the objects.

SHARING
The students share something they have written with another person or the group.

Lesson **129**

Pictures and Words

INTRODUCTION
Picture: Puzzle or _____
The teacher leads a brief discussion about the picture.

CHART DEVELOPMENT
Phase III—Sentences: The students volunteer words to label the picture, and the teacher writes the words on the chart. Students draw lines to connect parts of the picture to the words. The teacher writes a student-chosen title and at least one sentence on the chart.

COMPREHENSION FOCUS
The teacher develops comprehension of the picture by asking questions, many of which will begin with *what*.
The chart is displayed in the classroom.

Storytime

READ ALOUD
Rosie's Walk
by Pat Hutchins
or _____

DISCUSSION FOCUS
Make a map of Rosie's walk.

Writing

Five-Day Theme: Plants
or _____

INTRODUCTION
The teacher and the students have a conversation related to the theme.

WRITING ACTIVITIES
While the students are writing or drawing, the teacher meets with individuals or small groups to discuss the theme. The student's independent work may or may not relate to the theme. Each student's work is kept in a folder.

SHARING
The students share with another person or the group something they have written or drawn.

Alphabet

Letters: *Pp, Xx,* or _____

INTRODUCTION—OBJECT LABELING
The teacher introduces the letters and writes on the chalkboard student-volunteered names of objects in the classroom that contain one or both of the letters.

STUDENT ACTIVITY
The students write their favorite words from the chalkboard or their own words on strips of paper. The words are displayed near the objects.

SHARING
The students share something they have written with another person or the group.

Pictures and Words

INTRODUCTION
Picture: President or _____
   The teacher leads a brief discussion about the picture.

CHART DEVELOPMENT
Phase III—Sentences: The students volunteer words to label the picture, and the teacher writes the words on the chart. Students draw lines to connect parts of the picture to the words. The teacher writes a student-chosen title and at least one sentence on the chart.

COMPREHENSION FOCUS
The teacher develops comprehension of the picture by asking questions, many of which will begin with *who*.
   The chart is displayed in the classroom.

Storytime

READ ALOUD
Bean and Plant
by Christine Back
or _____

DISCUSSION FOCUS
Make a plan to plant a bean seed and compare its progress to the stages shown in the book.

Writing

Five-Day Theme: Plants
or _____

INTRODUCTION
The teacher leads a class discussion about points of interest generated during the first four days of the theme and introduces the student activity.

STUDENT ACTIVITY
Review the seed growth sequence from Storytime. Plant bean or other

appropriate seeds. Another good book to use is *The Tiny Seed* by Eric Carle.

SHARING
Students predict when they think their seeds will sprout.

Alphabet

Letters: *Gg, Yy,* or _____

INTRODUCTION—OBJECT LABELING
The teacher introduces the letters and writes on the chalkboard student-volunteered names of objects in the classroom that contain one or both of the letters.

STUDENT ACTIVITY
The students write their favorite words from the chalkboard or their own words on strips of paper. The words are displayed near the objects.

SHARING
The students share something they have written with another person or the group.

Lesson **131**

Pictures and Words

INTRODUCTION
Picture: Spring or _____
The teacher leads a brief discussion about the picture.

CHART DEVELOPMENT
Phase III—Sentences: The students volunteer words to label the picture, and the teacher writes the words on the chart. Students draw lines to connect parts of the picture to the words. The teacher writes a student-chosen title and at least one sentence on the chart.

COMPREHENSION FOCUS
The teacher develops comprehension of the picture by asking questions, many of which will begin with *when*.
The chart is displayed in the classroom.

Storytime

READ ALOUD
Bear-ly Bear-able Bear Jokes, Riddles, and Knock-Knocks
by Mort Gerberg
Grizzly Riddles
by Katy Hall
or _____

DISCUSSION FOCUS
Talk about jokes and riddles. Are jokes the same as riddles?

Writing

Five-Day Theme: Spring
or _____

INTRODUCTION
The teacher and the students have a conversation related to the theme. Conversations might include a reference to the Pictures and Words chart made earlier in the day.

WRITING ACTIVITIES
While the students are writing or drawing, the teacher meets with individuals or small groups to discuss the theme. The student's independent work may or may not relate to the theme. Each student's work is kept in a folder.

SHARING
The students share with another person or the group something they have written or drawn.

Alphabet

Letters: *Dd, Mm,* or _____

INTRODUCTION—OBJECT LABELING
The teacher introduces the letters and writes on the chalkboard student-volunteered names of objects in the classroom that contain one or both of the letters.

STUDENT ACTIVITY
The students write their favorite words from the chalkboard or their own words on strips of paper. The words are displayed near the objects.

SHARING
The students share something they have written with another person or the group.

Pictures and Words

INTRODUCTION
Picture: Sandwich or _____
  The teacher leads a brief discussion about the picture.

CHART DEVELOPMENT
Phase III—Sentences: The students volunteer words to label the picture, and the teacher writes the words on the chart. Students draw lines to connect parts of the picture to the words. The teacher writes a student-chosen title and at least one sentence on the chart.

COMPREHENSION FOCUS
The teacher develops comprehension of the picture by asking questions, many of which will begin with *how*.
  The chart is displayed in the classroom.

Storytime

READ ALOUD
The Giant Jam Sandwich
by J. V. Lord
or _____

DISCUSSION FOCUS
Discuss the problem of the wasps. Try to recreate the steps of the solution.

Writing

Five-Day Theme: Spring
or _____

INTRODUCTION
The teacher and the students have a conversation related to the theme.

WRITING ACTIVITIES
While the students are writing or drawing, the teacher meets with individuals or small groups to discuss the theme. The student's independent work may or may not relate to the theme. Each student's work is kept in a folder.

SHARING
The students share with another person or the group something they have written or drawn.

Alphabet

Letters: *Hh, Ww*, or _____

INTRODUCTION—OBJECT LABELING
The teacher introduces the letters and writes on the chalkboard student-volunteered names of objects in the classroom that contain one or both of the letters.

STUDENT ACTIVITY
The students write their favorite words from the chalkboard or their own words on strips of paper. The words are displayed near the objects.

SHARING
The students share something they have written with another person or the group.

Lesson **133**

Pictures and Words

INTRODUCTION
Picture: Breakfast foods or _____
   The teacher leads a brief discussion about the picture.

CHART DEVELOPMENT
Phase III—Sentences: The students volunteer words to label the picture, and the teacher writes the words on the chart. Students draw lines to connect parts of the picture to the words. The teacher writes a student-chosen title and at least one sentence on the chart.

COMPREHENSION FOCUS
The teacher develops comprehension of the picture by asking questions, many of which will begin with *when*.
   The chart is displayed in the classroom.

Storytime

READ ALOUD
Chickens Aren't the Only Ones
by Ruth Heller
or _____

DISCUSSION FOCUS
Children tell how the illustrations clarify the descriptions in the book.

Writing

Five-Day Theme: Spring
or _____

INTRODUCTION
The teacher and the students have a conversation related to the theme.

WRITING ACTIVITIES
While the students are writing or drawing, the teacher meets with individuals or small groups to discuss the theme. The student's independent work may or may not relate to the theme. Each student's work is kept in a folder.

SHARING
The students share with another person or the group something they have written or drawn.

Alphabet

Letter Cluster: *br* or _____

INTRODUCTION—BRAINSTORMING LESSON
The teacher introduces the letter cluster and writes student-volunteered words and illustrations of words containing the letters on the chalkboard.

STUDENT ACTIVITY
On their papers, students write
■ examples of the letters
■ their favorite words or illustrations from the chalkboard
■ other words or drawings

SHARING
The students share with another person or the group something they have written or drawn.
   Papers are dated and filed.

S u c c e s **S** u c c e s **S** u c c e s **S** u c c e s **S** u c c e s **S** u c c e s **S** u c c e s **S** u c c e s **S**

Lesson **134**

Pictures and Words

INTRODUCTION
Picture: Hair or _____
The teacher leads a brief discussion about the picture.

CHART DEVELOPMENT
Phase III—Sentences: The students volunteer words to label the picture, and the teacher writes the words on the chart. Students draw lines to connect parts of the picture to the words. The teacher writes a student-chosen title and at least one sentence on the chart.

COMPREHENSION FOCUS
The teacher develops comprehension of the picture by asking questions, many of which will begin with *how*.
The chart is displayed in the classroom.

Storytime

READ ALOUD
Green Eggs and Ham
by Dr. Seuss
or _____

DISCUSSION FOCUS
Talk about usual and unusual colors for everyday foods.

Writing

Five-Day Theme: Spring
or _____

INTRODUCTION
The teacher and the students have a conversation related to the theme.

WRITING ACTIVITIES
While the students are writing or drawing, the teacher meets with individuals or small groups to discuss the theme. The student's independent work may or may not relate to the theme. Each student's work is kept in a folder.

SHARING
The students share with another person or the group something they have written or drawn.

Alphabet

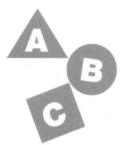

Letter Cluster: *br* or _____

INTRODUCTION—RESEARCH LESSON—Magazines
The teacher reviews the letter cluster. The teacher leads a discussion about objects that may be found in magazines that relate to the breakfast foods or

_____

STUDENT ACTIVITY
The students cut or tear related objects from magazines and glue them on individual papers or the class chart. Some of the objects may be labeled.

SHARING
The teacher and students discuss items on the class chart. The chart is displayed in the classroom.

233

Lesson **135**

Pictures and Words

INTRODUCTION
Picture: Crowd or _____

The teacher leads a brief discussion about the picture.

CHART DEVELOPMENT
Phase III—Sentences: The students volunteer words to label the picture, and the teacher writes the words on the chart. Lines are drawn to connect parts of the picture to the words. The teacher writes a student-chosen title and at least one sentence on the chart.

COMPREHENSION FOCUS
The teacher develops comprehension of the picture by asking questions, many of which will begin with *who*.

The chart is displayed in the classroom.

Storytime

READ ALOUD
The Flower Alphabet Book
by Jerry Palotta
or _____

DISCUSSION FOCUS
Notice which flowers in the book have the same color.

Writing

Five-Day Theme: Spring
or _____

INTRODUCTION
The teacher leads a class discussion about points of interest generated during the first four days of the theme and introduces the student activity.

STUDENT ACTIVITY
The students paint flowers and other signs of spring.

SHARING
The painting objects are cut out and displayed as a class mural.

Alphabet

Letter Cluster: *cr* or _____

INTRODUCTION—BRAINSTORMING LESSON
The teacher introduces the letter cluster and writes student-volunteered words and illustrations of words containing the letters on the chalkboard.

STUDENT ACTIVITY
On their papers, students write
■ examples of the letters
■ their favorite words or illustrations from the chalkboard
■ other words or drawings

SHARING
The students share with another person or the group something they have written or drawn.

Papers are dated and filed.

Pictures and Words

INTRODUCTION
Picture: Castles and dragons or _____

The teacher leads a brief discussion about the picture.

CHART DEVELOPMENT
Phase III—Sentences: The students volunteer words to label the picture, and the teacher writes the words on the chart.

Students draw lines to connect parts of the picture to the words. The teacher writes a student-chosen title and at least one sentence on the chart.

COMPREHENSION FOCUS
The teacher develops comprehension of the picture by asking questions, many of which will begin with _where_.

The chart is displayed in the classroom.

Storytime

READ ALOUD
How Is a Crayon Made?
by Oz Charles
or _____

DISCUSSION FOCUS
Discuss the steps in the manufacture of crayons.

Writing

Five-Day Theme: Castles and Dragons
or _____

INTRODUCTION
The teacher and the students have a conversation related to the theme. Conversations might include a reference to the Pictures and Words chart made earlier in the day.

WRITING ACTIVITIES
While the students are writing or drawing, the teacher meets with

individuals or small groups to discuss the theme. The student's independent work may or may not relate to the theme. Each student's work is kept in a folder.

SHARING
The students share with another person or the group something they have written or drawn.

Alphabet

Letter Cluster: _cr_ or _____

INTRODUCTION—STUDENT PROJECTS LESSON
The teacher reviews the letter cluster. The class discusses crayon-resist drawings.

STUDENT ACTIVITY
The students make their own crayon-resist drawings.

SHARING
The students take their projects home.

Lesson **137**

Pictures and Words

INTRODUCTION
Picture: Princess or _____
   The teacher leads a brief discussion about the picture.

CHART DEVELOPMENT
Phase III—Sentences: The students volunteer words to label the picture, and the teacher writes the words on the chart. Students draw lines to connect parts of the picture to the words. The teacher writes a student-chosen title and at least one sentence on the chart.

COMPREHENSION FOCUS
The teacher develops comprehension of the picture by asking questions, many of which will begin with *who*.
   The chart is displayed in the classroom.

Storytime

READ ALOUD
The Story of Ferdinand the Bull by Robert Lawson
or _____

DISCUSSION FOCUS
Does Ferdinand feel lonely?

Writing

Five-Day Theme: Castles and Dragons
or _____

INTRODUCTION
The teacher and the students have a conversation related to the theme.

WRITING ACTIVITIES
While the students are writing or drawing, the teacher meets with individuals or small groups to discuss the theme. The student's independent work may or may not relate to the theme. Each student's work is kept in a folder.

SHARING
The students share with another person or the group something they have written or drawn.

Alphabet

Letter Cluster: *pr* or _____

INTRODUCTION— BRAINSTORMING LESSON
The teacher introduces the letter cluster and writes student-volunteered words and illustrations of words containing the letters on the chalkboard.

STUDENT ACTIVITY
On their papers, students write
■ examples of the letters
■ their favorite words or illustrations from the chalkboard
■ other words or drawings

SHARING
The students share with another person or the group something they have written or drawn.
   Papers are dated and filed.

Pictures and Words

INTRODUCTION
Picture: Landscape or _____
    The teacher leads a brief discussion about the picture.

CHART DEVELOPMENT
Phase III—Sentences: The students volunteer words to label the picture, and the teacher writes the words on the chart. Students draw lines to connect parts of the picture to the words. The teacher writes a student-chosen title and at least one sentence on the chart.

COMPREHENSION FOCUS
The teacher develops comprehension of the picture by asking questions, many of which will begin with *what*.
    The chart is displayed in the classroom.

Storytime

READ ALOUD
Cinderella
(any version)
or _____

DISCUSSION FOCUS
Describe and compare the characters in the book.

Writing

Five-Day Theme: Castles and Dragons
or _____

INTRODUCTION
The teacher and the students have a conversation related to the theme.

WRITING ACTIVITIES
While the students are writing or drawing, the teacher meets with individuals or small groups to discuss the theme. The student's independent work may or may not relate to the theme. Each student's work is kept in a folder.

SHARING
The students share with another person or the group something they have written or drawn.

Alphabet

Letter Cluster: *pr* or _____

INTRODUCTION—RESEARCH LESSON—Magazines
The teacher reviews the letter cluster. The teacher leads a discussion about objects that may be found in magazines that relate to pretty things or _____

STUDENT ACTIVITY
The students cut or tear the letters or related objects from magazines and glue them on individual papers or the class chart. Some of the objects may be labeled.

SHARING
The teacher and students discuss items on the class chart. The chart is displayed in the classroom.

Lesson 139

Pictures and Words

INTRODUCTION
Picture: Something silly or _____
  The teacher leads a brief discussion about the picture.

CHART DEVELOPMENT
Phase III—Sentences: The students volunteer words to label the picture, and the teacher writes the words on the chart. Students draw lines to connect parts of the picture to the words. The teacher writes a student-chosen title and at least one sentence on the chart.

COMPREHENSION FOCUS
The teacher develops comprehension of the picture by asking questions, many of which will begin with *how*.
  The chart is displayed in the classroom.

Storytime

READ ALOUD
Shake My Sillies Out
by Raffi
or _____

DISCUSSION FOCUS
Sing or play the song. Act out the lyrics.

Writing

Five-Day Theme: Castles and Dragons
or _____

INTRODUCTION
The teacher and the students have a conversation related to the theme.

WRITING ACTIVITIES
While the students are writing or drawing, the teacher meets with individuals or small groups to discuss the theme. The student's independent work may or may not relate to the theme. Each student's work is kept in a folder.

SHARING
The students share with another person or the group something they have written or drawn.

Alphabet

Letter Cluster: *dr* or _____

INTRODUCTION— BRAINSTORMING LESSON
The teacher introduces the letter cluster and writes student-volunteered words and illustrations of words containing the letters on the chalkboard.

STUDENT ACTIVITY
On their papers, students write
■ examples of the letters
■ their favorite words or illustrations from the chalkboard
■ other words or drawings

SHARING
The students share with another person or the group something they have written or drawn.
  Papers are dated and filed.

Pictures and Words

INTRODUCTION
Picture: Tools or _____
The teacher leads a brief discussion about the picture.

CHART DEVELOPMENT
Phase III—Sentences: The students volunteer words to label the picture, and the teacher writes the words on the chart. Students draw lines to connect parts of the picture to the words. The teacher writes a student-chosen title and at least one sentence on the chart.

COMPREHENSION FOCUS
The teacher develops comprehension of the picture by asking questions, many of which will begin with *what*.
The chart is displayed in the classroom.

Storytime

READ ALOUD
Arthur's Baby
by Marc Brown
or _____

DISCUSSION FOCUS
How does Arthur feel about the baby?

Writing

Five-Day Theme: Castles and Dragons
or _____

INTRODUCTION
The teacher leads a class discussion about points of interest generated during the first four days of the theme and introduces the student activity.

STUDENT ACTIVITY
Read *Custard the Dragon*. Make a class book about a pet dragon.

SHARING
Read the student-made dragon book and place it with the classroom book collection.

Alphabet

Letter Cluster: *dr* or _____

INTRODUCTION—STUDENT PROJECTS LESSON
The teacher reviews the letter cluster. The class discusses construction of dragons out of assorted colors of construction paper.

STUDENT ACTIVITY
The students make their own version of a dragon.

SHARING
The students take their projects home.

Lesson **141**

Pictures and Words

INTRODUCTION
Picture: Frogs or _____
The teacher leads a brief discussion about the picture.

CHART DEVELOPMENT
Phase IV—Questions & Answers:
The students volunteer words to label the picture, and the teacher writes the words on the chart. Students draw lines to connect parts of the picture to the words. The teacher writes a student-chosen title, a sentence in the form of a question, and an answer on the chart.

COMPREHENSION FOCUS
The teacher develops comprehension of the picture by asking questions, many of which will begin with *where*.
The chart is displayed in the classroom.

Storytime

READ ALOUD
Good Dog Carl
by Alexandra Day
or _____

DISCUSSION FOCUS
Describe ways in which Carl was or was not helpful.

Writing

Five-Day Theme: Frogs
or _____

INTRODUCTION
The teacher and the students have a conversation related to the theme. Conversations might include a reference to the Pictures and Words chart made earlier in the day.

WRITING ACTIVITIES
While the students are writing or drawing, the teacher meets with individuals or small groups to discuss the theme. The student's independent work may or may not relate to the theme. Each student's work is kept in a folder.

SHARING
The students share with another person or the group something they have written or drawn.

Alphabet

Letter Cluster: *tr* or _____

INTRODUCTION—
BRAINSTORMING LESSON
The teacher introduces the letter cluster and writes student-volunteered words and illustrations of words containing the letters on the chalkboard.

STUDENT ACTIVITY
On their papers, students write
- examples of the letters
- their favorite words or illustrations from the chalkboard
- other words or drawings

SHARING
The students share with another person or the group something they have written or drawn.
Papers are dated and filed.

Lesson **142**

Pictures and Words

INTRODUCTION
Picture: Trains or _____
The teacher leads a brief discussion about the picture.

CHART DEVELOPMENT
Phase IV—Questions & Answers:
The students volunteer words to label the picture, and the teacher writes the words on the chart. Students draw lines to connect parts of the picture to the words. The teacher writes a student-chosen title, a sentence in the form of a question, and an answer on the chart.

COMPREHENSION FOCUS
The teacher develops comprehension of the picture by asking questions, many of which will begin with *when*.
The chart is displayed in the classroom.

Storytime

READ ALOUD
Ed Emberly's ABC
by Ed Emberly
or _____

DISCUSSION FOCUS
Choose one or two letters. Discuss all the ways in which Ed Emberly emphasized the letter (sounds and pictures).

Writing

Five-Day Theme: Frogs
or _____

INTRODUCTION
The teacher and the students have a conversation related to the theme.

WRITING ACTIVITIES
While the students are writing or drawing, the teacher meets with individuals or small groups to discuss the theme. The student's independent work may or may not relate to the theme. Each student's work is kept in a folder.

SHARING
The students share with another person or the group something they have written or drawn.

Alphabet

Letter Cluster: *tr* or _____

INTRODUCTION—RESEARCH LESSON—Magazines
The teacher reviews the letter cluster. The teacher leads a discussion about objects that may be found in magazines that relate to trains or _____

STUDENT ACTIVITY
The students cut or tear the letters or related objects from magazines and glue them on individual papers or the class chart. Some of the objects may be labeled.

SHARING
The teacher and students discuss items on the class chart. The chart is displayed in the classroom.

Lesson **143**

Pictures and Words

INTRODUCTION
Picture: Fruit or _____
The teacher leads a brief discussion about the picture.

CHART DEVELOPMENT
Phase IV—Questions & Answers:
The students volunteer words to label the picture, and the teacher writes the words on the chart. Students draw lines to connect parts of the picture to the words. The teacher writes a student-chosen title, a sentence in the form of a question, and an answer on the chart.

COMPREHENSION FOCUS
The teacher develops comprehension of the picture by asking questions, many of which will begin with *what*.
The chart is displayed in the classroom.

Storytime

READ ALOUD
The Mysterious Tadpole
by Stephen Kellogg
or _____

DISCUSSION FOCUS
Tell about the events that saved the "tadpole." Was this story real or make believe?

Writing

Five-Day Theme: Frogs
or _____

INTRODUCTION
The teacher and the students have a conversation related to the theme.

WRITING ACTIVITIES
While the students are writing or drawing, the teacher meets with individuals or small groups to discuss the theme. The student's independent work may or may not relate to the theme. Each student's work is kept in a folder.

SHARING
The students share with another person or the group something they have written or drawn.

Alphabet

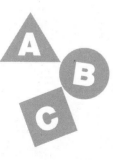

Letter Cluster: *fr* or _____

INTRODUCTION—
BRAINSTORMING LESSON
The teacher introduces the letter cluster and writes student-volunteered words and illustrations of words containing the letters on the chalkboard.

STUDENT ACTIVITY
On their papers, students write
■ examples of the letters
■ their favorite words or illustrations from the chalkboard
■ other words or drawings

SHARING
The students share with another person or the group something they have written or drawn.
Papers are dated and filed.

Pictures and Words

INTRODUCTION
Picture: Unicorn or _____
    The teacher leads a brief discussion about the picture.

CHART DEVELOPMENT
Phase IV—Questions & Answers:
The students volunteer words to label the picture, and the teacher writes the words on the chart. Students draw lines to connect parts of the picture to the words. The teacher writes a student-chosen title, a sentence in the form of a question, and an answer on the chart.

COMPREHENSION FOCUS
The teacher develops comprehension of the picture by asking questions, many of which will begin with *what*.
    The chart is displayed in the classroom.

Storytime

READ ALOUD
The Tale of Mr. Jeremy Fisher
by Beatrix Potter
or _____

DISCUSSION FOCUS
Make a list or talk about the places mentioned in the story.

Writing

Five-Day Theme: Frogs
or _____

INTRODUCTION
The teacher and the students have a conversation related to the theme.

WRITING ACTIVITIES
While the students are writing or drawing, the teacher meets with individuals or small groups to discuss the theme. The student's independent work may or may not relate to the theme. Each student's work is kept in a folder.

SHARING
The students share with another person or the group something they have written or drawn.

Alphabet

Letter Cluster: *fr* or _____

INTRODUCTION—STUDENT PROJECTS LESSON
The teacher reviews the letter cluster. The class discusses construction of frog puppets out of paper bags.

STUDENT ACTIVITY
The students make their own version of a frog puppet.

SHARING
The students take their projects home.

Lesson 145

Pictures and Words

INTRODUCTION
Picture: Being scared or _____
The teacher leads a brief discussion about the picture.

CHART DEVELOPMENT
Phase IV—Questions & Answers:
The students volunteer words to label the picture, and the teacher writes the words on the chart. Students draw lines to connect parts of the picture to the words. The teacher writes a student-chosen title, a sentence in the form of a question, and an answer on the chart.

COMPREHENSION FOCUS
The teacher develops comprehension of the picture by asking questions, many of which will begin with *why*.
The chart is displayed in the classroom.

Storytime

READ ALOUD
Jump, Frog, Jump!
by Robert Kalan
or _____

DISCUSSION FOCUS
How many action words can be heard in this story. Act out some of the words.

Writing

Five-Day Theme: Frogs
or _____

INTRODUCTION
The teacher leads a class discussion about points of interest generated during the first four days of the theme and introduces the student activity.

STUDENT ACTIVITY
Have a frog party. Serve "swamp water" punch and "butterfly" sandwiches. Play leapfrog and sing frog songs.

SHARING
The students tell another person or the group their favorite parts of the frog party.

Alphabet

Letter Cluster: *bl* or _____

**INTRODUCTION—
BRAINSTORMING LESSON**
The teacher introduces the letter cluster and writes student-volunteered words and illustrations of words containing the letters on the chalkboard.

STUDENT ACTIVITY
On their papers, students write
■ examples of the letters
■ their favorite words or illustrations from the chalkboard
■ other words or drawings

SHARING
The students share with another person or the group something they have written or drawn.
Papers are dated and filed.

244

Pictures and Words

INTRODUCTION
Picture: Circus or _____
   The teacher leads a brief discussion about the picture.

CHART DEVELOPMENT
Phase IV—Questions & Answers:
The students volunteer words to label the picture, and the teacher writes the words on the chart. Students draw lines to connect parts of the picture to the words. The teacher writes a student-chosen title, a sentence in the form of a question, and an answer on the chart.

COMPREHENSION FOCUS
The teacher develops comprehension of the picture by asking questions, many of which will begin with *what*.
   The chart is displayed in the classroom.

Storytime

READ ALOUD
Freight Train
by Donald Crews
or _____

DISCUSSION FOCUS
Talk about the colors mentioned in the book. Who is wearing these colors today?

Writing

Five-Day Theme: Circus
or _____

INTRODUCTION
The teacher and the students have a conversation related to the theme. Conversations might include a reference to the Pictures and Words chart made earlier in the day.

WRITING ACTIVITIES
While the students are writing or drawing, the teacher meets with individuals or small groups to discuss the theme. The student's independent work may or may not relate to the theme. Each student's work is kept in a folder.

SHARING
The students share with another person or the group something they have written or drawn.

Alphabet

Letter Cluster: *bl* or _____

INTRODUCTION—RESEARCH LESSON—Magazines
The teacher reviews the letter cluster. The teacher leads a discussion about objects that may be found in magazines that relate to the color blue or _____

STUDENT ACTIVITY
The students cut or tear the letters or related objects from magazines and glue them on individual papers or the class chart. Some of the objects may be labeled.

SHARING
The teacher and students discuss items on the class chart. The chart is displayed in the classroom.

Lesson **147**

Pictures and Words

INTRODUCTION
Picture: Seashells or _____
   The teacher leads a brief discussion about the picture.

CHART DEVELOPMENT
Phase IV—Questions & Answers:
The students volunteer words to label the picture, and the teacher writes the words on the chart. Students draw lines to connect parts of the picture to the words. The teacher writes a student-chosen title, a sentence in the form of a question, and an answer on the chart.

COMPREHENSION FOCUS
The teacher develops comprehension of the picture by asking questions, many of which will begin with *where*.
   The chart is displayed in the classroom.

Storytime

READ ALOUD
A House for Hermit Crab
by Eric Carle
or _____

DISCUSSION FOCUS
Discuss the sequence of the months of the year.

Writing

Five-Day Theme: Circus
or _____

INTRODUCTION
The teacher and the students have a conversation related to the theme.

WRITING ACTIVITIES
While the students are writing or drawing, the teacher meets with individuals or small groups to discuss the theme. The student's independent work may or may not relate to the theme. Each student's work is kept in a folder.

SHARING
The students share with another person or the group something they have written or drawn.

Alphabet

Letter Cluster: *cl* or _____

INTRODUCTION—BRAINSTORMING LESSON
The teacher introduces the letter cluster and writes student-volunteered words and illustrations of words containing the letters on the chalkboard.

STUDENT ACTIVITY
On their papers, students write
■ examples of the letters
■ their favorite words or illustrations from the chalkboard
■ other words or drawings

SHARING
The students share with another person or the group something they have written or drawn.
   Papers are dated and filed.

246

Pictures and Words

INTRODUCTION
Picture: City or _____

The teacher leads a brief discussion about the picture.

CHART DEVELOPMENT
Phase IV—Questions & Answers:
The students volunteer words to label the picture, and the teacher writes the words on the chart. Students draw lines to connect parts of the picture to the words. The teacher writes a student-chosen title, a sentence in the form of a question and an answer on the chart.

COMPREHENSION FOCUS
The teacher develops comprehension of the picture by asking questions, many of which will begin with *who*.

The chart is displayed in the classroom.

Storytime

READ ALOUD
The Little Island
by Margaret Wise Brown
or _____

DISCUSSION FOCUS
Talk about the seasonal changes on the little island. How do the illustrations show the change of seasons?

Writing

Five-Day Theme: Circus
or _____

INTRODUCTION
The teacher and the students have a conversation related to the theme.

WRITING ACTIVITIES
While the students are writing or drawing, the teacher meets with individuals or small groups to discuss the theme. The student's independent work may or may not relate to the theme. Each student's work is kept in a folder.

SHARING
The students share with another person or the group something they have written or drawn.

Alphabet

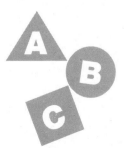

Letter Cluster: *cl* or _____

INTRODUCTION—STUDENT PROJECTS LESSON
The teacher reviews the letter cluster. The class discusses construction of a clown. They might use a paper plate, construction paper, and a balloon for the nose.

STUDENT ACTIVITY
The students make their own version of a clown.

SHARING
The students take their projects home.

Lesson 149

Pictures and Words

INTRODUCTION
Picture: Eyeglasses or _____
   The teacher leads a brief discussion about the picture.

CHART DEVELOPMENT
Phase IV—Questions & Answers:
The students volunteer words to label the picture, and the teacher writes the words on the chart. Students draw lines to connect parts of the picture to the words. The teacher writes a student-chosen title, a sentence in the form of a question, and an answer on the chart.

COMPREHENSION FOCUS
The teacher develops comprehension of the picture by asking questions, many of which will begin with *what*.
   The chart is displayed in the classroom.

Storytime

READ ALOUD
Spectacles
by Ellen Raskin
or _____

DISCUSSION FOCUS
Which of the five senses seems most important in this story?

Writing

Five-Day Theme: Circus
or _____

INTRODUCTION
The teacher and the students have a conversation related to the theme.

WRITING ACTIVITIES
While the students are writing or drawing, the teacher meets with individuals or small groups to discuss the theme. The student's independent work may or may not relate to the theme. Each student's work is kept in a folder.

SHARING
The students share with another person or the group something they have written or drawn.

Alphabet

Letter Cluster: *gl* or _____

INTRODUCTION—BRAINSTORMING LESSON
The teacher introduces the letter cluster and writes student-volunteered words and illustrations of other rhyming words on the chalkboard.

STUDENT ACTIVITY
On their papers, students write
■ examples of the letters
■ their favorite words or illustrations from the chalkboard
■ other words or drawings

SHARING
The students share with another person or the group something they have written or drawn.
   Papers are dated and filed.

Pictures and Words

INTRODUCTION
Picture: Popcorn or _____
   The teacher leads a brief discussion about the picture.

CHART DEVELOPMENT
Phase IV—Questions & Answers:
The students volunteer words to label the picture, and the teacher writes the words on the chart. Students draw lines to connect parts of the picture to the words. The teacher writes a student-chosen title, a sentence in the form of a question, and an answer on the chart.

COMPREHENSION FOCUS
The teacher develops comprehension of the picture by asking questions, many of which will begin with *how*.
   The chart is displayed in the classroom.

Storytime

READ ALOUD
Clifford Goes to the Circus
by Norman Bridwell
or _____

DISCUSSION FOCUS
Recall events in the story. If you were Clifford, which happenings would be *most* important to you?

Writing

Five-Day Theme: Circus
or _____

INTRODUCTION
The teacher leads a class discussion about points of interest generated during the first four days of the theme and introduces the student activity.

STUDENT ACTIVITIES
Small groups of students make up a circus act.

SHARING
The groups perform their circus acts for the class.

Alphabet

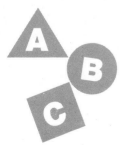

Letter Cluster: *gl* or _____

INTRODUCTION—RESEARCH
LESSON—Magazines
The teacher reviews the letter cluster. The teacher leads a discussion about objects that may be found in magazines that relate to things made of glass or

_____

STUDENT ACTIVITY
The students cut or tear the letters or related objects from magazines and glue them on individual papers or the class chart. Some of the objects may be labeled.

SHARING
The teacher and students discuss items on the class chart. The chart is displayed in the classroom.

Lesson **151**

Pictures and Words

INTRODUCTION
Picture: Environment or _____
   The teacher leads a brief discussion about the picture.

CHART DEVELOPMENT
Phase IV—Questions & Answers:
The students volunteer words to label the picture, and the teacher writes the words on the chart. Students draw lines to connect parts of the picture to the words. The teacher writes a student-chosen title, a sentence in the form of a question, and an answer on the chart.

COMPREHENSION FOCUS
The teacher develops comprehension of the picture by asking questions, many of which will begin with *where*.
   The chart is displayed in the classroom.

Storytime

READ ALOUD
A Zoo for Mr. Muster
by Arnold Lobel
or _____

DISCUSSION FOCUS
What jobs do the characters have? Who is the main character?

Writing

Five-Day Theme: Earth's Environment
or _____

INTRODUCTION
The teacher and the students have a conversation related to the theme. Conversations might include a reference to the Pictures and Words chart made earlier in the day.

WRITING ACTIVITIES
While the students are writing or drawing the teacher meets with individuals or small groups to discuss the theme. The student's independent work may or may not relate to the theme. Each student's work is kept in a folder.

SHARING
The students share with another person or the group something they have written or drawn.

Alphabet

Letter Cluster: *fl* or _____

INTRODUCTION—
BRAINSTORMING LESSON
The teacher introduces the letter cluster and writes student-volunteered words and illustrations of other rhyming words on the chalkboard.

STUDENT ACTIVITY
On their papers, students write
■ examples of the letters
■ their favorite words or illustrations from the chalkboard
■ other words or drawings

SHARING
The students share with another person or the group something they have written or drawn.
   Papers are dated and filed.

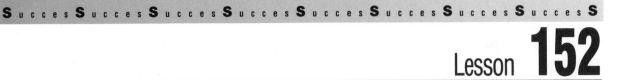
Pictures and Words

INTRODUCTION
Picture: Flags or _____
    The teacher leads a brief discussion about the picture.

CHART DEVELOPMENT
Phase IV—Questions & Answers:
The students volunteer words to label the picture, and the teacher writes the words on the chart. Students draw lines to connect parts of the picture to the words. The teacher writes a student-chosen title, a sentence in the form of a question, and an answer on the chart.

COMPREHENSION FOCUS
The teacher develops comprehension of the picture by asking questions, many of which will begin with *why*.
    The chart is displayed in the classroom.

Storytime

READ ALOUD
Patrick's Dinosaurs
by Carol Carrick
or _____

DISCUSSION FOCUS
Talk about what happens at the beginning of the story. What happens at the end?

Writing

Five-Day Theme: Earth's Environment
or _____

INTRODUCTION
The teacher and the students have a conversation related to the theme.

WRITING ACTIVITIES
While the students are writing or drawing, the teacher meets with individuals or small groups to discuss the theme. The student's independent work may or may not relate to the theme. Each student's work is kept in a folder.

SHARING
The students share with another person or the group something they have written or drawn.

Alphabet

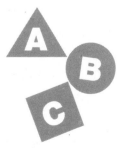

Letter Cluster: *fl* or _____

INTRODUCTION—STUDENT PROJECTS LESSON
The teacher reviews the letter cluster. The class discusses construction of a flag.

STUDENT ACTIVITY
The students make their own versions of a flag.

SHARING
The students take their projects home.

Lesson **153**

Pictures and Words

INTRODUCTION
Picture: Taste or _____
    The teacher leads a brief discussion about the picture.

CHART DEVELOPMENT
Phase IV—Questions & Answers:
The students volunteer words to label the picture, and the teacher writes the words on the chart. Students draw lines to connect parts of the picture to the words. The teacher writes a student-chosen title, a sentence in the form of a question, and an answer on the chart.

COMPREHENSION FOCUS
The teacher develops comprehension of the picture by asking questions, many of which will begin with *what*.
    The chart is displayed in the classroom.

Storytime

READ ALOUD
One Watermelon Seed
by Celia Cottridge
or _____

DISCUSSION FOCUS
Discuss size changes as things grow.

Writing

Five-Day Theme: Earth's Environment
or _____

INTRODUCTION
The teacher and the students have a conversation related to the theme.

WRITING ACTIVITIES
While the students are writing or drawing, the teacher meets with individuals or small groups to discuss the theme. The student's independent work may or may not relate to the theme. Each student's work is kept in a folder.

SHARING
The students share with another person or the group something they have written or drawn.

Alphabet

Letter Cluster: *pl* or _____

**INTRODUCTION—
BRAINSTORMING LESSON**
The teacher introduces the letter cluster and writes student-volunteered words and illustrations of words containing the letters on the chalkboard.

STUDENT ACTIVITY
On their papers, students write
■ examples of the letters
■ their favorite words or illustrations from the chalkboard
■ other words or drawings

SHARING
The students share with another person or the group something they have written or drawn.
    Papers are dated and filed.

252

Lesson **154**

Pictures and Words

INTRODUCTION
Picture: Rivers or _____
The teacher leads a brief discussion about the picture.

CHART DEVELOPMENT
Phase IV—Questions & Answers:
The students volunteer words to label the picture, and the teacher writes the words on the chart. Students draw lines to connect parts of the picture to the words. The teacher writes a student-chosen title, a sentence in the form of a question, and an answer on the chart.

COMPREHENSION FOCUS
The teacher develops comprehension of the picture by asking questions, many of which will begin with *where*.
The chart is displayed in the classroom.

Storytime

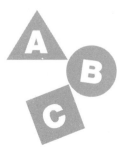

READ ALOUD
Child's Garden of Verses ("Where Go the Boats")
by Robert Louis Stevenson
or _____

DISCUSSION FOCUS
What do the words say about the river in this poem?

Writing

Five-Day Theme: Earth's Environment
or _____

INTRODUCTION
The teacher and the students have a conversation related to the theme.

WRITING ACTIVITIES
While the students are writing or drawing, the teacher meets with individuals or small groups to discuss the theme. The student's independent work may or may not relate to the theme. Each student's work is kept in a folder.

SHARING
The students share with another person or the group something they have written or drawn.

Alphabet

Letter Cluster: *pl* or _____

INTRODUCTION—RESEARCH LESSON—Magazines
The teacher introduces the letter cluster. The teacher leads a discussion about objects that may be found in magazines that relate to things you play with or

STUDENT ACTIVITY
The students cut or tear the letters or related objects from magazines and glue them on individual papers or the class chart. Some of the objects may be labeled.

SHARING
The teacher and students discuss items on the class chart. The chart is displayed in the classroom.

253

Lesson **155**

Pictures and Words

INTRODUCTION
Picture: Clothes or _____
   The teacher leads a brief discussion about the picture.

CHART DEVELOPMENT
Phase IV—Questions & Answers:
The students volunteer words to label the picture, and the teacher writes the words on the chart. Students draw lines to connect parts of the picture to the words. The teacher writes a student-chosen title, a sentence in the form of a question, and an answer on the chart.

COMPREHENSION FOCUS
The teacher develops comprehension of the picture by asking questions, many of which will begin with *who*.
   The chart is displayed in the classroom.

Storytime

READ ALOUD
Heron Street
by Ann Turner
or _____

DISCUSSION FOCUS
Talk about the changes from the beginning to the end of this book.

Writing

Five-Day Theme: Earth's Environment
or _____

INTRODUCTION
The teacher leads a class discussion about points of interest generated during the first four days of the theme and introduces the student activity.

STUDENT ACTIVITIES
Each student illustrates one way in which he or she will help the earth.

SHARING
The illustrations are posted on a bulletin board or published in a class book.

Alphabet

Letter Cluster: *st* or _____

INTRODUCTION—BRAINSTORMING LESSON
The teacher introduces the letter cluster and writes student-volunteered words and illustrations of words containing the letters on the chalkboard.

STUDENT ACTIVITY
On their papers, students write
■ examples of the letters
■ their favorite words or illustrations from the chalkboard
■ other words or drawings

SHARING
The students share with another person or the group something they have written or drawn.
   Papers are dated and filed.

Lesson **156**

Pictures and Words

INTRODUCTION
Picture: Snakes and reptiles or
_____

The teacher leads a brief discussion about the picture.

CHART DEVELOPMENT
Phase IV—Questions & Answers:
The students volunteer words to label the picture, and the teacher writes the words on the chart. Students draw lines to connect parts of the picture to the words. The teacher writes a student-chosen title, a sentence in the form of a question, and an answer on the chart.

COMPREHENSION FOCUS
The teacher develops comprehension of the picture by asking questions, many of which will begin with *what*.

The chart is displayed in the classroom.

Storytime

READ ALOUD
We're Going on a Bear Hunt
by Michael Rosen
or _____

DISCUSSION FOCUS
Discuss the events and how they are described in this story.

Writing

Five-Day Theme: Snakes and Reptiles
or _____

INTRODUCTION
The teacher and the students have a conversation related to the theme. Conversations might include a reference to the Pictures and Words chart made earlier in the day.

WRITING ACTIVITIES
While the students are writing or drawing, the teacher meets with individuals or small groups to discuss the theme. The student's independent work may or may not relate to the theme. Each student's work is kept in a folder.

SHARING
The students share with another person or the group something they have written or drawn.

Alphabet

Letter Cluster: *st* or _____

INTRODUCTION—STUDENT PROJECTS LESSON
The teacher introduces the letter cluster. The class discusses construction of a paper stop sign.

STUDENT ACTIVITY
The students make their own version of a stop sign.

SHARING
The students take their projects home.

Lesson **157**

Pictures and Words

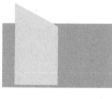

INTRODUCTION
Picture: Sleep or _____
  The teacher leads a brief discussion about the picture.

CHART DEVELOPMENT
Phase IV—Questions & Answers:
The students volunteer words to label the picture, and the teacher writes the words on the chart. Students draw lines to connect parts of the picture to the words. The teacher writes a student-chosen title, a sentence in the form of a question, and an answer on the chart.

COMPREHENSION FOCUS
The teacher develops comprehension of the picture by asking questions, many of which will begin with *when*.
  The chart is displayed in the classroom.

Storytime

READ ALOUD
Lullaby by Joan Aragon
Night in the Country
by Cynthia Rylant
Animals of the Night
by Merry Banks
or _____

DISCUSSION FOCUS
Talk about the way that one of these books goes from evening, through the night, until morning.

Writing

Five-Day Theme: Snakes and Reptiles
or _____

INTRODUCTION
The teacher and the students have a conversation related to the theme.

WRITING ACTIVITIES
While the students are writing or drawing, the teacher meets with individuals or small groups to discuss the theme. The student's independent work may or may not relate to the theme. Each student's work is kept in a folder.

SHARING
The students share with another person or the group something they have written or drawn.

Alphabet

Letter Cluster: *sl* or _____

INTRODUCTION—BRAINSTORMING LESSON
The teacher introduces the letter cluster and writes student-volunteered words and illustrations of words containing the letters on the chalkboard.

STUDENT ACTIVITY
On their papers, students write
■ examples of the letters
■ their favorite words or illustrations from the chalkboard
■ other words or drawings

SHARING
The students share with another person or the group something they have written or drawn.
  Papers are dated and filed.

Pictures and Words

INTRODUCTION
Picture: Hamburgers or _____
The teacher leads a brief discussion about the picture.

CHART DEVELOPMENT
Phase IV—Questions & Answers:
The students volunteer words to label the picture, and the teacher writes the words on the chart. Students draw lines to connect parts of the picture to the words. The teacher writes a student-chosen title, a sentence in the form of a question, and an answer on the chart.

COMPREHENSION FOCUS
The teacher develops comprehension of the picture by asking questions, many of which will begin with *how*.
The chart is displayed in the classroom.

Storytime

READ ALOUD
The Hare and the Tortoise
(any version)
or _____

DISCUSSION FOCUS
Make a Venn diagram of the characteristics of the hare and the tortoise.

Writing

Five-Day Theme: Snakes and Reptiles
or _____

INTRODUCTION
The teacher and the students have a conversation related to the theme.

WRITING ACTIVITIES
While the students are writing or drawing, the teacher meets with individuals or small groups to discuss the theme. The student's independent work may or may not relate to the theme. Each student's work is kept in a folder.

SHARING
The students share with another person or the group something they have written or drawn.

Alphabet

Letter Cluster: *sl* or _____

INTRODUCTION—RESEARCH
LESSON—Magazines
The teacher reviews the letter cluster. The teacher leads a discussion about objects that may be found in magazines that relate to slow things or _____

STUDENT ACTIVITY
The students cut or tear the letters or related objects from magazines and glue them on individual papers or the class chart. Some of the objects may be labeled.

SHARING
The teacher and students discuss items on the class chart. The chart is displayed in the classroom.

Lesson 159

Pictures and Words

INTRODUCTION
Picture: Snail or _____

The teacher leads a brief discussion about the picture.

CHART DEVELOPMENT
Phase IV—Questions & Answers:
The students volunteer words to label the picture, and the teacher writes the words on the chart. Students draw lines to connect parts of the picture to the words. The teacher writes a student-chosen title, a sentence in the form of a question, and an answer on the chart.

COMPREHENSION FOCUS
The teacher develops comprehension of the picture by asking questions, many of which will begin with *where*.

The chart is displayed in the classroom.

Storytime

READ ALOUD
The Runaway Bunny
by Margaret Wise Brown
or _____

DISCUSSION FOCUS
Talk about the story first from the mother's point of view and then discuss the point of view of the little bunny.

Writing

Five-Day Theme: Snakes and Reptiles
or _____

INTRODUCTION
The teacher and the students have a conversation related to the theme.

WRITING ACTIVITIES
While the students are writing or drawing, the teacher meets with individuals or small groups to discuss the theme. The student's independent work may or may not relate to the theme. Each student's work is kept in a folder.

SHARING
The students share with another person or the group something they have written or drawn.

Alphabet

Letter Cluster: *sn* or _____

INTRODUCTION—BRAINSTORMING LESSON
The teacher introduces the letter cluster and writes student-volunteered words and illustrations of words containing the letters on the chalkboard.

STUDENT ACTIVITY
On their papers, students write
- examples of the letters
- their favorite words or illustrations from the chalkboard
- other words or drawings

SHARING
The students share with another person or the group something they have written or drawn.

Papers are dated and filed.

Lesson 160

Pictures and Words

INTRODUCTION
Picture: Lights or _____
The teacher leads a brief discussion about the picture.

CHART DEVELOPMENT
Phase IV—Questions and Answers: The students volunteer words to label the picture, and the teacher writes the words on the chart. Students draw lines to connect parts of the picture to the words. The teacher writes a student-chosen title, a sentence in the form of a question, and an answer on the chart.

COMPREHENSION FOCUS
The teacher develops comprehension of the picture by asking questions, many of which will begin with *when*.
The chart is displayed in the classroom.

Storytime

READ ALOUD
ABC Bunny
by Wanda Grag
or _____

DISCUSSION FOCUS
How did the artist make the pictures for this book? Do you like black and white illustrations?

Writing

Five-Day Theme: Snakes and Reptiles
or _____

INTRODUCTION
The teacher leads a class discussion about points of interest generated during the first four days of the theme and introduces the student activity.

STUDENT ACTIVITY
The students make snake cookies.

SHARING
Eat the cookies!

Alphabet

Letter Cluster: *sn* or _____

INTRODUCTION—STUDENT PROJECTS LESSON
The teacher reviews the letter cluster. The class discusses construction of snakes.

STUDENT ACTIVITY
The students make their own version of a snake.

SHARING
The students take their projects home.

259

Lesson **161**

Pictures and Words

INTRODUCTION
Picture: Insects and spiders or _____

The teacher leads a brief discussion about the picture.

CHART DEVELOPMENT
Phase IV—Questions & Answers:
The students volunteer words to label the picture, and the teacher writes the words on the chart. Students draw lines to connect parts of the picture to the words. The teacher writes a student-chosen title, a sentence in the form of a question, and an answer on the chart.

COMPREHENSION FOCUS
The teacher develops comprehension of the picture by asking questions, many of which will begin with _what_.

The chart is displayed in the classroom.

Storytime

READ ALOUD
Crictor
by Tomi Ungerer
or _____

DISCUSSION FOCUS
Some of the ways that Crictor was helpful involved shape. Discuss.

Writing

Five-Day Theme: Insects and Spiders or _____

INTRODUCTION
The teacher and the students have a conversation related to the theme. Conversations might include a reference to the Pictures and Words chart made earlier in the day.

WRITING ACTIVITIES
While the students are writing or drawing, the teacher meets with individuals or small groups to discuss the theme. The student's independent work may or may not relate to the theme. Each student's work is kept in a folder.

SHARING
The students share with another person or the group something they have written or drawn.

Alphabet

Letter Cluster: _sm_ or _____

INTRODUCTION—
BRAINSTORMING LESSON
The teacher introduces the letter cluster and writes student-volunteered words and illustrations of words containing the letters on the chalkboard.

STUDENT ACTIVITY
On their papers, students write
■ examples of the letters
■ their favorite words or illustrations from the chalkboard
■ other words or drawings

SHARING
The students share with another person or the group something they have written or drawn.

Papers are dated and filed.

Pictures and Words

INTRODUCTION
Picture: Worried Person or _____
The teacher leads a brief discussion about the picture.

CHART DEVELOPMENT
Phase IV—Questions & Answers:
The students volunteer words to label the picture, and the teacher writes the words on the chart. Students draw lines to connect parts of the picture to the words. The teacher writes a student-chosen title, a sentence in the form of a question, and an answer on the chart.

COMPREHENSION FOCUS
The teacher develops comprehension of the picture by asking questions, many of which will begin with *why*.
The chart is displayed in the classroom.

Storytime

READ ALOUD
Is It Larger? Is It Smaller?
by Tana Hoban
or _____

DISCUSSION FOCUS
Find and list the small objects in this book.

Writing

Five-Day Theme: Insects and Spiders
or _____

INTRODUCTION
The teacher and the students have a conversation related to the theme.

WRITING ACTIVITIES
While the students are writing or drawing, the teacher meets with individuals or small groups to discuss the theme. The student's independent work may or may not relate to the theme. Each student's work is kept in a folder.

SHARING
The students share with another person or the group something they have written or drawn.

Alphabet

Letter Cluster: *sm* or _____

INTRODUCTION—RESEARCH LESSON—Magazines
The teacher reviews the letter cluster. The teacher leads a discussion about objects that may be found in magazines that relate to small things or _____

STUDENT ACTIVITY
The students cut or tear the letters or related objects from magazines and glue them on individual papers or the class chart. Some of the objects may be labeled.

SHARING
The teacher and students discuss items on the class chart. The chart is displayed in the classroom.

Lesson 163

Pictures and Words

INTRODUCTION
Picture: Meat or _____
The teacher leads a brief discussion about the picture.

CHART DEVELOPMENT
Phase IV—Questions & Answers:
The students volunteer words to label the picture, and the teacher writes the words on the chart. Students draw lines to connect parts of the picture to the words. The teacher writes a student-chosen title, a sentence in the form of a question and an answer on the chart.

COMPREHENSION FOCUS
The teacher develops comprehension of the picture by asking questions, many of which will begin with *what*.
The chart is displayed in the classroom.

Storytime

READ ALOUD
The Very Hungry Caterpillar
by Eric Carle
or _____

DISCUSSION FOCUS
How did Eric Carle use sizes in this story?

Writing

Five-Day Theme: Insects and Spiders or _____

INTRODUCTION
The teacher and the students have a conversation related to the theme.

WRITING ACTIVITIES
While the students are writing or drawing, the teacher meets with individuals or small groups to discuss the theme. The student's independent work may or may not relate to the theme. Each student's work is kept in a folder.

SHARING
The students share with another person or the group something they have written or drawn.

Alphabet

Letter Cluster: *sp* or _____

INTRODUCTION—BRAINSTORMING LESSON
The teacher introduces the letter cluster and writes student-volunteered words and illustrations of words containing the letters on the chalkboard.

STUDENT ACTIVITY
On their papers, students write
■ examples of the letters
■ their favorite words or illustrations from the chalkboard
■ other words or drawings

SHARING
The students share with another person or the group something they have written or drawn.
Papers are dated and filed.

Pictures and Words

INTRODUCTION
Picture: Coins or _____
The teacher leads a brief discussion about the picture.

CHART DEVELOPMENT
Phase IV—Questions & Answers:
The students volunteer words to label the picture, and the teacher writes the words on the chart. Students draw lines to connect parts of the picture to the words. The teacher writes a student-chosen title, a sentence in the form of a question, and an answer on the chart.

COMPREHENSION FOCUS
The teacher develops comprehension of the picture by asking questions, many of which will begin with *how*.
The chart is displayed in the classroom.

Storytime

READ ALOUD
The Very Quiet Cricket
by Eric Carle
or _____

DISCUSSION FOCUS
How did Eric Carle use sounds and words for sounds in this book?

Writing

Five-Day Theme: Insects and Spiders
or _____

INTRODUCTION
The teacher and the students have a conversation related to the theme.

WRITING ACTIVITIES
While the students are writing or drawing, the teacher meets with individuals or small groups to discuss the theme. The student's independent work may or may not relate to the theme. Each student's work is kept in a folder.

SHARING
The students share with another person or the group something they have written or drawn.

Alphabet

Letter Cluster: *sp* or _____

INTRODUCTION—STUDENT PROJECTS LESSON
The teacher reviews the letter cluster. The class discusses construction of a spider. They might use an egg carton section and pipe cleaners.

STUDENT ACTIVITY
The students make their own version of a spider.

SHARING
The students take their projects home.

Lesson 165

Pictures and Words

INTRODUCTION
Picture: Teeth or _____
   The teacher leads a brief discussion about the picture.

CHART DEVELOPMENT
Phase IV—Questions & Answers:
The students volunteer words to label the picture, and the teacher writes the words on the chart. Students draw lines to connect parts of the picture to the words. The teacher writes a student-chosen title, a sentence in the form of a question, and an answer on the chart.

COMPREHENSION FOCUS
The teacher develops comprehension of the picture by asking questions, many of which will begin with *who*.
   The chart is displayed in the classroom.

Storytime

READ ALOUD
The Very Busy Spider
by Eric Carle
or _____

DISCUSSION FOCUS
How did Eric Carle show pattern and sequence in this book?

Writing

Five-Day Theme: Insects and Spiders
or _____

INTRODUCTION
The teacher leads a class discussion about the points of interest generated during the first four days of the theme and introduces the student activity.

STUDENT ACTIVITY
Make a class book in the manner of *The Very Busy Spider* by Eric Carle. Trace the lines of the spider web with a thin line of white glue. The glue will dry clear and add texture to the web.

SHARING
Read the bound book to the class and place it with the classroom book collection.

Alphabet

Letter Cluster: *sc/sk* or _____

INTRODUCTION—BRAINSTORMING LESSON
The teacher introduces the letter cluster and writes student-volunteered words and illustrations of words containing the letters on the chalkboard.

STUDENT ACTIVITY
On their papers, students write
■ examples of the letters
■ their favorite words or illustrations from the chalkboard
■ other words or drawings

SHARING
The students share with another person or the group something they have written or drawn.
   Papers are dated and filed.

Lesson 166

Pictures and Words

INTRODUCTION
Picture: City Animals or _____
   The teacher leads a brief discussion about the picture.

CHART DEVELOPMENT
Phase IV—Questions & Answers:
The students volunteer words to label the picture, and the teacher writes the words on the chart. Students draw lines to connect parts of the picture to the words. The teacher writes a student-chosen title, a sentence in the form of a question, and an answer on the chart.

COMPREHENSION FOCUS
The teacher develops comprehension of the picture by asking questions, many of which will begin with *what*.
   The chart is displayed in the classroom.

Storytime

READ ALOUD
Parade
by Donald Crews
or _____

DISCUSSION FOCUS
Talk about time of day in relation to the sequence of the parade story.

Writing

Five-Day Theme: City Animals
or _____

INTRODUCTION
The teacher and the students have a conversation related to the theme. Conversations might include a reference to the Pictures and Words chart made earlier in the day.

WRITING ACTIVITIES
While the students are writing or drawing, the teacher meets with individuals or small groups to discuss the theme. The student's independent work may or may not relate to the theme. Each student's work is kept in a folder.

SHARING
The students share with another person or the group something they have written or drawn.

Alphabet

Letter Cluster: *sc/sk* or _____

INTRODUCTION—RESEARCH LESSON—Magazines
The teacher reviews the letter cluster. The teacher leads a discussion about objects that may be found in magazines that relate to scary things or _____

STUDENT ACTIVITY
The students cut or tear the letters or related objects from magazines and glue them on individual papers or the class chart. Some of the objects may be labeled.

SHARING
The teacher and students discuss items on the class chart. The chart is displayed in the classroom.

Lesson 167

Pictures and Words

INTRODUCTION
Picture: Jellybeans or _____
The teacher leads a brief discussion about the picture.

CHART DEVELOPMENT
Phase IV—Questions & Answers:
The students volunteer words to label the picture, and the teacher writes the words on the chart. Students draw lines to connect parts of the picture to the words. The teacher writes a student-chosen title, a sentence in the form of a question, and an answer on the chart.

COMPREHENSION FOCUS
The teacher develops comprehension of the picture by asking questions, many of which will begin with *when*.
The chart is displayed in the classroom.

Storytime

READ ALOUD
When Sheep Cannot Sleep
by Satoshi Kitamura
or _____

DISCUSSION FOCUS
What kinds of counting can we do in this book? Are there any number words?

Writing

Five-Day Theme: City Animals
or _____

INTRODUCTION
The teacher and the students have a conversation related to the theme.

WRITING ACTIVITIES
While the students are writing or drawing, the teacher meets with individuals or small groups to discuss the theme. The student's independent work may or may not relate to the theme. Each student's work is kept in a folder.

SHARING
The students share with another person or the group something they have written or drawn.

Alphabet

Letter Cluster: *sh* or _____

INTRODUCTION—BRAINSTORMING LESSON
The teacher introduces the letter cluster and writes student-volunteered words and illustrations of words containing the letters on the chalkboard.

STUDENT ACTIVITY
On their papers, students write
- examples of the letters
- their favorite words or illustrations from the chalkboard
- other words or drawings

SHARING
The students share with another person or the group something they have written or drawn.
Papers are dated and filed.

Lesson **168**

Pictures and Words

INTRODUCTION
Picture: Shark or _____
   The teacher leads a brief discussion about the picture.

CHART DEVELOPMENT
Phase IV—Questions & Answers:
The students volunteer words to label the picture, and the teacher writes the words on the chart. Students draw lines to connect parts of the picture to the words. The teacher writes a student-chosen title, a sentence in the form of a question, and an answer on the chart.

COMPREHENSION FOCUS
The teacher develops comprehension of the picture by asking questions, many of which will begin with *where*.
   The chart is displayed in the classroom.

Storytime

READ ALOUD
Henny Penny
(any two versions)
or _____

DISCUSSION FOCUS
Choose an event in the book. Compare that event in two versions of the story.

Writing

Five-Day Theme: City Animals
or _____

INTRODUCTION
The teacher and the students have a conversation related to the theme.

WRITING ACTIVITIES
While the students are writing or drawing, the teacher meets with individuals or small groups to discuss the theme. The student's independent work may or may not relate to the theme. Each student's work is kept in a folder.

SHARING
The students share with another person or the group something they have written or drawn.

Alphabet

Letter Cluster: *sh* or _____

INTRODUCTION—STUDENT PROJECTS LESSON
The teacher reviews the letter cluster. The class discusses construction of a shark with a movable jaw made out of construction paper and a brad.

STUDENT ACTIVITY
The students make their own version of a shark.

SHARING
The students take their projects home.

Lesson **169**

Pictures and Words

INTRODUCTION
Picture: Swimming Pool or _____
   The teacher leads a brief discussion about the picture.

CHART DEVELOPMENT
Phase IV—Questions & Answers:
The students volunteer words to label the picture, and the teacher writes the words on the chart. Students draw lines to connect parts of the picture to the words. The teacher writes a student-chosen title, a sentence in the form of a question, and an answer on the chart.

COMPREHENSION FOCUS
The teacher develops comprehension of the picture by asking questions, many of which will begin with *who*.
   The chart is displayed in the classroom.

Storytime

READ ALOUD
A Children's Zoo
by Tana Hoban
or _____

DISCUSSION FOCUS
Talk about the animals in the book. Reread favorites.

Writing

Five-Day Theme: City Animals
or _____

INTRODUCTION
The teacher and the students have a conversation related to the theme.

WRITING ACTIVITIES
While the students are writing or drawing, the teacher meets with individuals or small groups to discuss the theme. The student's independent work may or may not relate to the theme. Each student's work is kept in a folder.

SHARING
The students share with another person or the group something they have written or drawn.

Alphabet

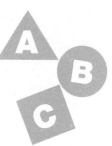

Letter Cluster: *sw* or _____

**INTRODUCTION—
BRAINSTORMING LESSON**
The teacher introduces the letter cluster and writes student-volunteered words and illustrations of words containing the letters on the chalkboard.

STUDENT ACTIVITY
On their papers, students write
■ examples of the letters
■ their favorite words or illustrations from the chalkboard
■ other words or drawings

SHARING
The students share with another person or the group something they have written or drawn.
   Papers are dated and filed.

Pictures and Words

INTRODUCTION
Picture: Shoes or _____
The teacher leads a brief discussion about the picture.

CHART DEVELOPMENT
Phase IV—Questions & Answers:
The students volunteer words to label the picture, and the teacher writes the words on the chart. Students draw lines to connect parts of the picture to the words. The teacher writes a student-chosen title, a sentence in the form of a question, and an answer on the chart.

COMPREHENSION FOCUS
The teacher develops comprehension of the picture by asking questions, many of which will begin with *what*.
The chart is displayed in the classroom.

Storytime

READ ALOUD
Shoes
by Elizabeth Winthrop
Alligator Shoes
by Arthur Dorros
or _____

DISCUSSION FOCUS
Tell about your favorite shoes. Then read about a special kind of shoe from the book. What kinds of shoes are there?

Writing

Five-Day Theme: City Animals
or _____

INTRODUCTION
The teacher leads a class discussion about points of interest generated during the first four days of the theme and introduces the student activity.

STUDENT ACTIVITY
Take a trip to the zoo or a pet store. An alternate choice would be to see a film or video about the zoo or pet store.

SHARING
The students tell the class about their favorite city animal.

Alphabet

Letter Cluster: *sw* or _____

INTRODUCTION—RESEARCH LESSON—Magazines
The teacher reviews the letter cluster. The teacher leads a discussion about objects that may be found in magazines that relate to sweet things or _____

STUDENT ACTIVITY
The students cut or tear the letters or related objects from magazines and glue them on individual papers or the class chart. Some of the objects may be labeled.

SHARING
The teacher and students discuss items on the class chart. The chart is displayed in the classroom.

Lesson **171**

Pictures and Words

INTRODUCTION
Picture: Country animals or _____

The teacher leads a brief discussion about the picture.

CHART DEVELOPMENT
Phase IV—Questions & Answers:
The students volunteer words to label the picture, and the teacher writes the words on the chart. Students draw lines to connect parts of the picture to the words. The teacher writes a student-chosen title, a sentence in the form of a question, and an answer on the chart.

COMPREHENSION FOCUS
The teacher develops comprehension of the picture by asking questions, many of which will begin with *what*.

The chart is displayed in the classroom.

Storytime

READ ALOUD
Humphrey's Bear
by Jan Wahl
or _____

DISCUSSION FOCUS
Can favorite things help us go to sleep?

Writing

Five-Day Theme: Country Animals
or _____

INTRODUCTION
The teacher and the students have a conversation related to the theme. Conversations might include a reference to the Pictures and Words chart made earlier in the day.

WRITING ACTIVITIES
While the students are writing or drawing, the teacher meets with individuals or small groups to discuss the theme. The student's independent work may or may not relate to the theme. Each student's work is kept in a folder.

SHARING
The students share with another person or the group something they have written or drawn.

Alphabet

Letter Cluster: *ck* or _____

INTRODUCTION—BRAINSTORMING LESSON
The teacher introduces the letter cluster and writes student-volunteered words and illustrations of words containing the letters on the chalkboard.

STUDENT ACTIVITY
On their papers, students write
■ examples of the letters
■ their favorite words or illustrations from the chalkboard
■ other words or drawings

SHARING
The students share with another person or the group something they have written or drawn.

Papers are dated and filed.

Pictures and Words

INTRODUCTION
Picture: Clocks or _____
   The teacher leads a brief discussion about the picture.

CHART DEVELOPMENT
Phase IV—Questions & Answers:
The students volunteer words to label the picture, and the teacher writes the words on the chart. Students draw lines to connect parts of the picture to the words. The teacher writes a student-chosen title, a sentence in the form of a question, and an answer on the chart.

COMPREHENSION FOCUS
The teacher develops comprehension of the picture by asking questions, many of which will begin with *when*.
   The chart is displayed in the classroom.

Storytime

READ ALOUD
Five Minutes Peace
by Jill Murphy
or _____

DISCUSSION FOCUS
What made this story funny?

Writing

Five-Day Theme: Country Animals
or _____

INTRODUCTION
The teacher and the students have a conversation related to the theme.

WRITING ACTIVITIES
While the students are writing or drawing the teacher meets with individuals or small groups to discuss the theme. The student's independent work may or may not relate to the theme. Each student's work is kept in a folder.

SHARING
The students share with another person or the group something they have written or drawn.

Alphabet

Letter Cluster: *ck* or _____

INTRODUCTION—STUDENT PROJECTS LESSON
The teacher reviews the letter cluster. The class discusses construction of a clock. They might use a paper plate with a brad to attach movable hands.

STUDENT ACTIVITY
The students make their own version of a clock.

SHARING
The students take their projects home.

Lesson 173

Pictures and Words

INTRODUCTION
Picture: Kings and queens or
_____

The teacher leads a brief discussion about the picture.

CHART DEVELOPMENT
Phase IV—Questions & Answers:
The students volunteer words to label the picture, and the teacher writes the words on the chart. Students draw lines to connect parts of the picture to the words. The teacher writes a student-chosen title, a sentence in the form of a question, and an answer on the chart.

COMPREHENSION FOCUS
The teacher develops comprehension of the picture by asking questions, many of which will begin with _who_.

The chart is displayed in the classroom.

Storytime

READ ALOUD
The Big Sneeze
by Ruth Brown
or _____

DISCUSSION FOCUS
List the characters and have the students choose some attributes to sort them by.

Writing

Five-Day Theme: Country Animals
or _____

INTRODUCTION
The teacher and the students have a conversation related to the theme.

WRITING ACTIVITIES
While the students are writing or drawing, the teacher meets with individuals or small groups to discuss the theme. The student's independent work may or may not relate to the theme. Each student's work is kept in a folder.

SHARING
The students share with another person or the group something they have written or drawn.

Alphabet

Letter Cluster: _th_ or _____

INTRODUCTION— BRAINSTORMING LESSON
The teacher introduces the letter cluster and writes student-volunteered words and illustrations of words containing the letters on the chalkboard.

STUDENT ACTIVITY
On their papers, students write
■ examples of the letters
■ their favorite words or illustrations from the chalkboard
■ other words or drawings

SHARING
The students share with another person or the group something they have written or drawn.

Papers are dated and filed.

Pictures and Words

INTRODUCTION
Picture: Fog or _____
  The teacher leads a brief discussion about the picture.

CHART DEVELOPMENT
Phase IV—Questions & Answers:
The students volunteer words to label the picture, and the teacher writes the words on the chart. Students draw lines to connect parts of the picture to the words. The teacher writes a student-chosen title, a sentence in the form of a question, and an answer on the chart.

COMPREHENSION FOCUS
The teacher develops comprehension of the picture by asking questions, many of which will begin with *where*.
  The chart is displayed in the classroom.

Storytime

READ ALOUD
Hide and Seek Fog
by Roger Duvoisin
or _____

DISCUSSION FOCUS
Look at one or more of the illustrations and discuss what could be seen, heard, smelled, felt, or tasted.

Writing

Five-Day Theme: Country Animals
or _____

INTRODUCTION
The teacher and the students have a conversation related to the theme.

WRITING ACTIVITIES
While the students are writing or drawing, the teacher meets with individuals or small groups to discuss the theme. The student's independent work may or may not relate to the theme. Each student's work is kept in a folder.

SHARING
The students share with another person or the group something they have written or drawn.

Alphabet

Letter Cluster: *th* or _____

INTRODUCTION—RESEARCH LESSON—Magazines
The teacher reviews the letter cluster. The teacher leads a discussion about objects that may be found in magazines that relate to thick or thin things.

STUDENT ACTIVITY
The students cut or tear the letters or related objects from magazines and glue them on individual papers or the class chart. Some of the objects may be labeled.

SHARING
The teacher and students discuss items on the class chart. The chart is displayed in the classroom.

Lesson 175

Pictures and Words

INTRODUCTION
Picture: Textures or _____
   The teacher leads a brief discussion about the picture.

CHART DEVELOPMENT
Phase IV—Questions & Answers:
The students volunteer words to label the picture, and the teacher writes the words on the chart. Students draw lines to connect parts of the picture to the words. The teacher writes a student-chosen title, a sentence in the form of a question, and an answer on the chart.

COMPREHENSION FOCUS
The teacher develops comprehension of the picture by asking questions, many of which will begin with *how*.
   The chart is displayed in the classroom.

Storytime

READ ALOUD
Farm Noises
by Jane Miller
or _____

DISCUSSION FOCUS
Read for a second time and talk about the places on a farm. Call attention to the background in the pictures.

Writing

Five-Day Theme: Country Animals
or _____

INTRODUCTION
The teacher leads a class discussion about points of interest generated during the first four days of the theme and introduces the student activity.

STUDENT ACTIVITY
Each student draws a country animal. The illustrations are bound into a class book.

SHARING
Read the bound class book and place it with the classroom book collection.

Alphabet

Letter Cluster: *ch* or _____

INTRODUCTION—
BRAINSTORMING LESSON
The teacher introduces the letter cluster and writes student-volunteered words and illustrations of words containing the letters on the chalkboard.

STUDENT ACTIVITY
On their papers, students write
■ examples of the letters
■ their favorite words or illustrations from the chalkboard
■ other words or drawings

SHARING
The students share with another person or group something they have written or drawn.
   Papers are dated and filed.

274

Pictures and Words

INTRODUCTION
Picture: Summer or _____
    The teacher leads a brief discussion about the picture.

CHART DEVELOPMENT
Phase IV—Questions & Answers:
The students volunteer words to label the picture, and the teacher writes the words on the chart. Students draw lines to connect parts of the picture to the words. The teacher writes a student-chosen title, a sentence in the form of a question and an answer on the chart.

COMPREHENSION FOCUS
The teacher develops comprehension of the picture by asking questions, many of which will begin with *when*.
    The chart is displayed in the classroom.

Storytime

READ ALOUD
Grandma Gets Grumpy
by Anna Hines
or _____

DISCUSSION FOCUS
How did Grandma feel when things got out of hand?

Writing

Five-Day Theme: Summer
or _____

INTRODUCTION
The teacher and the students have a conversation related to the theme. Conversations might include a reference to the Pictures and Words chart made earlier in the day.

WRITING ACTIVITIES
While the students are writing or drawing the teacher meets with individuals or small groups to discuss the theme. The student's independent work may or may not relate to the theme. Each student's work is kept in a folder.

SHARING
The students share with another person or the group something they have written or drawn.

Alphabet

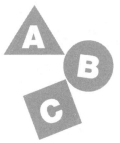

Letter Cluster: *ch* or _____

INTRODUCTION—STUDENT PROJECTS LESSON
The teacher reviews the letter cluster. The class discusses construction of a chain made from strips of paper.

STUDENT ACTIVITY
The students make their own version of a chain.

SHARING
The students take their projects home.

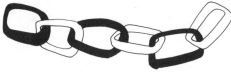

Lesson 177

Pictures and Words

INTRODUCTION
Picture: Tent or _____
   The teacher leads a brief discussion about the picture.

CHART DEVELOPMENT
Phase IV—Questions & Answers:
The students volunteer words to label the picture, and the teacher writes the words on the chart. Students draw lines to connect parts of the picture to the words. The teacher writes a student-chosen title, a sentence in the form of a question and an answer on the chart.

COMPREHENSION FOCUS
The teacher develops comprehension of the picture by asking questions, many of which will begin with *where*.
   The chart is displayed in the classroom.

Storytime

READ ALOUD
Do Not Disturb
by Nancy Tafuri
or _____

DISCUSSION FOCUS
What happens when people trespass in an animal's territory?

Writing

Five-Day Theme: Summer
or _____

INTRODUCTION
The teacher and the students have a conversation related to the theme.

WRITING ACTIVITIES
While the students are writing or drawing the teacher meets with individuals or small groups to discuss the theme. The student's independent work may or may not relate to the theme. Each student's work is kept in a folder.

SHARING
The students share with another person or the group something they have written or drawn.

Alphabet

Letter Cluster: *wh* or _____

INTRODUCTION—
BRAINSTORMING LESSON
The teacher introduces the letter cluster and writes student-volunteered words and illustrations of words containing the letters on the chalkboard.

STUDENT ACTIVITY
On their papers, students write
■ examples of the letters
■ their favorite words or illustrations from the chalkboard
■ other words or drawings

SHARING
The students share with another person or the group something they have written or drawn.
   Papers are dated and filed.

Pictures and Words

INTRODUCTION
Picture: Beach or _____
   The teacher leads a brief discussion about the picture.

CHART DEVELOPMENT
Phase IV—Questions & Answers:
The students volunteer words to label the picture, and the teacher writes the words on the chart. Students draw lines to connect parts of the picture to the words. The teacher writes a student-chosen title, a sentence in the form of a question, and an answer on the chart.

COMPREHENSION FOCUS
The teacher develops comprehension of the picture by asking questions, many of which will begin with *who*.
   The chart is displayed in the classroom.

Storytime

READ ALOUD
Wheel Away
by Dayle Ann Dodds
or _____

DISCUSSION FOCUS
This book is based on a song. Are there rhyming words in the song?

Writing

Five-Day Theme: Summer
or _____

INTRODUCTION
The teacher and the students have a conversation related to the theme.

WRITING ACTIVITIES
While the students are writing or drawing, the teacher meets with individuals or small groups to discuss the theme. The student's independent work may or may not relate to the theme. Each student's work is kept in a folder.

SHARING
The students share with another person or the group something they have written or drawn.

Alphabet

Letter Cluster: *wh* or _____

INTRODUCTION—RESEARCH LESSON—Magazines
The teacher reviews the letter cluster. The teacher leads a discussion about objects that may be found in magazines that relate to things with wheels or _____

STUDENT ACTIVITY
The students cut or tear the letters or related objects from magazines and glue them on individual papers or the class chart. Some of the objects may be labeled.

SHARING
The teacher and students discuss items on the class chart. The chart is displayed in the classroom.

Lesson 179

Pictures and Words

INTRODUCTION
Picture: Strawberries or _____
   The teacher leads a brief discussion about the picture.

CHART DEVELOPMENT
Phase IV—Questions & Answers:
The students volunteer words to label the picture, and the teacher writes the words on the chart. Students draw lines to connect parts of the picture to the words. The teacher writes a student-chosen title, a sentence in the form of a question, and an answer on the chart.

COMPREHENSION FOCUS
The teacher develops comprehension of the picture by asking questions, many of which will begin with _what._
   The chart is displayed in the classroom.

Storytime

READ ALOUD
The Little Mouse, The Ripe Red Strawberry and the Big Hungry Bear
by Don and Audrey Wood
or _____

DISCUSSION FOCUS
Talk about the relative size of the main characters.

Writing

Five-Day Theme: Summer
or _____

INTRODUCTION
The teacher and the students have a conversation related to the theme.

WRITING ACTIVITIES
While the students are writing or drawing, the teacher meets with individuals or small groups to discuss the theme. The student's independent work may or may not relate to the theme. Each student's work is kept in a folder.

SHARING
The students share with another person or the group something they have written or drawn.

Alphabet

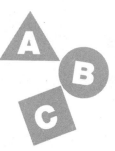

Letter Cluster: _tw_ or _____

INTRODUCTION—BRAINSTORMING LESSON
The teacher introduces the letter cluster and writes student-volunteered words and illustrations of words containing the letters on the chalkboard.

STUDENT ACTIVITY
On their papers, students write
■ examples of the letters
■ their favorite words or illustrations from the chalkboard
■ other words or drawings

SHARING
The students share with another person or the group something they have written or drawn.
   Papers are dated and filed.

278

Pictures and Words

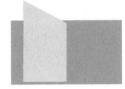

INTRODUCTION
Picture: Sailboats or _____
   The teacher leads a brief discussion about the picture.

CHART DEVELOPMENT
Phase IV—Questions & Answers:
The students volunteer words to label the picture, and the teacher writes the words on the chart. Students draw lines to connect parts of the picture to the words. The teacher writes a student-chosen title, a sentence in the form of a question, and an answer on the chart.

COMPREHENSION FOCUS
The teacher develops comprehension of the picture by asking questions, many of which will begin with *where*.
   The chart is displayed in the classroom.

Storytime

READ ALOUD
Best Friends
by Stephen Kellogg
Do You Want To Be My Friend?
by Eric Carle
or _____

DISCUSSION FOCUS
Talk about friends. Do friends always make you feel good? Did this story have a happy ending?

Writing

Five-Day Theme: Summer
or _____

INTRODUCTION
The teacher leads a class discussion about points of interest generated during the first four days of the theme and introduces the student activity.

STUDENT ACTIVITY
Each student makes an autograph book.

SHARING
The students have classmates sign their autograph book at an autograph party.

Alphabet

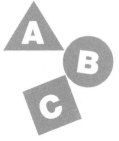

Letter Cluster: *tw* or _____

INTRODUCTION—STUDENT PROJECTS LESSON
The teacher reviews the letter cluster. The class discusses construction of twirlers made from tissue paper streamers on sticks.

STUDENT ACTIVITY
The students make their own version of a twirler.

SHARING
The students take their projects home.

▶ Appendix

Pictures for the Pictures and Words Module

1	* school	39	gorilla	77	teachers	114	cereal	152	flags
2	school bus	40	dessert	78	bedroom	115	happy	153	taste
3	animals	41	* monsters	79	shopping	116	* sports	154	rivers
4	furniture	42	yo-yos	80	candy	117	rose	155	clothes
5	food	43	cooking	81	* money	118	hearts	156	* snakes/reptiles
6	* children	44	umbrella	82	rabbits	119	"Angus"	157	sleep
7	adults	45	sky	83	fox	120	airport	158	hamburgers
8	feet	46	* nursery rhymes	84	girls	121	* map	159	snail
9	automobiles	47	zebra	85	mother	122	locks	160	lights
10	houses	48	plants	86	* cartoon	123	clouds	161	* insects/spiders
11	* family	49	hands	87	playground	124	state map	162	worried person
12	fire fighters	50	Mother Goose	88	basketball player	125	athletes	163	meats
13	bubble gum	51	* weather	89	Donald Duck	126	* plants	164	coins
14	rain	52	radio	90	house	127	tractor	165	teeth
15	dentist	53	nickels	91	* Winter	128	ants	166	* city animals
16	* Fall	54	mice	92	forest	129	puzzle	167	jellybeans
17	circles	55	rainbow	93	pigs	130	president	168	shark
18	bears	56	* space	94	lollipops	131	* Spring	169	swimming pool
19	ponds	57	hats	95	dogs	132	sandwich	170	shoes
20	football player	58	cats	96	* dinosaurs	133	breakfast food	171	* country animals
21	* birds	59	ice cream	97	fish	134	hair	172	clocks
22	boats	60	crying	98	hot dogs	135	crowd	173	kings/queens
23	kitchens	61	* grandparents	99	man	136	* castle/dragons	174	fog
24	airplanes	62	elephants	100	swamp	137	princess	175	textures
25	hearing	63	crops	101	* meal	138	landscape	176	* Summer
26	* transportation	64	ocean	102	horses	139	something silly	177	tent
27	police officer	65	octopus	103	stars	140	tools	178	beach
28	eyes	66	* rocks	104	cows	141	* frogs	179	strawberries
29	chairs	67	cartoon character	105	buildings	142	trains	180	sailboats
30	desert	68	vegetables	106	* machines	143	fruit		
31	* bedtime	69	kites	107	seeing	144	unicorn		
32	water	70	doctors	108	desk	145	being scared		
33	astronauts	71	* five senses	109	T.V. star	146	* circus		
34	pirate	72	sweaters	110	fire	147	seashells		
35	tennis shoes	73	squares	111	* community helpers	148	city		
36	* safety	74	mountains	112	boats	149	eyeglasses		
37	rectangles	75	elves	113	pebbles	150	popcorn		
38	wizard	76	* toys			151	* environment		

Suggested Themes for Writing

Lessons	Theme	Lessons	Theme	Lessons	Theme	Additional Themes
1–5	School	71–75	5 Senses	141–145	Frogs	Friends
6–10	All About Me	76–80	Toys	146–150	Circus	Zoo
11–15	My Family	81–85	Money	151–155	Earth & Environment	Fish
15–20	Fall	86–90	Cartoons	156–160	Snakes & Amphibians	Holidays
21–25	Birds	91–95	Winter	161–165	Insects & Spiders	Oceans
26–30	Transportation	96–100	Dinosaurs	166–170	City Animals	Monsters
31–35	Bedtime	101–105	Food Groups	171–175	Country Animals	Television
36–40	Safety	106–110	Machines	175–180	Summer	Computers
41–45	Scary Things	111–115	Community Helpers			Favorite Places
46–50	Nursery Rhymes	116–120	Sports & Games			Fairy Tales
51–55	Weather	121–125	Maps & States			Jokes
56–60	Space	126–130	Plants			Feelings
61–65	Grandparents	131–135	Spring			Energy
66–70	Rocks	136–140	Castles & Dragons			Presidents

Suggested Book Titles and Discussion Foci For Storytime

1. *The Story About Ping,* Clare H. Bishop. Putnam, 1938. (cause/effect)
2. *School Bus,* Donald Crews. Greenwillow, 1984. (sequence)
3. *Leo the Late Bloomer,* Robert Kraus. Crowell Jr., 1987. (emotions)
4. *Action Alphabet,* Marty Neumeier, Byron Glaser. Greenwillow, 1988. (prior knowledge)
   We Read: A to Z, Donald Crews. Greenwillow, 1984. (prior knowledge)
5. *My Teacher Sleeps in School,* Leatie Weiss. Puffin, 1985. (places)
6. *Box Turtle at Long Pond,* William T. George. Greenwillow, 1989. (description)
7. *Annabelle Swift, Kindergartner,* Amy Schwartz. Orchard, 1988. (character)
8. *Feet!,* Peter Parnall. Macmillan, 1988. (sizes)
9. *Swimmy,* Leo Lionni. Knopf, 1987. (colors)
10. *Don't Forget the Bacon,* Pat Hutchins. Greenwillow, 1976. (sequence)
11. *Jennie's Hat,* Ezra Jack Keats. Harper Trophy, 1985. (describing words)
12. *Harry the Dirty Dog,* Gene Zion. Harper Trophy, 1976. (character)
    Clifford the Big Red Dog, Norman Bridwell. Scholastic, 1985. (character)
13. *The Tale of Benjamin Bunny,* Beatrix Potter. Warne, 1987. (character)
14. *Rain, Rain Rivers,* Uri Shulevitz. Farrar, Straus & Giroux, 1969. (colors)
15. *Be Nice to Spiders,* Margaret Bloy Graham. Harper Jr., 1967. (humor)
16. *Apples and Pumpkins,* Anne Rockwell. Macmillan, 1989. (sequence)
17. *Inch by Inch,* Leo Lionni. Astor-Honor, 1962. (places)
18. *Jesse Bear, What Will You Wear?,* Nancy White Carlstrom. Macmillan. 1986. (rhyming)
19. *Jam,* Margaret Mahy, W. Helen Craig. Little, 1986. (sequence)
20. *Frederick,* Leo Lionni. Knopf, 1987. (time)
21. *The Little House,* Virginia Lee Burton. Houghton Mifflin, 1978. (time)
22. *Feathers for Lunch,* Lois Ehlert. Harcourt Brace Jovanovich, 1990. (colors)
23. *Alligators All Around,* Maurice Sendak. Harper Jr., 1962. (humor)
    Pierre, Maurice Sendak. Harper Jr., 1962. (humor)
24. *Ten, Nine, Eight,* Molly Bang. Greenwillow, 1983. (prior knowledge)
25. *What Is a Bird?,* Ron Hirschi. Walker, 1987. (living things)
    Home for a Bird, Ron Hirschi. Walker, 1987. (living things)
26. *Little Bear,* Elsie Holmelund Minarik. Harper Trophy, 1978.
    Flossie and the Fox, Patricia McKissack. Dial, 1986. (feelings)
27. *Mother Goose,* Tomie dePaola. Putnam, 1985. (rhyming words)
28. *The Bear's Bicycle,* David McPhail. Little, Brown, 1975. (prior knowledge)
29. *Brown Bear, Brown Bear,* Bill Martin, Jr. Holt, 1983. (colors)
30. *Trucks,* Byron Barton. Crowell Jr., 1986. (descriptions)
    Trucks, Gail Gibbons. Crowell, 1981. (descriptions)
31. *Roll Over! A Counting Song,* Merle Peek. Houghton Mifflin, 1981. (cause/effect)
32. *Arthur's Valentine,* Marc Brown. Little, Brown, 1988. (characters)
33. *I Want to Be an Astronaut,* Byron Barton. Crowell Jr., 1988. (important events)
34. *Beneath a Blue Umbrella,* Jack Prelutsky. Greenwillow, 1990. (rhyming)
35. *Ira Sleeps Over,* Bernard Waber. Houghton Mifflin, 1983. (emotions)
36. *Funny Bones,* Allan Ahlberg. Greenwillow, 1981. (descriptions)
37. *Willy the Wimp,* Anthony Browne. Knopf, 1985. (cause/effect)
38. *Caps for Sale,* Esphyr Slobodkina. Harper, 1947. (comparing)
39. *The Gorilla Did It,* Barbara Hazen. Athenaem, 1974. (cause/effect)
40. *Yummers!,* James Marshall. Houghton Mifflin, 1973. (humor)
41. *Where the Wild Things Are,* Maurice Sendak. Harper Trophy, 1988 (description)
42. *Napping House,* Don and Audrey Wood. Harcourt Brace Jovanovich, 1984. (sequence)
43. *Blueberries for Sal,* Robert McCloskey. Viking, 1948. (comparing characters)
44. *I Hear a Noise,* Diane Goode. Dutton, 1988. (characters)
45. *Teeny Tiny,* Jill Bennett. Putnam, 1986. (funny words or phrases)
    A Dark, Dark Tale, Ruth Brown. Putnam, 1986. (funny words or phrases)
46. *If You Give a Mouse a Cookie,* L. J. Numeroff. Harper, 1985. (pattern)
47. *Millions of Cats,* Wanda Gàg. Putnam, 1977. (cause/effect)
48. *Zella Zack and Zodiac,* Bill Peet. Houghton Mifflin, 1986. (rhyming words)
49. *Here Are My Hands,* Bill Martin, Jr., John Archambault. Holt, 1989. (prior knowledge)
50. *Whistle for Willie,* Ezra Jack Keats. Viking, 1964. (emotions/feelings)
51. *Three Billy Goats Gruff,* Janet Steven. Harcourt Brace Jovanovich, 1987. (sizes)
52. *Cloudy with a Chance of Meatballs,* Judi Barrett. Macmillan, 1978. (humor)
53. *Where Do Horses Live?,* Ron Hirschi. Walker, 1990. (places)
54. *Whose Mouse Are You?,* Robert Kraus. Macmillan, 1970. (characters)
55. *A Rainbow of My Own,* Don Freeman. Viking, 1966. (color)

56. *New Kid on the Block,* Jack Prelutsky. Greenwillow, 1984. (rhyming)
57. *Earthlets,* Tony Ross. Dutton, 1989. (humor)
58. *Rotten Ralph,* Jack Gantos. Houghton Mifflin, 1976 (cause/effect)
59. *The Caterpillar and the Polliwog,* Jack Kent. Simon & Schuster, 1982. (sequence)
60. *Rocket in my Pocket,* Carl Withers. Holt, 1988. (rhyming)
61. *The Chick and the Duckling,* Mirra Ginsburg. Macmillan, 1972. (cause/effect)
62. *Too Much Noise,* Ann McGovern. Houghton Mifflin, 1960. (animals)
63. *Wilfred Gordon McDonald Partridge,* Mem Fox. Kane-Miller, 1989. (emotions)
64. *George and Martha,* James Marshall. Houghton Mifflin, 1972. (important events)
    One Fine Day, Nonny Hogrogian. Macmillan, 1971. (important events)
65. *Color Zoo,* Lois Ehlert. Harper, 1989. (colors/shapes)
66. *Play with Me,* Marie Hall Ets. Viking, 1955. (sequence)
67. *Everybody Needs a Rock,* Byrd Baylor. Macmillan, 1985. (places)
68. *Growing Vegetable Soup,* Lois Ehlert. Harcourt Brace Jovanovich, 1990. (sequence)
69. *Anno's Counting Book,* Mitsumasa Anno. Crowell Jr., 1977. (objects)
70. *Rock Collecting,* Roma Gans. Harper Trophy, 1987. (places)
71. *Goggles,* Ezra Jack Keats. Macmillan, 1987. (important events)
72. *No Roses for Harry,* Gene Zion. Harper Trophy, 1976. (feelings)
73. *Shapes, Shapes, Shapes,* Tana Hoban. Greenwillow, 1986. (shapes)
74. *Salty Dog,* Gloria Rand. Holt, 1989. (animals)
75. *My Five Senses,* Aliki. Harper Trophy, 1990. (five senses)
76. *Poetry, Sing a Song of Popcorn,* Scholastic, 1988. (objects)
77. *The Patchwork Quilt,* Valerie Flournoy. Dial, 1985. (patterns)
    The Quilt, Ann Jonas. Greenwillow, 1984. (patterns)
78. *Alexander and the Wind-up Mouse,* Leo Lionni. Pantheon, 1969. (feelings)
79. *Corduroy,* Don Freeman. Viking, 1968. (emotions/feelings)
80. *Hi Cat!,* Ezra Jack Keats. Aladdin, 1988. (animals)
81. *Fast-Slow High-Low,* Peter Spier. Doubleday, 1988. (opposites)
    Dry or Wet, Bruce McMillan. Lathrop, 1988. (opposites)
82. *Who Said Red?,* Mary Serfozo. Macmillan, 1988. (colors)
83. *Mike Mulligan and His Steam Shovel,* Virginia Lee Burton. Houghton Mifflin, 1939. (cause/effect)
84. *Madeline,* Ludwig Bemelmans. Puffin, 1977. (important events)
85. *A Chair for My Mother,* Vera B. Williams. Greenwillow, 1982. (sequence)
86. *Curious George,* H. A. Rey. Houghton Mifflin, 1973. (characters)
87. *It's Mine, It's Mine,* Leo Lionni. Knopf, 1986. (cause/effect)
88. *Sun Up, Sun Down,* Gail Gibbons. Harcourt Brace Jovanovich, 1983. (time)
89. *Jack and the Beanstalk,* Beatrice DeRegniers. Aladdin, 1990. (objects)
90. *How a House Is Built,* Gail Gibbons. Holiday House, 1990. (sequence)
91. *Happy Birthday Moon,* Frank Asch. Simon & Schuster, 1981. (character)
92. *The Mitten,* Jan Brett. Putnam, 1990. (sequence)
    The Mitten, Alvin Tressett. Lothrop, 1964. (sequence)
93. *Small Pig,* Arnold Lobel. Harper, 1969. (important events)
94. *Amelia Bedelia,* Peggy Parish. Harper, 1983. (humor)
95. *The Snowy Day,* Ezra Jack Keats. Viking, 1962. (seasons)
96. *Chicken Soup with Rice,* Maurice Sendak. Harper, 1962 (seasons)
97. *Fish Eyes,* Lois Ehlert. Harcourt Brace Jovanovich, 1990. (colors/sizes)
98. *Dinosaurs, Dinosaurs,* Byron Barton. Crowell Jr., 1989.
    Dinosaurs, Gail Gibbons. Holiday, 1987. (colors)
99. *The Mixed-Up Chameleon,* Eric Carle. Harper, 1988. (animals)
100. *Bones, Bones, Dinosaur Bones,* Byron Barton. Crowell, 1990. (sizes)
101. *The Planets in Our Solar System,* Franklyn Branley. Harper Trophy, 1987. (sizes)
102. *Flying,* Donald Crews. Greenwillow, 1986.
    Flying, Gail Gibbons. Holiday House, 1989. (important events)
103. *Will's Mammoth,* Rafe Martin. Putnam, 1989. (descriptions)
104. *The Milk Makers,* Gail Gibbons. Macmillan, 1985. (places)
105. *Little Red Hen,* Paul Galdone. Clarion, 1979. (cause/effect)
106. *Q Is for Duck,* Mary Elting, Michael Folsom. Clarion, 1980. (humor)
107. *Look! Look! Look!,* Tana Hoban. Greenwillow, 1988. (objects)
108. *Machines at Work,* Byron Barton. Crowell, 1987. (descriptions)
    Machines, Ann Harlow Rockwell. Greenwillow, 1985. (descriptions)
    Dig, Drill, Dump, Fill, Tana Hoban. Greenwillow, 1975. (descriptions)
109. *Sheep in a Jeep,* Nancy Shaw. Houghton Mifflin, 1986. (rhyming)
110. *The Book of Foolish Machinery,* Donna Page. Scholastic, 1988. (funny words)
111. *A Letter to Amy,* Ezra Jack Keats. Harper Trophy, 1984. (emotions)

112.   *It's a Perfect Day,* Abigail Pizer. Harper, 1990. (animals)
113.   *Sylvester and the Magic Pebble,* William Steig. Simon & Schuster, 1969. (emotions)
114.   *Switch On, Switch Off,* Melvin Berger. Harper Trophy, 1990. (cause/effect)
115.   *The Post Office Book,* Gail Gibbons. Crowell, 1982. (sequence)
116.   *George Shrinks,* William Joyce. Harper Jr., 1985. (sizes)
117.   *Each Peach Pear Plum,* Janet and Allan Ahlberg. Viking, 1979. (rhyming)
118.   *Where Does the Brown Bear Go?,* Nicki Weiss. Penguin, 1990. (characters)
119.   *Angus Lost,* Marjorie Flack. Doubleday, 1989. (characters)
120.   *Dinosaur Bob,* William Joyce. Harper, 1988. (size)
121.   *Have You Seen My Duckling?,* Nancy Tafuri. Penguin, 1986. (number)
122.   *The Doorbell Rang,* Pat Huchins. Greenwillow, 1986. (sequence)
123.   *It Looked Like Spilt Milk,* Charles G. Shaw. Harper, 1988. (object)
124.   *Bread and Jam for Frances,* Russell Hoban. Harper, 1964. (descriptions)
125.   *Puzzle Maps U.S.A.,* Nancy Clouse. Holt, 1990. (places)
126.   *The Carrot Seed,* Ruth Kraus. Harper, 1945. (characters)
127.   *Planting a Rainbow,* Lois Ehlert. Harcourt Brace Jovanovich, 1988. (colors)
128.   *Ant Cities,* Arthur Dorros. Harper Trophy, 1988. (description)
129.   *Rosie's Walk,* Pat Hutchins. Macmillan, 1968. (description)
130.   *Bean and Plant,* Christine Back. Silver Burdett, 1986. (sequence)
131.   *Bearly Bear-able Baseball Riddles, Jokes and Knock-Knocks,* Mort Gerbert. Scholastic, 1989.
       Grizzly Riddles, Katy Hall. Dial, 1989. (humor)
132.   *Giant Jam Sandwich,* J. V. Lord. Houghton Mifflin, 1975. (sequence)
133.   *Chickens Aren't the Only Ones,* Ruth Heller. Putnam, 1981. (description)
134.   *Green Eggs and Ham,* Dr. Seuss. Random, 1960. (colors)
135.   *The Flower Alphabet Book,* Jerry Palotta. Charlesbridge. 1989. (colors)
136.   *How Is a Crayon Made?,* Oz Charles. Simon & Schuster, 1988. (sequence)
137.   *The Story of Ferdinand,* Robert Lawson, Munro Leaf, Viking, 1936. (feelings)
138.   *Cinderella,* Charles Perrault, Marcia Brown. Aladdin, 1988. (characters)
139.   *Shake My Sillies Out,* Raffi. McKay, 1990. (prior knowledge)
140.   *Arthur's Baby,* Marc Brown. Little, 1987. (emotions)
141.   *Good Dog Carl,* Ruth Brown. Green Tiger Press, 1985. (description)
142.   *Ed Emberly's ABC,* Ed Emberly. Little, 1978. (description)
143.   *The Mysterious Tadpole,* Stephen Kellogg. Dial, 1979. (important events)
144.   *The Tale of Mr. Jeremy Fisher,* Beatrix Potter. Warne, 1987. (places)
145.   *Jump, Frog, Jump!,* Robert Kalin. Scholastic, 1981. (action words)
146.   *Freight Train,* Donald Crews. Greenwillow, 1978. (colors)
147.   *A House for Hermit Crab,* Eric Carle. Picture Book Studio, 1987. (sequence)
148.   *The Little Island,* Golden MacDonald. Doubleday, 1946. (time)
149.   *Spectacles,* Ellen Raskin. Macmillan, 1988. (five senses)
150.   *Clifford at the Circus,* Norman Bridwell. Scholastic, 1985. (important events)
151.   *A Zoo for Mr. Muster,* Arnold Lobel. Harper, 1962. (characters)
152.   *Patrick's Dinosaurs,* Carol Carrick. Houghton Mifflin, 1983. (sequence)
153.   *One Watermelon Seed,* Celia Lottridge. Oxford University Press, 1990. (sizes)
154.   *Child's Garden of Verses* (Poem: "Where Go the Boats"), Robert Louis Stevenson. Macmillan,
       1981. (description)
155.   *Heron Street,* Ann Turner. Harper, 1989. (cause/effect)
156.   *We're Going on a Bear Hunt,* Michael Rosen. Macmillan, 1989. (description)
157.   *Lullabye,* Joan Aragon. Chronicle, 1989. (time)
       Night in the Country, Cynthia Rylant. Bradbury, 1986. (time)
       Animals of the Night, Merry Banks. Scribner's, 1990. (time)
158.   *The Hare and the Tortoise,* Brian Wildsmith. Oxford, 1987. (comparing characters)
159.   *The Runaway Bunny,* Margaret Wise Brown. Harper, 1972. (emotions)
160.   *ABC Bunny,* Wanda Gàg. Putnam, 1978. (colors)
       A Farmer's Alphabet, Mary A. Zarian. Godine, 1981. (colors)
161.   *Crictor,* Tomi Ungerer. Harper Trophy, 1983. (shapes)
162.   *Is It Larger? Is It Smaller?,* Tana Hoban. Greenwillow, 1985. (sizes)
163.   *The Very Hungry Caterpillar,* Eric Carle. Philomel, 1981. (sizes)
164.   *The Very Quiet Cricket,* Eric Carle. Philomel, 1990. (sounds)
165.   *The Very Busy Spider,* Eric Carle. Philomel, 1989. (sequence)
166.   *Parade,* Donald Crews. Greenwillow, 1983. (time)
167.   *When Sheep Cannot Sleep,* Satoshi Kitamura. Farrar, Straus & Giroux, 1986. (numbers)
168.   *Henny Penny,* Paul Galdone. Clarion, 1979. (important events)
169.   *A Children's Zoo,* Tana Hoban. Greenwillow, 1985. (descriptive words)
170.   *Shoes,* Elizabeth Winthrop. Harper, 1988. (descriptions)

Alligator Shoes, Arthur Dorros. Dutton, 1982. (descriptions)
171. *Humphrey's Bear,* Jan Wahl. Holt, 1987. (emotions)
172. *Five Minutes Peace,* Jill Murphy. Putnam, 1986. (humor)
173. *The Big Sneeze,* Ruth Brown. Lothrop, 1985. (five senses)
174. *Hide and Seek Fog,* Roger Duvoisin. Morrow, 1988. (five senses)
175. *Farm Noises,* Jane Miller. Simon & Schuster, 1989. (places)
176. *Grandma Gets Grumpy,* Anna G. Hines. Clarion, 1988. (emotions)
177. *Do Not Disturb,* Nancy Tafuri. Greenwillow, 1987. (cause/effect)
178. *Wheel Away,* Dayle Ann Dodds. Harper, 1989. (rhyming)
179. *The Little Mouse, The Bright Red Strawberry and the Big Hungry Bear,* Don & Audrey Wood. Playspaces, 1990. (sizes/comparing characters)
180. *Best Friends,* Stephen Kellogg. Dial, 1986. (emotions/feelings)
     Do You Want to Be My Friend?, Eric Carle. Philomel, 1988. (emotions/feelings)

ALPHABET MODULE LESSONS
Upper- and Lower-Case Letters

Lesson		
1	Letter *Ll*	Brainstorming
2	"	SP—ladybugs
3	"	R—magazines
4	Letter *Tt*	Brainstorming
5	"	R—magazines
6	"	SP—turtles
7	Letter *Ff*	Brainstorming
8	"	R—newspapers
9	"	SP—fish
10	Letter *Hh*	Brainstorming
11	"	SP—hats
12	"	R—magazines
13	Letter *Dd*	Brainstorming
14	"	SP—ducks
15	"	R—magazines
16	Letter *Ii*	Brainstorming
17	"	SP—inchworms
18	"	R—newspapers
19	Letter *Jj*	Brainstorming
20	"	R—magazines
21	"	SP—jack-in-the-box
22	Letter *Aa*	Brainstorming
23	"	SP—alligators
24	"	R—magazines
25	Letter *Pp*	Brainstorming
26	"	SP—puppets
27	"	R—newspapers
28	Letter *Bb*	Brainstorming
29	"	SP—brown bears
30	"	R—magazines
31	Letter *Vv*	Brainstorming
32	"	SP—valentines
33	"	R—magazines
34	Letter *Xx*	Brainstorming
35	"	R—newspapers
36	"	SP—x-rays
37	Letter *Ww*	Brainstorming
38	"	SP—wishing wands
39	""	R—magazines
40	Letter *Yy*	Brainstorming
41	"	SP—yellow yarn designs
42	"	R—magazines

Lesson		
43	Letter *Uu*	Brainstorming
44	"	SP—umbrellas
45	"	R—newspapers
46	Letter *Zz*	Brainstorming
47	"	SP—zebras
48	"	R—magazines
49	Letter *Mm*	Brainstorming
50	"	R—magazines
51	"	SP—monsters
52	Letter *Nn*	Brainstorming
53	"	SP—noodle necklace
54	"	R—newspapers
55	Letter *Rr*	Brainstorming
56	"	SP—rainbows
57	"	R—magazines
58	Letter *Cc*	Brainstorming
59	"	SP—caterpillars
60	"	R—magazines
61	Letter *Ee*	Brainstorming
62	"	SP—elephants
63	"	R—newspapers
64	Letter *Oo*	Brainstorming
65	"	SP—oval octopus
66	"	R—magazines
67	Letter *KK*	Brainstorming
68	"	R—magazines
69	"	SP—kites
70	Letter *Gg*	Brainstorming
71	"	SP—green goggles
72	"	R—newspapers
73	Letter *Ss*	Brainstorming
74	"	SP—sailboats
75	"	R—magazines
76	Letter *Qq*	Brainstorming
77	"	SP—quilts
78	"	R—magazines

R = Research
SP = Student Projects

Rhyming Words

79	Rhyme—mat	Brainstorming
80	"	SP—cat

Lesson		
81	Rhyme—bed	Brainstorming
82	"	R—magazines—red things
83	Rhyme—fox	Brainstorming
84	"	SP—decorate a box
85	Rhyme—drill	Brainstorming
86	"	R—magazines—things that can spill
87	Rhyme—fun	Brainstorming
88	"	SP—suns
89	Rhyme—quack	Brainstorming
90	"	R—magazines—black things
91	Rhyme—well	Brainstorming
92	"	SP—bells
93	Rhyme—trick	Brainstorming
94	"	R—magazines—things that are quick
95	Rhyme—dog	Brainstorming
96	"	SP—foggy scene
97	Rhyme—rug	Brainstorming
98	"	R—magazines—bug related things
99	Rhyme—man	Brainstorming
100	"	SP—fans
101	Rhyme—jet	Brainstorming
102	"	R—magazines—pets
103	Rhyme—star	Brainstorming
104	"	SP—car
105	Rhyme—rake	Brainstorming
106	"	R—magazines—things you bake
107	Rhyme—hook	Brainstorming
108	"	SP—miniature books
109	Rhyme—sheep	Brainstorming
110	"	R—magazines—sleep related things
111	Rhyme—float	Brainstorming
112	"	SP—boats
113	Rhyme—right	Brainstorming
114	"	R—magazines—things with lights
115	Rhyme—play	Brainstorming
116	"	SP—clay sculptures
117	Rhyme—rose	Brainstorming
118	"	R—magazines—things a nose smells
119	Rhyme—ring	Brainstorming
120	"	SP—string art
121	Rhyme—clock	Brainstorming
122	"	R—magazines—things with locks

R = Research
SP = Student Projects

Object Labeling

123	Letters b–n	Object labeling
124	Letters c–l	"
125	Letters j–s	"
126	Letters r–k	"
127	Letters f–v	"
128	Letters t–q	"
129	Letters p–x	"
130	Letters g–y	"
131	Letters d–m	"
132	Letters h–w	"

Letter Clusters

Lesson		
133	Cluster br	Brainstorming
134	"	R—magazines—breakfast foods
135	Cluster cr	Brainstorming
136	"	SP—crayon resist art
137	Cluster pr	Brainstorming
138	"	R—magazines—pretty things
139	Cluster dr	Brainstorming
140	"	SP—dragons
141	Cluster tr	Brainstorming
142	"	R—magazines—things related to trains
143	Cluster fr	Brainstorming
144	"	SP—frogs
145	Cluster bl	Brainstorming
146	"	R—magazines—black or blue objects
147	Cluster cl	Brainstorming
148	"	SP—clowns
149	Cluster gl	Brainstorming
150	"	R—magazines—things made of glass
151	Cluster fl	Brainstorming
152	"	SP—flags
153	Cluster pl	Brainstorming
154	"	R—magazines—things you play with
155	Cluster st	Brainstorming
156	"	SP—stop signs
157	Cluster sl	Brainstorming
158	"	R—magazines—slow things
159	Cluster sn	Brainstorming
160	"	SP—snakes
161	Cluster sm	Brainstorming
162	"	R—magazines—small objects
163	Cluster sp	Brainstorming
164	"	SP—spiders
165	Cluster sc–sk	Brainstorming
166	"	R—magazines—scary things
167	Cluster sh	Brainstorming
168	"	SP—sharks
169	Cluster sw	Brainstorming
170	"	R—magazines—sweet things
171	Cluster ck	Brainstorming
172	"	SP—clocks
173	Cluster th	Brainstorming
174	"	SP—magazines—thick or thin things
175	Cluster ch	Brainstorming
176	"	SP—chains
177	Cluster wh	Brainstorming
178	"	R—magazines—things with wheels
179	Cluster tw	Brainstorming
180	"	SP—twirlers

R = Research
SP = Student Projects

▶ Index